MERSEY MARINERS

Bob Evans

D1386604

Change of Name

In 2000 The Mersey Mission to Seamen became The Mersey Mission to Seafarers. This was to reflect the changes in the shipping industry which encourages seafarers of both genders and also the role of the Mission to all those who go down to the sea in ships.

For D'rene
and the
Family

First published 1997
Reprinted and updated 2002

Published 2002 by Countyvise Limited, 14 Appin Road, Birkenhead, Merseyside CH41 9HH in conjunction with the author R.A. Evans

Copyright © 1997 R.A. Evans

The right of R.A. Evans to be identified as the author of this work has been asserted by her in accordance with the Copyright, Design and Patents Act 1988.

British Library Cataloguing in Publication Data.
A catalogue record for this book is available from the British Library.

ISBN 1 901231 05 4

My boat is so small
Your sea so vast
Dear Lord
protect me.

Front Cover: *The painting of Sorlandet is by the author, from a photo-graph on the R.N.L.I.'s 1997 Calendar. This full-rigged ship was built in 1927 and now trains cadets for the Norwegian Merchant Navy.*

Contents

Chapter One	Roots	1
Chapter Two	The Early Chaplains	13
Chapter Three	The Gordon Smith Institute	26
Chapter Four	The Liverpool Sailors' Home	38
Chapter Five	Around the Sailors' Home	56
Chapter Six	The Mersey Mission to Seamen	66
Chapter Seven	The Apostleship of the Sea	87
Chapter Eight	The Orphans	107
Chapter Nine	Runcorn and Widnes and Garston	121
Chapter Ten	Poor Jack	133
Chapter Eleven	Strikes	144
Chapter Twelve	The Scandinavian Churches	171
Chapter Thirteen	The Akbar	180
Chapter Fourteen	The Clarence	195
Chapter Fifteen	The Indefatigable	202
Chapter Sixteen	H.M.S. Conway	217
Chapter Seventeen	H.M.S. Eaglet	232
Chapter Eighteen	Summerlands and the Ocean Club	245
Chapter Nineteen	The Chinese Seafarers	258
Chapter Twenty	The Mercantile Marine Service Association	265
Chapter Twenty-One	The British Sailors' Society	276

Foreword

by Len Holder

'Though it is a little out of fashion, there is much care and valour in this Welshman ...'

Shakespeare (Henry V)

Bob's first book 'A Dog Collar in the Docks' was full of humour and compassion. It centered on people and their differing attitudes to life. This second book is about caring for mariners in the wider context of local welfare organisations.

Some readers may know about one or more of the institutions in this book, but few will know them all. The book is well balanced and gives a brief but fair insight into each. Reading the chapter on the Liverpool Sailors' Home, reminded me of their shop, and a story I was told about a 'new boy' about to go to sea, whose mother still tied his shoe laces! I bet he had a hard time, but no doubt the sea will have made him grow up quickly and become self-assured and confident. I am sure readers will have many memories triggered by this book, particularly memories of many remarkable people.

Life in the Mersey's training ships was tough and the regimes of the reformatory ships of earlier years were sometimes very cruel. The narrative takes you through the experiences of some of the orphans and others who 'benefitted' from the training. No wonder some wanted to escape!

We are introduced to mariners who served their country with selfless courage in war and later in peace time and need to be cared for in poor health and old age. Memorial services are welcomed as a reminder, but life's needs go on from day to day. This is an aspect of caring which was important in history and still is today.

The welfare organisations are evidence of the fact that when people work together, the achievement of the group is greater than the sum of the individual contributions. This is reflected in the achievements of the Apostleship of the Sea, the British Sailors' Society, the Mercantile Marine Service Association (now NUMAST), the Mersey Mission to Seamen and all the other bodies that are still working together in support of seafarers' welfare.

Organisations such as the Scandinavian and German churches are, and have for a long time, been here in Liverpool to provide a special welcome for their countrymen. Caring and welfare also covers Chinese and other ethnic groups who have served at sea and settled here.

Wherever mariners come from, Merseyside has always provided a welcome. Like any other major seaport, the Mersey has its seamy and criminal side. It is all part of the picture and Bob gives us insights into the shameful and sordid activities of some of the local boarding house keepers and pimps. However, as Bob tells us, there were usually people around who would stand against injustice, cruelty and crime and give the mariner a shoulder to lean on. The hospitality of Merseyside works both ways. Wherever you go in the shipping world, north, east, west or south right across the globe, there are usually people who know Liverpool and make you welcome.

If, like me, you are interested in the history of local seafaring and have felt that one day you should stir yourself and look back in time, there is no need to rush to the records office or archives. Bob has done the hard work for us and acts as our guide. He is a gifted and natural story teller and has provided a valuable reference book. He would have made a good history teacher, because many who read this book - myself included - will want to follow his lead and go and find out more from the sources he has unearthed.

As a history of mariners on Merseyside, it puts a lot of today's problems into context. By looking at past hardships we appreciate the present and can look forward to the future.

L.A.Holder
Chairman, Mersey Mission to Seamen Committee.

Preface

The full title for this book should have been 'Mersey Mariners - Who Cares?' or it might have been 'Mersey Mariners - Who Cares!' Many people in the last two centuries have cared about the well-being of the seafarer and this book is the story of that caring. Obviously the script is partially autobiographical, partially old fashioned history, sometimes lifted from fading memories and sometimes unbelievable.

William A McLeod in his Boatswain's Manual, produced in 1944, may help us with John Curry's poem, 'Portrait of Liverpool Jack'. Every young apprentice pilot would have possessed a copy. '*Worming.* A method of filling in groves between the strands of a rope with marlin or other small stuff. Once used on fire bucket handles and manropes on accommodation ladders. *Parcelled.* This served the double purpose of keeping weather out of a wire, and helps to level off any unevenness near the region of a splice. *Serving.* This is the finishing touch which makes all the difference between a neat job and an eyesore.' The details were very detailed! The poem was first conceived and papered in 1970 in the Mission. The newly introduced and rather daring 'Page Three Girl' in the Daily Mirror must have been a nostalgic topic for many an old Liverpool Jack. John Curry is Chairman of the Liverpool Pilots·and a time-served friend. Many thanks and keep on writing!

Nothing could be written about Mersey Mariners without reference to the two volumes (1883 and 1886) on the story of Liverpool produced by J.A. Picton and also the 'History of Liverpool' (1852) by T Baines. The excellent book, 'The Sea Chaplains' published by the Oxford Illustrated Press and written by Gordon Taylor has become the definitive source for information about Naval Chaplains. Margaret Simey's 'Charity Rediscovered' reveals the last century's response to the need of the poor people of Liverpool and paints a vivid picture of society. A.R.B. Robinson (1987). has researched the life of Thring in his fascinating work entitled 'Chaplain on the Mersey' (1859 - 67). Another invaluable book was written in 1947 by Maurice R Kingsford entitled 'The Life and Influence of

William Henry Giles Kingston'; he also published 'The Mersey Mission to Seamen 1856-1956'. I am much indebted to J.C. Drummond and Anne Wilbraham's 'The Englishman's Food', published by Jonathan Cape and to my good friend, Doctor Eric Sherwood-Jones for his advice on much of the detail in the chapter 'Poor Jack'. E.L. Taplin's 'Liverpool Dockers and Seamen, 1870-1890', published by the University of Hull in 1974 is invaluable for details of the strikes in Liverpool. Another source for strike details was 'Strike 1911' by Harold Hickins, published in volume 113, 1961, of the Historical Society of Lancashire and Cheshire. Liverpool University Press published in 1992 John Belcham's 'Popular Politics, Riot and Labour, Essays in Liverpool History (1790-1940)'. Much information was also found in the archives of the Liverpool Post and Echo. Gladys Mary Coles's fascinating collection of prose and poetry in 'Both Sides of the River' (published by Headland of West Kirby in 1993) pointed the way to many sources of information. The Nugent Care Society carries on the work of its famous founder. The research of ship-board work-songs by Stan Hugil resulted in his book, 'Shanties from the Seven Seas'. Whilst many shanties are common knowledge, Stan has raised them to art-form and saved them for posterity. As far as possible sources have been acknowledged in the script and omissions are not intentional. The staff of the Liverpool Central Libraries Record Office and Local History Office helped with cheerful patience. Members of all the Welfare Societies and Organisations were ever helpful, although I hasten to add that opinions are my own. Captain Graham Grenfell performed computer miracles with the illustrations.

It is not possible to record the names of all the friends who produced snippets and articles from endless, often nameless, sources. But a special 'thank you' to Dorothy Tucker who provided the details of her husband's escapades during the last war. Captain Edward John Tucker was a friend and like so many is no longer with us. Also I thank Tim McCoy who gave of his time and his memories. So many Liverpool men were fortunate to have survived their war experiences and I suspect that far too many stories are lost and should have been recorded. Captain Bill Williams (Conway 1939 - 41) suggested the title for this book and gave me hours of his time and experience. The manuscript has been read and nautically prodded by Captain Len Holder and I am grateful to him and his wife Ann for their encouragement and for the on-going support of the committee of the Mersey Mission to Seamen, which enabled this book to be published. Each member of my family has buttressed my endeavours and, of course, D'rene has never failed me. The blemishes, mistakes, misjudgements and omissions are entirely mine... with apologies. Actually, I have thoroughly enjoyed the research and, above all, talking to so many Mersey Mariners who have remained good friends as the years have tumbled along.

My final thoughts are that each chapter deserves a book ... many exist ... and that so much more needs to be written.

A ship once arrived at Seattle and someone on the quayside shouted, 'Is there anyone aboard from Liverpool?' There came a prompt reply from the deck. 'How do you think we got here!' The Mersey Mariners are in most cases now old and gray, but without them the world would have been a lesser place. They deserve our thanks.

Bob Evans

Acknowledgements

Amongst those who contributed to, and supported, the Mersey Mission to Seafarers in the reprint of this edition of the book, special thanks are due to the following persons and organisations:

Atlantic Container Line Agencies (U.K.) Ltd
Bahr Behrend & Co. Ltd
Coastal Container Line Limited
Len and Ann Holder
Khong Shen Ping
Eric and Grace Knowles
David and Ann Lowry
Liverpool Pilots' Association
Liverpool Pilots' Association (Retired Division)
Liverpool Ship Owners' and Port Users' Association
Mersey Docks and Harbour Company
S. Norton & Co. Ltd
Alan Stimson
Wijsmuller Marine Ltd

The Mersey Mission to Seafarers also acknowledges the continuing support for its work by individuals and organisations, in particular Liverpool Sailors' Home Trust, NUMAST, King George's Fund for Sailors, the International Transport Workers' Federation, The Merchant Navy Welfare Board, The Shipwrecked Mariners' Society etc, and the many other individuals and organisations who support welfare work for seafarers through the Mersey Mission to Seafarers.

Portrait of Liverpool Jack

What do you fancy
You old shell-backed Scouser,
A bit of tit
Or the favourite
In the three-thirty at Catterick?

Saw you there in the Mission.
I sipped my coffee,
You thumbed the Daily Mirror,
Peering at pages
Over booze-red nose.

Your marlin-spiked fingers,
Wormed, and parcelled and served
The world over.
In Shanghai, Honolulu and Bombay,
They thrilled the girls
In the most gentle
Of sailors' manners,
Exploring secret parts
With climaxtic touch.

You wily man
With tanned skin of a rhinoceros,
Blackhead pitted,
What a wealth of experience!

John Curry

1.
Roots

You stand upon the highway of the sea
Where in ships, your children, come and go
In splendour at the full of every flow,
Bound to and from whatever ports may be.

John Masefield

When you fly over Liverpool, you look down upon a green city with its trees and parks, but you cannot ignore the Mersey. Its course is almost due north and south. The story of Liverpool evolved from the development of its waterfront which was to become a major port in Europe, creating a gateway into the world and a meeting place for the nations of the world. At the centre of that story were the seafarers, used and, more often, abused by all about them. No wonder in the last century he was called Poor Jack!

In Roman times, the Mersey was of little account and we had no harbour in Liverpool. The river was like a large lake with a small sea outlet and vast reaches of water stretching inland to Runcorn. The Ribble was the most important port in the area.

Probably the earliest mention of the River Mersey is in the reign of Ethelred in 1004. No-one is certain of the derivation of the name, but it might have a connection with the Kingdom of Mercia as the river formed the northern boundary.

Liverpool was in the hundred of West Derby which boasted six settlements and Liverpool was one of them. It would have been not much more than a small group of medieval serfs, living in hovels and fishing for survival in the creek or pool. 'Lever' was the word for rushes; hence, possibly, a 'pool of rushes', leverpool - Liverpool. However, these are only theories.

The probable founder of the port and borough of Liverpool was King John. The conquest of Ireland demanded a port to service the north. Bristol and Milford Haven were suitable for the attack on the south of Ireland, but as the Ribble was unusable and the Dee, which had been well used in Roman and Saxon times, was now too shallow for the transportation of troops, Shotwick on the Dee had been developed and a castle had been built to protect the area from the Welsh. However, Liverpool was about to be discovered.

In the year, 1206, King John visited Lancashire and on February 26th he was at Lancaster and on the 28th at Chester. This suggests that he probably passed through Liverpool. The result was that in the August of the following year the King entered into formal possession and presented a Charter to Henry Fitzwarin of Lancaster. The document was signed in Winchester, witnessed by Earls and barons and countersigned by the Archdeacon of Wales. The Charter stated that,

'... we have granted to all our faithful people who shall have taken burgages at Lytherpul, that they shall have all the liberties and free customs in the town of Lytherpul which any free borough on the sea hath in our land ...'.

Liverpool was launched.

The houses were probably built of oak frames and filled with wattle and clay and the oak would have come from the West Derby woods. A stone Town Hall was built for business to be transacted and also a Chapel of Ease to the mother Church at Walton. Meanwhile, commercially, use was made of Liverpool for shipping stores and troops to Ireland.

A new Charter was granted in 1229, at a cost of £6 13s 6d, by Henry III. John had created a free trade area, but twenty two years had passed and vested interests had taken over. Unsurprisingly, the burgesses wished to keep all the good things to themselves and they set up an exclusive and protectionist society. A closed guild was established. Duty was imposed upon the ships and a tax was even placed upon the seamen when they came ashore!

Between the years 1232 and 1237, Liverpool Castle was built in a prominent position with a slope down to the beach on three sides. On the north, a road ran from the Castle gate. The town was garrisoned and grew in importance

By the end of the century some 840 people lived in Liverpool. The Crown Rights were £10 per annum; Bristol was paying £266 13s 4d. Liverpool, at least, had started.

In the fourteenth century, Liverpool became a small medieval town with wind and water mills, a ferry across the Mersey, an annual fair and a weekly market.

The ferry was probably run by the monks at Birkenhead Priory. To call the ferry a wood fire would have been lit on the rocks ... 'to put up a boat smoke'.

The boat would have been made of wicker-work, a coracle, and would have required some faith by the travellers!

In 1335, six ships of war were impressed and, with a complement of soldiers and mariners, they were victualled with all that was essential for the King to remove any Scottish ships from the sea as he was intent on invading Scotland. The King paid the bills. In 1348, Liverpool even sent one ship to help with the siege of Calais.

The first mention of a mayor was in May 19th, 1356, when he was instructed by the King to invest £10 in land

> 'to encourage the performance of divine service for the souls of the faithful deceased in the Chapel of the Blessed Virgin Mary and St. Nicholas at Liverpool'.

The port continued to service ships for the war in Ireland; eighty ships of thirty tons and upwards were seized in other ports and sent to Liverpool.

By the middle of the fourteenth century Bubonic plague came to Cornwall and the West. This was called the Black Death and Liverpool was to be decimated. It was impossible to carry the bodies to the church at Walton, so the Bishop of Lichfield granted permission for a grave yard to be made around the Chapel of Our Lady and St. Nicholas. At least a third of the population died.

Yet another Charter was presented to the burgesses in the fifteenth century by Henry IV and this strengthened their monopoly. They controlled all the courts and dictated all punishments. The knightly families of Stanley of Lathom and Molyneaux of Sefton controlled the castles and the fortunes of the locality.

England was torn apart by war, pestilence and famine and no place suffered more than Lancashire. The Wars of the Roses resulted in untilled land and a falling population. So Liverpool lost trade. The eventual success of the White Rose increased the dynasty of the Stanleys and Molyneaux under Edward IV in 1461. The Stanleys held the Borough of Liverpool. The Molyneaux controlled the forests and parks of West Derby and the Constableship of the Castle of Liverpool.

In 1484, an unknown Richard Cook 'in consideration of the good and faithful service' was granted by Richard III:

'the ferry over the water of the Mersey between the town of Lythepole and the County of Chester for his life, without any account therfor to be rendered or anything therfor to be paid'.

However, when Henry VII secured the Duchy of Lancaster in 1485, Richard Cook promptly lost his rights and had to pay 60 shillings a year to the Crown.

These were the years of the great sea journeys of Christopher Columbus (1492) and John Cabot (1497) to the Americas and of ships finding the way to the Guinea Coasts of Africa.

Henry VIII paid special notice to Liverpool, not out of sympathy for the plight of the inhabitants, but because their contributions to the exchequer had fallen. A commission was appointed to investigate this state of affairs in 1515, but no record of the report exists.

Power was moving from the land and its feudal system into the hands of the burghers and the middle class. Above all, at this time, there was a growing demand for English wool and woollens.

'Villages decayed, tenants were evicted, commons closed', wrote Sir Thomas Moore in 1518. John Leland, the King's Antiquary, after a visit to Liverpool, wrote in his Journal in about 1535, that 'Lyrpole, alias Lyverpoole, a pavid Towne, hath but a chapel, Walton three miles off, not far from the se, is a Paroche Chirch. The King hath a Castelet and the Erle of Darbe a Stone House there. Irisch Marchountes cum much hither as a good Haven'. He writes about linen yarn spun in Ireland and brought to Liverpool to be woven in Manchester. This was the start of an industry, which eventually dominated Lancashire.

Liverpool was having a hard time. Dreadful epidemics struck in 1540, 1548 and 1558. The total population was probably 1,000 and over half died in the first two plagues. It seems likely that another two hundred died in 1558. No wonder the town was referred to as a 'poor and decayed' place!

In 1561, a tremendous hurricane destroyed the jetty and breakwater of the haven. Robert Corbett, the mayor, called a meeting on Sunday, 5th November, at which it was decided to build a new haven. On the Monday, one labourer went to the pool and began the work. On Tuesday, every house in Castle Street sent a labourer. On Wednesday, every house in Dale Street sent a man. The records continue.

> 'Thursday then next after the Juggler Street: with the More Street, Mylne Street, Chapell Street, every house sending a labourer and this order continued until St. Nicholas's Day then next after gratis'.

The total capital was 13s 9d.

It was estimated that twelve vessels belonged to the port with a total tonnage of 223, navigated by 75 seamen.

In 1567, a cockpit was erected at public expense and in 1576 horse races were established on the sea shore to be run on Ascension Day; one of the prizes was a silver bell presented by Mr Ed Torbock. Liverpool was looking up!

William Camden, in his first copy of 'Britannia', published in 1586, made this statement.

'From Warrington the Mersey grows broader, and soon after contracts itself again, but at last opens with a wide mouth very commodious for trade, and then runs into the sea, near Litherpoole, in Saxon Literpole, commonly Lirpoole, called (as 'tis thought) from the water spread like a fern there. It is the most convenient and frequented place for setting sail into Ireland'.

Trade was increasing. In 1570, the income of the Corporation was £20 14s 8d. In 1580, it had reached £86 13s 2d. The Liverpool custom dues in 1586 produced the sum of £272 3s 0d, whilst Chester, Conway and Beaumaris together yielded only £211 4s 8d.

In 1588, came the Spanish Armada and both Lancashire and Cheshire took a full patriotic share in the defence of the country. Beacons were prepared at Everton, Billinge and Rivington, ready to be lit and spread the alarm. The first news of the sailing of the Armada was brought to England by a Liverpool merchant and mariner, Humphrey Brooke, when he returned home from St. Jean de Luz in France.

The sixteenth century closed with the prospects of Liverpool much improved. Trade was increasing with Ireland and the Lancashire industries were beginning to expand. The revenue of the customs had grown and so had the population. But, the place was really still small and had changed but little over the past two hundred years.

No-one could really describe Liverpool at the start of the seventeenth century with any hopes of prosperity. However, it was to be a century of change. There were now twenty four ships with a total tonnage of 462; this had doubled in thirty years. Chester trailed behind with fifteen ships.

The Civil War found Liverpool divided with the majority of the council committed to the Royalists and the majority of the inhabitants favouring the Parliament. Mayor John Walker, with Royal consent, did his utmost to fortify the town with earthworks, gates, bars across the street and a ditch all round, twelve yards wide and three yards deep. In 1642, a small garrison of Royalists occupied the castle.

Wigan fell to the Parliamentarians on Easter Eve, 1643, but they were then defeated by the Earl of Derby at Stockton Heath, a mile south of Warrington. The respite was short. The Royalists were forced to retreat to Liverpool Castle and failed to retain it. So, Liverpool came under martial law and was controlled by the Parliamentary forces.

The Parliamentary Governor of Liverpool was Colonel John Moore and, mainly at his expense, ships were fitted out to cruise against the enemy, to blockade Dublin and to cut off the Royalist supplies for their army in Ireland.

Early in 1644, Prince Rupert made his headquarters in Everton Village, erected his batteries in Lime Street and proceeded to bombard the castle for eighteen days. Colonel Moore, realising that he could not hold on much longer, embarked most of his men in ships and escaped. Prince Rupert stayed for less than a week and then departed to York. A few days later Moore was back, the Royalists mutinied, took their own officers and surrendered. The Civil War for the people of Liverpool was over.

Colonel Thomas Birch was appointed Parliamentary Governor and promptly moved into the castle. The ferry boats were restored to the Corporation and relief was sought from the Parliament to restore the town and support the widows and orphans. Parliament allowed five hundred tons of timber for the repair of ruined houses to be taken from the woods of the neighbouring gentry, with lead from the ruins of Lathom House, the home of the Earl of Derby. The Rector of Walton, who was a Royalist, had his tithes sequestrated and one hundred pounds was set aside to be used in Liverpool.

In 1651, the Royalists made a last effort in Lancashire under the Earl of Derby. Cromwell was supreme and encouraged Colonel Thomas Birch to send ships from the Mersey to cut off the supplies and to prevent the arrival of the Earl of Derby from the Isle of Man. At last, at the Battle of Wigan, the Royalists were finally routed, the Civil War in Lancashire was really over. Cromwell remained in control for the next nine years

The first attempt at street lighting is recorded in 1654.

> 'Two lanterns, with two candles burning every night in the dark moon, be set at the High Cross and at the White Cross ... in every night till past eight of the clock.'

That same year, the fortifications were taken down, the gates removed, the mud walls levelled and Dale Street bridge repaired. During the Commonwealth, the town became a parish in its own right. However, the military governor was not popular. There were objections to the presence of the soldiers. After eleven years, the restoration of Charles II in 1660 was welcomed.

Manufacturing was increasing in Lancashire and Yorkshire, foreign trade was growing and the facilities of the Mersey were ready for development. By the close of the century, the port would possess a third of the trade of the country and pay the King upwards of £50,000 a year in customs.

Building increased, new roads were laid on the estate of Edward Moore (son of John Moore) and named Fenwick Street and James Street. Around this time a sugar baker from London built a four storey building to boil and dry sugar and Liverpool quickly became the sugar refining centre in the country. This naturally led to trade with Barbados. Linen and butter and other produce were taken to the West Indies in return for sugar and tobacco. In addition, the coal and pottery produced in Whiston and Prescot became part of the export trade.

The Sailors' Church

By 1670, Liverpool boasted sixty five ships, but the total tonnage was only 2,600. A great help was the development of Manchester, especially the production of cotton cloth. West Indies cotton came into Liverpool and Lancashire became the centre for the cotton trade. Apart from the Parish Church of Our Lady and St Nicholas, the Corporation built St Peter's to meet the needs of the growing population. A new Town Hall was built in 1673. Liverpool was coming of age with a population of some five thousand.

At the end of the seventeenth century, the seaward approach to Liverpool was a maze of marsh and shifting shoals; the landward approach was an equal confusion of marsh and heath. The tide rose and fell some thirty feet, with strong currents and frequent gales, but the height of the tide allowed ships to reach the Pool. However, the port was not able to meet the new demands of the ships. Action was required, if the trade with the Americas and West Africa was to flourish

Thomas Steers was brought from London to survey the land for a dock in the Pool. Steers proposed to enclose the Pool with a sea wall and the plan was approved by Parliament in 1709. Ten years passed before the scheme was completed. This new dock had room for over eighty ships and was a success. This appears to have been the first wet dock built in England; the first dock constructed in London was in 1802 ... a century after Liverpool! A new Custom House was built. Next came Salthouse Dock in 1753 to handle the Cheshire salt trade.

These were the first commercial docks in Britain and the town grew around these ventures. A charity school, the Bluecoat Hospital, was created. The new docks attracted ancillary trade ... sugar refineries, copper works, salt works, timber yards and ship building.

Steers first dock was eventually filled in to provide the new site for the Custom House, which did not survive the Second World War. In a comparatively short time, the Liverpool docks had an unbroken sea frontage of granite for seven miles, a water area of 324 acres and a lineal quayage of 22 miles; on the Cheshire side, the Birkenhead docks contained 159 acres of water area and a lineal quayage of nine miles.

After 1750, there was a dramatic increase in tonnage in Liverpool. Above all, it was the presence of salt, which proved a ready export to America, that was to dominate trade for a century. Coal was essential to the growing industries and was readily available, eventually becoming a large export trade in its own right. So, there was established a cycle of sugar and tobacco imports balancing coal and salt exports. This was a solid basis for the future of the port.

Transport was the catalyst ... the Leeds and Liverpool Canal, the Manchester Canal, the Shropshire Union to Birmingham and the Grand Canal. All these made available the coal from Lancashire, the salt of Cheshire, the coal and iron of South Yorkshire, the textiles of Manchester and the West Riding, the pottery of Staffordshire and the hardware of Birmingham. Liverpool was the only port to enjoy such wealth from its hinterland.

At the start of the nineteenth century, the Rev. James Aspinall, M.A., the Vicar of St. Michael's in the City and of St. Luke's, wrote under the name of An Old Stager and gave a pen picture of the Liverpool of his childhood.

'The docks ended with George's at one extremity and the Queen's at the other. There was a battery near the latter and another near the former. Farther north was a large fort of some thirty guns, and halfway towards Bootle, a smaller one with nine. The town on one side hardly extended beyond Colquitt-street. The greater part of Upper Duke-street was not built. Cornwallis-street, the large house which Mr. Morall erected, the ground on which St. Michael's Church stands, all were fields at the time of which we speak. There was a picturesque-looking mill at the top end of Duke-street, and behind Rodney-street we had a narrow lane, with a high bank overgrown with roses. Russell-street, Seymour-street, and all beyond were still free from bricks. Lime-street was bounded by a field, in which many a time we watched rough lads chasing cocks on Shrove Tuesday for a prize.'

At the start of the nineteenth century, the roads were in a sad state. The canals were the only answer. In time the roads were improved and a twenty four hour coach service was established between Liverpool and London. That was not fast enough. The Liverpool to Manchester railway was started in 1826 and finished in 1830, mainly at the request of the Liverpool corn merchants. The canals, the roads and the railways really expanded to cope with the shipping industry ... industry it had become!

There was American and, especially, Canadian timber, West Indian sugar and, above all, Virginian tobacco ... all these dominated the evolving shipping industry. Parliament abolished the East India Company monopoly in 1813 and that of the China trade in 1833. Shipping companies came into being. Cunard instituted in 1840 the first regular steamer across the Atlantic. Pacific Steam Navigation Company opened trade with South America. John Holt, the Guinea Coast Line, worked the rivers of Nigeria. The Brocklebank Line carried tobacco and traded East and West. The Ocean Steamship Company (the Blue Funnel Line) was established in 1865 and this led to trade with the Far East and eventually with Australia.

Charles Booth was a corn merchant in Warrington and his sons Alfred and Charles opened up the trade with Brazil. John Bibby started with ships sailing from Parkgate to Dublin, but developed trade to Alexandria and then across the North Atlantic. The move from sail to iron and steam led to a great growth of shipping companies with the result that, by the end of the century, Liverpool ships traded with almost every corner of the five continents.

The Custom House

At the centre of the Liverpool scene are the now famous Liver Building, the Cunard Building and the Mersey Docks and Harbour Company Building and, of course, the Landing Stage. The buildings belong to the turn of this century and the stage was built first.

In the 1830's there had been two little stages in use, one for river traffic and another for channel·steamers, but neither had been more than sixty feet in length. They were obviously too small and in 1846 the George's stage was completed and moored into position.

The George's stage was five hundred feet long and, christened the Leviathan of the Mersey, it was regarded as one of the wonders of the age. But about ten years later the Prince's stage was produced, one thousand and two feet in length and eighty-two feet in width. This was a great advance although at low tide the slope of the bridges was so steep that the horses could not use the stages. The George's basin was in between these two stages and as it had no lock gates, it was the ideal refuge for small craft to sit on the mud until the next tide.

The ultimate plan was to fill in the basin and join the two stages together with a new piece about five hundred feet long. This was when a workman fixing the gas pipes under the stage lit a candle and the complete stage was destroyed.

Benjamin Blower in 1878 tells the story.

> 'The Landing stage in its present magnificence is the outcome of the experience gained through many previous structures. It is a large open deck 2063 feet long and 80 broad; built on pontoons, and connected with the pier by seven bridges. When nearly completed, and the townspeople were looking forward to a grand gala day at the opening, on July 28 1874, it was accidentally set on fire by a gas-fitter, who was working underneath. Burning on the under surface, the stage was in flames from one end to the other in an incredibly short space of time. So great was the smoke that a gentlemen who lived at Speke, nine miles off, mounted his horse, and rode to Liverpool, thinking the town was all in flames. The building ... was in two hours reduced to a mass of charred ruins. The estimated damage was £250,000. It has now risen again like a Phoenix out of its ashes.
>
> 'Throughout the day, there are multitudes of passers over, from the gayest lady, to the veriest ragged urchin who can pay his penny. Also, early and late can be seen the care-encumbered merchant, and the wild speculators. Then on the north end are

groups of emigrants, fathers and mothers with anxious countenances, taking care of their goods and chattels; while the children play with the bright new tin cans provided for the voyage. Friends are parting, who know that thousands of miles of 'weary waves' will intervene ere they meet again. A mother with brim-full heart is parting with her Sailor Boy. Now hurry down the busy voyagers, with piles of luggage, to be conveyed by the tenders, to the ocean steamers, waiting for the tide. The time of sailing has at length arrived; and there is a tear in the stout-hearted sailor's eye, as he waves his adieu to his not less sorrowful friends ashore.

'There are excellent refreshment rooms, sheds for shelter from the weather, places for left luggage, etc, etc.

'Simpson's Bowl. During the recent famine in India, Mr. Simpson, the manager, conceived the happy idea of placing an open bowl on the stage, where the passer-by may cast in his mite. The benevolent effort succeeded beyond all expectations. In thirty-one days £203 1s.3d. was dropped in.

'Now again the 'Bowl' has done good service for the poor distressed Miners of South Wales; not only does it contain money in all forms, both papers and coin, but around it are heaped boxes, bales, and bundles containing all descriptions of articles of food and clothing. It was closed March 3, 1878, having collected money and goods to the value of £1723 18s. 3/d.'

The replacement stage remained until 1975 and undulated in all weathers for a hundred years. Finally modern technology arrived and a shorter cellular structure replaced it. Sadly in February 1976, there was a Force Ten gale and the technological wonder sunk!

The rise and decline of the Liverpool landing stages almost exactly reflect the stature of the port. Today the river seems almost devoid of shipping as the vessels are handled in Royal Seaforth docks, away from the centre of the city and the present stage remains to service the 'ferry across the Mersey'.

Out of these roots evolved the need to care for the seafarer, both to protect him from himself and from those who tried to exploit him. A Shipping Bill in 1850 controlled the shipping and discharge of crews. In 1851, Schools for Nautical Instruction were opened and the following year the Board of Trade adopted and expanded the scheme. Much was to follow. This path of caring was also taken up by the Churches and Seafaring Charities on Merseyside. The record of this care is the story of the Port of Liverpool, the ships, the sailors and the people. It is a story of a waterfront ... but, above all, the tale the Mersey Mariners.

2.
The Early Chaplains

'The same God you have at shore is ours at sea.'

Seamen's Protestation 1642

No-one can argue that when Paul in about the year 60 'broke bread' aboard ship, he might well be regarded as the first Christian to minister to seafarers. Occasional references to chaplains involved in the Crusades and thereafter indicate that they were attached to particular ships, but not on any regular basis. A naval fleet, as such, did not exist until the middle of the sixteenth century. However, records suggest that a clergyman might be found aboard vessels on their voyages of discovery.

We read that in 1147, when an expedition left Dartmouth for Lisbon in the reign of King Stephen, one of the articles of agreement was 'That on board each ship shall be a priest, and the same observances as in parishes on shore.'

The explorers of the New World and the fleet which beat the Spanish Armada made the daily service of Almighty God the first article of agreement with crews.

Sebastian Cabota, Governor of the Company of Merchant Adventurers, in 1553 gave instructions to the captains:

'... that Morning and Evening Prayer, with other common services appointed by the King's Majestie, and lawes of this realm, to be read and saide in every ship dayly by the Minister in the Admirall, and the marchant, or some other person learned in other ships, and the Bible or paraphrases to be read devoutly and Christianly to God's honour, and for his grace to be obtained, and had by humble and heartie praier of the Navigants accordingly.'

In 1578, on his third voyage of discovery, the articles of Captain Martyn Frobisher began:

> 'Imprimus ... to banish swearinge, dice, cardes playinge and all filthie talk, and to serve God twice a daie with the ordinaire service usuall in the Church of England.'

When the Puritan Government of Oliver Cromwell came into power, the Book of Common Prayer was banished from public or private use, whether on land or sea. However, the sailors refused to do without it; so Parliament was forced to issue a 'Supply of Prayers for the ships of this kingdom that want Ministers to pray with them.' This supply of prayers was proved to be mainly unsuitable as they really dealt with politics and little else.

This Prayer Book probably was not really used very much aboard ships, so the abolition of the Book of Common Prayer by Cromwell in reality led to the cessation of Divine Service altogether.

The Seamen's protestation of 1642 during the Civil War makes a stand for their rights as Christians.

> 'Be pleased to understand; although we have no churches, we say our prayers as well as you; and the same God you have at shore is ours at sea: whom we will serve, although not so decently as we would, being for the most part of our daies restrained from a church, to dwell upon the seas for your better securitie.'
>
> (G. Penn, The Memorials of Sir William Penn, 1833.)

Samuel Pepys in 1673 organised an Act of Parliament 'For the Regulation and Better Government of His Majesty's Ships at Sea' ... and the opening article was:

> 'First, all Commanders, Captains and other Officers at Sea, shall cause the Public Worship of Almighty God according to the Liturgy of the Church of England, to be solemnly, orderly and reverently performed in their respective ships; and the Prayers and Preaching by the respective Chaplains in Holy Orders of the respective ships be performed diligently; and that the Lord's Day be observed according to Law.'
>
> (Kealy's Chaplains of the Royal Navy 1626 - 1903.)

The story of Naval Chaplains is well recorded by Gordon Taylor in his excellent book 'The Sea Chaplains'. A quotation speaks for all the men who have served in the Royal Navy as Chaplains. It was 1941, when the *Prince of Wales* and the *Hood* were about to engage the German battleship *Bismark* and the cruiser *Prinz Eugen*. This is the account of the episode.

> "We were waiting for the order to fire" said one young man. "We knew it would come at any moment and we were ready. Then,

instead of the order, we heard the Padre reading a prayer. But we got the order to fire soon after."

'I had already heard that story from the Chaplain, the Rev. W.G. Parker. Just before action was joined he was called to the bridge by Captain Leach.

"Padre, we are going into action," said the Captain, "and we shall need help. I want you to read a prayer to the ship's company. Can you remember that prayer which begins, 'O God, thou knowest how busy I am ... ?"

"Yes, sir," replied the Padre. "It's called Sir Jacob Astley's prayer before Edgehill, and I have the words in my cabin."

"Go, then, and fetch it quickly," said the Captain, "There's not much time."

'While the battleship, steaming into action, was taut with expectancy, every nerve stretched to meet the explosion of the fourteen-inch guns, instead of the order to fire there came to every corner of the ship, from the engine-room to crow's nest, the sound of the Chaplain's voice, saying:

"O Lord, Thou knowest how busy we must be today, if we forget Thee, do not Thou forget us; for Christ's sake. Amen".

'Then the guns fired.'

It appears that Acts of Worship aboard merchant ships were not unusual and some vessels carried chaplains. The Society for the Propagation of the Gospel, founded in 1701, included instructions that missionaries were to say the Daily Service. However, by the nineteenth century, the Mercantile Marine had almost dropped the custom.

Chaplains aboard merchant ships became almost non-existent, until a number of British Companies in recent years appointed chaplains to minister on the cruise-ships. I was asked to serve a number of occasions in this way by Canadian Pacific and P and O. There were fourteen passenger ships calling into Liverpool when I started my ministry in the port and I serviced all the altars aboard; this enabled travelling priests to celebrate communion, but the ship's captain always conducted the main public service each Sunday at sea.

The idea that captains were able to perform marriages aboard their vessels probably arose from the liaisons between young people on the overlong voyages. A public acknowledgement before the captain that a couple wished to be recognised as 'man and wife' would be seen as an actual marriage ... to be legalised when on shore.

The real caring for the seafarer by the churches and other bodies developed as a shore-based operation, not just in Liverpool but in other ports. This did not begin in earnest until the start of the nineteenth century. There is a need to look at the work in other ports in order to put Liverpool into perspective.

In 1812, a Non-Conformist Captain of a Tyne coal carrying ship inaugurated services for his own crew on their trips to London. He invited other crews, alongside in the Thames, to join him in worship. This initiative led to the work of the Non-Conformists in 1819 and that developed into the British and Foreign Sailors' Society in 1833.

The man who did the most for seafarers in the nineteenth century was without doubt the Baptist Minister, the Reverend George Charles Smith. His achievements are remarkable ... the first floating chapel for sailors was established in 1819 on the Thames; the first Mariners' Church (1824), the first asylum for destitute seamen (1826), the first Temperance Society in England (1828), the first Sailors' Home (1829). Much more was achieved by this remarkable man, including the editing of The Sailors' Magazine (1827). His influence is examined more closely in the chapter on the Gordon Smith Institute. He was a great man.

The Non-Conformists inaugurated the Liverpool Seamen's Friend Society on the 12th September, 1820. This was to lead eventually to the creation in Liverpool of the Gordon Smith Institute in 1900.

A number of men are essential to the telling of this story ... Elliot, Ashley, Childs, Scoresby and Kingston ... and all influenced what was to happen in Liverpool.

Captain Robert James Elliot, R.N., worked in the Sailors' Home in Dock Street in the East End of London from 1827 until 1845. His main task was to visit ships and his main objective was to find crews and place them aboard ships himself and thus safeguard the seafarer from exploitation. His opponents called him a 'crimp' and he received many threats to his life, but he was successful and did much to clean up the port of London.

The next person of influence was the Reverend Doctor John Ashley. The story of his initiative has almost become a legend. In 1835 he returned from work in Ireland and went on holiday to Clevedon in Somerset before taking up his new parish. The story goes that with his son he was looking across to Wales at the islands of Steep Holme and Flat Holme in the Bristol Channel and the child is reputed to have asked: "How do the people there go to Church?" That question was to be answered by Ashley by his actions. Apparently, Ashley was to visit those islands a number of times afterwards in order to minister to the light-keepers and the farmers.

My first real contact with the Missions to Seamen was in 1954 on a visit to Flatholm with the Padre from Cardiff. We sailed from Barry Dock. The welcome from the lighthouse keepers was tremendous and without doubt this was the event which sparked my involvement with the care of the seafarer.

When Ashley visited the islands, he counted over four hundred vessels anchored off the Welsh coast. On his first visit to one of these waiting ships, he was appalled at the conditions and much cheered by the welcome that he was given. As a result he abandoned his new parish and decided to devote his time to this work in the Bristol Channel.

Fortunately he had private means from a family plantation in the West Indies and bought a cutter, called *Eirene* (peace), fitted her with a chapel, hired a crew and began his work in the Bristol Channel.

In 1837, Ashley wrote to the Archbishop of Canterbury, and was advised to found the Bristol Channel Mission; in 1845 this was renamed the Bristol Channel Seamen's Mission. Sadly this Mission was not viable, lacking financial support in spite of Ashley's remarkable work. In 1850, Ashley's health broke and the Mission closed. He had visited some fourteen thousand ships, sold five thousand Bibles and established a lending library. It had been a fantastic achievement.

The next important name was the Reverend T.C. Childs, who worked in Plymouth from 1846 to 1852, calling on every emigrant ship. Childs, like Ashley, also financed himself until the Society for the Promotion of Christian Knowledge helped him with a grant. He did not form a Mission Society in Plymouth, but informally depended upon friends and voluntary help. S.P.C.K., undoubtedly inspired by Childs, was to appoint a chaplain to work in Liverpool in 1849 in order to visit the emigrant-carrying ships in the port.

Perhaps the greatest contribution of Childs was his friendship with W.H.G. Kingston and his appeal to Kingston 'to endeavour to form a Society in London' ... this request was to have a direct impact upon Liverpool.

William H.G. Kingston was brought up in Oporto and as his father was the head of a a firm, shipping port wine, he quickly made contact with the seafarer. By the age of nine he had crossed the Bay of Biscay six times. His love of the sea led him to write stories. 'Peter the Whaler' was regarded highly when it was first produced and many such tales were to follow. This was the man who was to found the Mersey Mission to Seamen.

William Kingston led the campaign to create a national society and thus co-ordinate the activities which already existed in various ports. Kingston became the Honorary Secretary of the Missions to Seamen Afloat, at Home and Abroad. The first meeting of this Society was in London on the 20th February 1856. That same year he was to visit Liverpool.

Much had already been achieved in Liverpool. As we discovered the Non-Conformists were the first to begin working on the Mersey. The Liverpool Seamen's Friend Society and Bethel Union had been founded on the 12th September, 1820. They established a Floating Chapel, the two-decked ship '*The William*'. In 1900 this old Society was to build the Gordon Smith Institute and that particular work will have a chapter to itself.

However, long before Kingston was to come to Liverpool, the Church of England had not been idle on Merseyside. The first Church of England Chaplain in Liverpool was the Reverend Dr. William Scoresby, M.A., D.D., F.R.S. (1789 - 1857).

(Left) William Scoresby, Chaplain, 1927-32
(Right) The Scoresby Stamps R.R.S. William Scoresby (1926-46)

18

At the age of eleven, he had run away to sea on his father's ship. He was to become a fine sea-captain and an Arctic explorer. Moreover, he became a scientist whose writings were translated into many languages. There has even been a Falkland Island stamp with an illustration of the Royal Research ship, *'The William Scoresby'*. He was elected Fellow of the Royal Societies of England and Scotland; and Cambridge honoured him as Doctor of Divinity.

Scoresby gave up all that exciting life in order to be ordained. After a brief curacy in Bridlington, he came to Liverpool to found a Mariners' Church in May, 1827. Obviously, the movement to establish work amongst seafarers in Liverpool had been under way for some time. When asked to take up the post he replied:

"I cannot but feel that there seems to be drawing of me to that great object; my early habits of life, my intimate knowledge with the sailor with his habits of thought, prejudices, language, and possessions, my admission into Holy Orders at such a season - and all seem to me as many links of a chain connecting me with the Mariners' Church."

In 1826, the Government had presented to Liverpool an old ship-of-the-line, *H.M.S. Tees,* which had seen action with Nelson and was once commanded by Captain Marryat, the author of 'Mr. Midshipman Easy', for use as a Mariners' Floating Church. The *Tees* had been towed from Plymouth to Liverpool by H.M.Frigate *Pyramus* (42 guns) in the previous November and was moored in George's Dock.

In the Liverpool Chronicle of 12th May, 1827, had appeared the following notice:

'His Majesty's Frigate Tees having been fitted up for the Floating Church for the accommodation of Seafaring People, etc., is to be opened on Thursday, 17th May, on which occasion seats will be reserved for the subscribers, and the remainder will be thrown open to the public at large. Divine Service will commence at Twelve o'clock. N.B. The Tees is moored at the South West corner of George's Dock.'

The address was given by the Reverend R.P. Buddicom, A.M., F.A.S., the Minister of St. George's Church, Everton. As befitted the age, the sermon was dramatically long and was well laced with 'hell-fire and brimstone'. The text was innocuous enough ... 'Hast Thou not reserved a blessing for me?' He then described the seafarers of the day.

'They are engaged in a profession habitually conversant with peril and death. They walk continually on the very confines of eternity.

Waves and storms, rocks and quicksands, climate and battle, often summon them, with awful suddenness, to meet their God.'

Buddicom next described the sins of the flesh and talked of the men who are 'conversant with ribaldry, profaneness and infidelity.' There was much more on that theme.

At last, he came to the new minister, Scoresby, and made much of the need for the Established Church to support the seafarer. There follows a quotation from Scoresby's 'Journal of a Voyage to the Northern Whale Fishery', published in 1822. Scoresby stated 'that religion, when real, gives confidence and courage to the sailor, rather than destroys his hardihood and bravery.'

Finally, Buddicom mentioned that the preparation of the ship cost at least £800 and '... of this sum, £500 has been raised and paid.' I suspect that most of the congregation would have felt that Scoresby might have been better placed to give the address ... he was an internationally known character. Unsurprisingly, he was to be very successful in his short ministry on Merseyside.

Sadly, Scoresby has left little information about his time in Liverpool, except to indicate that he was much concerned with 'visits to the extensive docks in order to make myself acquainted, as far as circumstances allowed, with the numerous captains frequenting this port.' His preaching was very much for the seafarer and based upon his experiences. His wife proved a problem. 'She had only been a few months in Liverpool, when her ordinary health altogether gave way, and was only recruited, under the divine blessing, by a summer's residence in Ireland.' Scoresby adds that during his last year in the Mariners' Church, his wife was to spend all her time in Ireland.

In 1831, Scoresby wrote a book entitled 'Discourses to Seamen'. In the preface are these words.

' ... as but little suitable accommodation is to be found in our Churches and Chapels for the numerous seamen frequenting the more considerable seaports - the providing of Churches, and other places of Worship, expressly for them, has become a characteristic feature in the operations of the various Societies established for their spiritual benefit. In the bestowment of this boon of gratitude, the Dissenters of Britain had the distinguished honour of taking the lead, and through their vigorous exertions, with the co-operation, in many instances, of members of the Established Church, several 'Arks', or 'Floating Chapels', were early fitted up for the use of Seamen.

'The first place of worship appointed for this purpose, under the form and discipline of the Established Church, was the 'Episcopal Floating Chapel' in Dublin; next followed the 'Mariners' Church' at Liverpool, with similar institutions in Hull, Plymouth, London, and Cork.'

Scoresby was to remain as Chaplain in the Mariners' Church for only five years, but a man of his standing must have made a great impression and certainly he paved the way for the work which lay ahead. He established the need for the chaplain to visit the seafarer aboard his ship and the need to inform the public of the plight of so many of these men. These priorities have not changed today.

Interior of the Mariners' Church

Scoresby was to continue his researches and in 1856 he made a voyage to Australia on the steamer *Royal Charter*. He died in 1857. His name stands out firmly in the annals of Arctic and Antarctic research.

Scoresby was almost impossible to replace. His successor was the Reverend William Maynard. He worked for forty years in the docks. As might be expected, the influence of the Mariners' Church declined with the departure of Scoresby, but Maynard worked assiduously amongst the seafarers as this extract from the Mersey Mission Records reveals. Maynard produced a list of 'Boarding Houses that I can with some degree of confidence recommend as suitable for any seaman who wishes to be comfortably and honestly dealt with.' Obviously, Maynard, as an Anglican

Chaplain, was to work with the Mersey Mission to Seamen, which was to be founded some twenty years after he had started. Maynard died in January, 1875. His contribution was almost totally under-estimated.

In 1879 the Trustees of the Mariners' Church begged 'to hand over to the Mission (Mersey Mission to Seamen) the Floating Church now lying in the Birkenhead Docks.' We assume that this was done and that, as it had fallen into disrepair, the Floating Church was then sold to be broken up.

There can be no doubt that the Mariners' Church owed its allegiance to Church of England. Gore's Directory of Liverpool for 1859 states:

'Mariners' Church Society. Established 1826. Bishop of Chester, Patron; Adam Hodgson, Vice-President. The Rector of Liverpool, T.B. Horsfall, M.P., C.S. Parker, Adam Hodgson and Thomas Forsyth, Esq., Trustees. Mr. Thomas Tyrer, Secretary; the Reverend W. Maynard, Chaplain; the Reverend W. Maynard and Thomas D. Anderson, Secretaries.'

There are conflicting statements about the end of the *Tees*. One account refers to her sinking in the George's Dock, 7th June, 1872. Yet, the Mariners' Church Society in 1879 talks of '... the Floating Church lying in Birkenhead Docks.'

Whilst, as we shall see, the Mersey Mission to Seamen was formally founded in 1856, it is obvious that the continuity of Church of England's care for seafarers on Merseyside goes back to 1826 and to the Mariners' Church Society and to the name of Scoresby.

An article in Sea Breezes (1946) tells a little more about that Mariners' Church.

'The interior was fitted with pews and benches, all regulation style; a powerful little organ, and what was surely most appropriate on a ship, a three-decker pulpit, the upper portion high enough to command the gallery above.'

A picture of the interior is also printed and the article continues:

'It is just over seventy years since the gentleman who lent me the pictures ceased his connection with the church, that being but a few months before she sank on June 7th, 1872, (sic) after 45 years of unique service. Although built of prime English oak she suffered very seriously from dry rot in her old age.

'Captain T. Mercer Griffiths told the story that in 1865, when he was a cadet on the Conway, the boys used to be taken regularly to the Cornwallis Street Baths and he, with one or two others, would slip away and go on board the Mariners' Church, as they were fond of the old caretaker. He was a most affable individual and often entertained them with exciting stories about Collingwood and Nelson. Now and then he would show them a handful of 'fungus', as he designated the dry rot from the hull below. He used to tell them tales of the pumping which had to be done and he predicted for the ancient maritime warrior an untimely end. Help at the pumps could be readily obtained from willing outsiders, whose reward would be a stiff 'peg' of something warm and comfortable from one of a solid block of seven adjoining public houses which, on the other side of the road, faced this strange, floating religious edifice.

'The old ship,' says another authority,

'was nicknamed the 'flogging' Tees by the sailors of those days, on account of the severe treatment meted out to her Jack Tars for very trivial offences by the popular novelist and gallant sailor, Captain Marryat. The caretaker, 'old Joe', lived in the schoolroom at the corner of Irwell Street and Mann Island. For a fee of one penny he would allow trippers to inspect a portion of the church, which was increased to twopence if they viewed the more historic parts, the money being devoted to the upkeep of the day and Sunday schools.'

'Opposite the Mariners' Church were the seven notorious public houses. These second-rate taverns, at one time amongst the chief haunts of the Press Gang, have only recently been demolished in order that the Dock Board could erect, in their stead, a fine modern building.'

The editor of Sea Breezes does not reveal who the author, T.E.E., was or his sources.

W.H.G. Kingston, having founded the Missions to Seamen in London in the February of 1856, continued to extend his vision. He was a busy man. From his pamphlet, 'A Cruise on the Mersey', we read that he set about organising similar Missions to Seamen in Dublin, Kingstown, Cork, Queenstown, Milford Haven and Liverpool. The nucleus of the work in these ports was obviously always there and Kingston must have organised ahead of his visits to meet the people with influence. The final words of the pamphlet 'Cruise on the Mersey' reveals the intention.

'We have arranged also a flag with an appropriate device. On the public it depends with God's Grace how soon that banner may be seen flying in every port and roadstead of the Kingdom. Let us hope that in many a one it may be hoisted ere this summer be over.'

The figure on the flag was meant to represent the Angel of Revelation, Chapter 14, verse 6. 'And I saw another angel fly in the midst of heaven, having the everlasting gospel to preach unto them that dwell on the earth, and to every nation; and kindred, and tongue, and people.'

Kingston wasted no time on his journeys. An extract from his wife's diary, dated December 3rd 1856, tells the story well.

'Half an hour after came William from London and Fleetwood, and Belfast and Newry and Dublin, and Limerick and Cork - very cold and hungry and well and merry - thawed him and fed him.'

His whirlwind visit to Liverpool was effective! From Mrs Kingston's diary, we read that he was in London on Friday, 21st November 1856, and spent Saturday and Sunday in Liverpool before departing for Ireland on the Monday. It was long enough to found the Mersey Mission to Seamen. A provisional committee was elected on the Saturday and the first official meeting of the Committee was called for Monday 24th, November.

In the middle of this organising, Kingston found time for his 'Cruise on the Mersey'.

'At about three o'clock the Rev. J.N. Gillman and I, with a bag full of tracts in English, Spanish, Portuguese, French, Italian, and Greek accompanied by the Rev. J. Welsh (S.P.C.K, Emigration Chaplain) embarked from Liverpool in Mr. Cotesworth's boat, with two hands, and pulled for the Boanerges, a large ship of 1,350 tons, lying off the west end of the town.' Kingston then goes on to describe the adventures of that afternoon with many stories.

'The first to whom I spoke was a Spaniard. Opening my bag I offered him some Spanish tracts. It was pleasant to see the eager way in which he accepted them. He instantly went under the poop by himself, and began to read them. Near him stood another swarthy man at work. Thinking that he also was a Spaniard, I offered him some Spanish tracts.

"No understand", he replied, after looking at them intently.

"Of what nation are you then?", I asked.

"Me Grego", he answered.

"Here, here then", I replied, diving into my bag and producing some Greek tracts. "How do you like these?"

"Good, good, very good", he exclaimed.'

On the Sunday morning before another day on the river, Kingston attended the Mariners' Church, which had been founded by Scoresby and still sat in George's Dock.

'I found Mr. Maynard, the Chaplain, and begged him to give me some printed notices of the church and school to put on board the ships we might visit. He took me over the church, once a 28-gun ship. The hold makes the body, the gun deck with the centre cut out forms a gallery, with a very high skylight, which ventilates it well. There is a second gallery in the fore and after part, while the captain's cabin makes the vestry. It is very neatly painted in grained wood; nothing indeed could be better: yet more landsmen than sailors frequent it.'

His conclusion was simple.

'One immediate result of our cruise was the evidence we were able to offer of the abundance of work which a chaplain might obtain on the waters of the Mersey. I say a chaplain, but I believe that six chaplains and six colporteurs, with as many boats, would find ample scope for their ministrations among the seafaring population on the River Mersey and its banks.'

Kingston made it quite clear that he wished to work with the Mariners' Church. Not only had he worshiped there on the Sunday of his Liverpool visit, but he had also asked Maynard for notices to place aboard the ships during his 'Cruise on the Mersey'. With hindsight, it is surprising that the Mariners' Church, which was firmly a Church of England foundation, had not been formally merged with the Mersey Mission to Seamen in 1856.

This was the man who founded the Mersey Mission in one week end. It was not surprising that exactly one hundred years later, the Mission's new headquarters in James Street was named Kingston House ... although it might with almost equal justification have been called Scoresby House!

Whilst Elliot and Ashley and Child and Kingston led to the formation of what was to become the Mersey Mission to Seamen, other work in the port was well under way.

Most important of all on Merseyside, the Liverpool Sailors' Home pioneered much of the early caring for the seafarers and this work was to be well supported by the Mersey Mission to Seamen, the Gordon Smith Institute, the Apostleship of the Sea and the Scandinavian Churches. This is a story which started at the beginning of the nineteenth century and continues and will flourish into the twenty-first century.

3.
The Gordon Smith Institute

Will your anchor hold in the storms of life,
When the clouds unfold their wings of strife?
When the strong tides lift, and the cables strain,
Will your anchor drift, or firm remain?

Few people realised that the Society which built the Gordon Smith Institute for Seamen in Paradise Street was actually founded in 1820, just five years after the Battle of Waterloo. It was the second oldest Society of its kind in Britain, the oldest being the British Sailors' Society in London, which was founded in 1818. The Liverpool Society was formed to promote 'the present comfort and future happiness of seamen and their families and of other persons connected with shipping.' The work was carried out in a number of centres in the dock area in Liverpool. In 1881 the Committee decided to develop what was to be called the Gordon Smith Institute and it was completed in 1900. The correct name of this organisation was the Liverpool Seamen and Migrants Friend Society and Bethel Union. Its roots are found outside Liverpool.

The early days are linked with one man ... his influence was to reach Liverpool. He was the Rev. George Charles Smith, commonly known as Bosun Smith. He was born in 1782 in Castle Street, off Leicester Square, in London. At the age of fourteen Smith was apprenticed to an American Captain. That same year he was in the West Indies and, caught by a 'press gang', he spent twelve months with the Royal Navy. The following year, he became a midshipman in the *Agamemnon* and served in the North Sea Fleet. In 1801, Smith was in the Battle of Copenhagen under the command of Nelson. Such was his seafaring background.

The next information that we have reveals that, during a stay in Reading, he visited a chapel there and was converted to Christianity. His life was turned upside down and as a result his influence was to spread far and wide ... and of course that was to include Liverpool.

In 1804, Smith began training for the ministry under the care of a Baptist minister in Devonport. For four years he studied, spending much time with the sailors in Plymouth. His first call as a minister was to a chapel in Penzance and there he began his letter writing service for seafarers. Correspondence was to keep him in touch with hundreds of men and their families. He was to build six other chapels in and around Penzance and, through his open-air preaching, he helped found the Home Missionary Society.

In 1819, Smith opened a Floating Chapel on the River Thames. He then did the same in Liverpool, Bristol, Hull and other ports. His work, his energy and his vision were tremendous. In 1822, he founded the Thames Waterman's Friend Society. In 1823, he started the Merchant Seaman's Orphan Asylum for boys. In 1824, he built the first Mariners' Church. He took over a disused Danish Church in Wellclose Square, by the London Docks. It became the first church if its kind in the country. There were terrible storms that year and with others, in order to help the widows and orphans, he set up a relief fund which led to the formation of the Shipwrecked Mariners' Society. Today that Society still plays an important part in caring for the seafarer and his family ... the Mersey Mission to Seamen acts as agent in the North West. Pastor Smith's concern was not restricted to the seafarer. He started the City Mission Society to work in the courts and back streets of London; from this evolved visits to Prisons and Workhouses and open-air preaching. Without doubt, the Reverend Charles George Smith set the pattern for the work amongst seafarers which evolved in the nineteenth century.

There is a story told of him which illustrates both his wit and tact. Most of this information comes from a tract found in the Liverpool Reference Library ... with no author indicated, but with the title 'The Seamen's Christian Friend Society.'

> 'He used to preach at the open-air fair at Bristol. He used to stand in front of St. James Church where most of the stalls and shows were situated, and where the greatest crowd would gather. They were very noisy gatherings. On this occasion the Town Magistrate had charged a Constable to stop his preaching. His open-air work was much opposed by the authorities and he was often in trouble with the police. He took his stand at the time he said he would, and the Constable told him that he was not to preach.

"Well", he said. "Will you allow me to tell the people why I cannot preach?"

To this the Constable agreed. Bosun Smith began.

"My friends I came here intending to preach to you from these solemn words, 'Flee from the wrath to come' ... I meant to have told you whose wrath you should flee from. But my friend here says I must not. I meant to have told you why you should flee from this wrath to come. But I am forbidden by the Constable, and I obey orders. I meant to have told you to whom you should flee from this wrath to come - even to the Lord Jesus Christ, the Saviour of the poor lost sinners. But I cannot do what I would for the Constable says "No!"

'In this way he managed to preach the whole of the sermon. And when he had finished he said, "Now Mr. Constable, you will not, I am sure, object to my properly dismissing these people?"

"Oh dear me, no; certainly not, Sir."

"Then", said the Bosun "Let us sing, Praise God from whom all blessings flow." And when this had been well and truly sung by the crowd he offered up a brief but impressive prayer and with a smile full of meaning he received the thanks of the Constable for being so good as to comply with his instructions without giving any trouble.'

In 1828, the Reverend George Charles Smith opened an Asylum for Destitute and Starving Sailors and, in the same year, the first Temperance Society in England. When London's Old Brunswick Theatre fell down, Smith was there to help with the injured and to recover the dead. That was when he decided to buy the site and build a Sailors' Home. The next year, he collected £3,000 and the home was built. He was a prolific writer, having started a Sailors' Magazine in 1827. He died in Penzance in 1863, with no money but a world full of friends. He was a great man and his work sent ripples out into the seafaring world.

It was the influence of Smith, which led the Non-Conformists in Liverpool to be the first in the field. The Liverpool Seamen's Friend Society was founded on the 12th September 1820. From this came the inspiration to establish the first Floating Chapel in Liverpool. The vessel they acquired was the two-decked ship, *The William*. She was a whaler and the date was 1821.

The William had been built by John Sutton at Liverpool for Richard Kent and was launched on March 2, 1775. This was the first ship built in Liverpool for the Greenland Fishery. She was to lay in King's Dock until about 1850 and, by that time, had incurred dock dues for twenty-eight years, amounting to £1,277. This was an exciting and positive start for the work of caring for Mersey Mariners.

E. Baines in his Directory of Lancashire in 1824 describes *The William*.

'A floating Chapel in a converted ship anchored in a valuable mooring space in Salthouse Dock. This large nautical sanctuary was formed out of the ship The William, of 447 tons, which was purchased by the Seamen's Friend Society and Bethel Union, on 6th October, 1821, for the sum of £940, and the expense of the ship, and fitting it up as a neat and commodious chapel, after deducting the money received on the sale of the original stores, was £1,051. Accommodation is here afforded to upwards of a 1,000 persons, and ever since the chapel opened, on 16th May, 1822, the attendance has been satisfactory to the benevolent individuals to whose piety and zeal the seamen are indebted for this accommodation.'

She was sometimes called the Bethel Ship. The primary concern of the Liverpool Seamen's Friend Society and Bethel Union was to do with 'mission', but that naturally led to concern about the total welfare of the seafarer.

The committee was fifty-five strong and almost entirely composed of evangelical clergy. One of the early members painted a picture of the water-front as he saw it.

"Alas! British sailors have not always presented to the view of foreigners the most favourable specimen of morality and religion of this country. They are a shame and a reproach!

"We have been grieved and discouraged by seeing how drunkenness, in many instances, prevails amongst the Seamen. One seaman acknowledged that he had not been sober for one night in three weeks. Some ships are floating hells!"

Over a decade, the Society established three Bethels ... the North Bethel in Bath Street, the South Bethel in Wellington Road and the Fo'castle in Wapping. The agents worked from these rooms and were responsible to the committee.

A selection from agents' reports well illustrate the problems with which they grappled. We shall confine ourselves to a few brief extracts, referring to the Floating Chapel, the Bethel Meetings, the Lodging Houses, and the Registry Office.

August. (1841)

'During the past month the several meetings have been attended by about 3,171 persons, great numbers of them seamen, who appear to take a deep interest in our weekly meetings, and several of them engage in prayer.

'The Fellowship Meetings, as usual are very encouraging. Captains, mates, and seamen, both American and English, have together, with the deepest interest, expressed their gratitude to God for what has been done for them.

'Several of our pious captains have recently left. Captains Young, Cox, and Reed, all desired an interest in our prayers, that the blessing of God may rest upon them.

'Several captains and seamen are anxious to have a Sailors' Home in connection with this Society.'

(Note: The Rev George Charles Smith had already opened such a Home in London, which would have been known by all seamen over the world. The Liverpool Sailors' Home was to be opened by a new Society in 1844. The demand was becoming evident.)

September. (1841)

'During the past month the meetings have been better attended than usual, a great number of seamen having been present. Several captains have assisted by giving addresses. The Sabbath evenings, as usual, have been well attended, the room being crowded to excess, a large number always remaining at the prayer meeting, which is held after the service. The Wednesday evening has secured a large attendance; sometimes twenty have spoken of their experience, and some very encouraging statements have been made of the good done by the Society's labours.'

The Registrar's Report for August. (1844)

'The office has been better supplied during the past month, and I have received from several masters of ships, lately returned from sea, very agreeable reports of the conduct of seamen taken from this office whilst in foreign ports.'

The Registrar's Report for September. (1844)

'During the past month, several excellent reports have been received from masters of ships, who have taken crews from the Liverpool Seamen's Friend Society, testifying to the good character of the crews which have been under their command. Still there are difficulties with some of the seamen.'

(Obviously the Society was waging a successful battle against the Liverpool Crimps by supplying ship's crews. A crimp was a lodging house keeper who swindled the seafarer and then 'sold' him to a ship's master. This self-imposed task of providing an agency to protect the seafarer was also to be adopted by the Liverpool Sailors' Home, which by this date was newly opened.)

There then follows a list of libraries placed aboard ships and another list of returned libraries. In one section of the 1841 Annual Report there is a relevant note.

October Library Report. (1841)

'The agent states that during his visit to Bolton, on behalf of the Society, Mr. Hamilton made the Society a present of 114 volumes to the Library. Another kind friend, the Rev. Mr. Bury, of Kendal, presented to the Society, for the use of the Library, 'The Lives of the Reformers', in twelve volumes. To these must be added, other friends who, by similar donations, have contributed considerably to the usefulness of the Liverpool Seamen's Friend Society. These will be found a great acquisition to the Society, as it will be enabled to administer more extensively to the mental and spiritual improvement of the Seamen. At the moment nothing further relating to the Library calls for particular attention.'

(Such books would hardly be accepted today!)

Lodging House Committee's Report. (February 1841)

'About 60 houses have been visited, supplied with tracts and notices of our services. We have also prayed with several of the families, and many have been induced to attend the Bethel Room and Floating Chapel.

'Also I have had some very encouraging and delightful visits among the shipping. I have been on board nearly every ship in five of the docks, and circulated 1,500 tracts among seamen.'

Lodging House Committee's Report. (December 31st 1840)

'Many seamen with whom the Agent has conversed during the last month seem to have a desire for the establishment of a sailors' home in the Port of Liverpool, as in many other places in the kingdom. One poor old sailor whom the agent met with, told him that he had been compelled to leave the boarding-house that he had gone to when he had arrived at the port, under painful circumstances. He belonged to London, and had reserved two pounds with which to visit his native place. On the morning of the day which he had fixed for the journey, and when he was about to set off, the person of the house came to him, knowing that he had the money, and asked him for a loan of it for a few hours. Anxious to oblige her, he gave her the amount, expecting that it would be returned in a few hours. The day passed over, but no money was forthcoming; and from day to day she put him off, until weeks had elapsed, and then she demanded payment for lodging. Having no money, he was compelled to leave the house, and take refuge in the Night Asylum, and as his clothes were kept for the debt, excepting what he had on, he could not get a ship, and on the day when he met with the Agent he had had nothing to eat.'

Lodging House Committee's Report. (March 1840)

'I met a Captain belonging to Jersey, who had been shipwrecked, and left penniless. When in those circumstances, he had been recommended to, and kindly received and provided for by the Sailors' Home in London. Although this occurred several years ago, when he was a common sailor, he had not forgotten their kindness; and, as a proof of it, gave me two pounds as a donation to the Society.'

There was much correspondence - Bosun Smith would have encouraged it - and some extracts are revealing.

A letter to one of the Bethel agents, Robert Day, was from a sailor, who, with two of his messmates, had been in the habit of attending the Bethel Room when in port. He says:

'Dear Brother,

I have sad news to tell you indeed. We went out of Salthouse Dock on the Wednesday evening, and sailed from the river on Thursday morning, bound for Gloucester. On Friday morning, about one o'clock, we were about twenty miles from Barseys; the wind came on very strong, and the night was very dark. The wind was E.S.E. We had a square sail set, but at that time took it in. Cole was to leeward, getting the sail clear of the cathead, and we suppose the wind got under the sail and lifted him overboard; but we saw him not - it was very dark. My brother was at the helm. He saw something pass the lee-quarter, and cried out, "What is that overboard?"' I cried out for Cole, but he answered me not, for he was gone overboard. Oh, how dreadful was the thought! We tried to rescue his precious life, but all in vain; we could render him no assistance at all; and now the poor dear young man is lying in a watery grave. Oh! dear brother, pray for us, and warn poor sailors to prepare for such an awful change. I hope our loss is his eternal gain; and that the Lord will prepare us to meet him in heaven.'

'Valparaiso, June 12th, 1844.

I feel a longing desire to be with you again. I trust that the Lord had blessed you in your bodily health since the summer has set in. It is now dead of winter with us. Please to give my kind regards to Mrs ... and all your family. I trust they are doing well.

'Perhaps I ought to tell you that this is a dry and barren land, where little or no water is. There is a clergyman of the Church of England stationed here. I believe he is a very good man, but I am sorry to say he has seen but little fruit of his labour. I trust it may, at least, be as bread cast upon the waters, to be seen after many days. Darkness covers the land, and gross darkness the minds of the people. Oh! for brighter days, when darkness and superstition shall be chased from the face of the earth, and when the glory of the Lord shall shine triumphantly!'

The work of the Liverpool Seamen's Friend Society was to continue in the same way up to the end of the nineteenth century. The use of Bethels seemed appropriate to the aims of the Society.

Others were thinking along different paths. Robert Owen, who formed a model industrial community at New Lanark in Scotland and pioneered co-operative societies in this country opened a co-operative store in Gateacre, Liverpool. The first exhibition of Co-operative productions was held in Liverpool in 1832. Owen and the great social leader John Finch were great friends. On the 16th February, 1831, Finch sent a circular to Owen proposing the establishment of a hostel for seamen in Liverpool to be run on co-operative lines. It was a startling proposition, well in advance of its day.

'To rent or purchase a large building, convertible into proper apartments for store-rooms for provisions, clothing, and sea-stores; a savings bank, library, school, lecture, reading and dining rooms, and other conveniences for boarding and lodging at least 500 seamen, and to raise, by subscription, a sufficient sum of money to furnish and stock the building for these purposes. The seamen to pay such a sum weekly, for board and lodging, as will cover the expenses.'

This was a remarkable vision. It was proposed to buy in bulk and sell at cheap prices. Shipping companies who gave advance notes would be guaranteed their money. Finch also added in his circular to Owen that 'every seaman was to attend a place of worship on Sundays, at least once a day, or pay a fine.' This is a little surprising because Finch had written a letter, which was published in the Liverpool Mercury on the 14th January, 1831 (one month before the production of the circular), claiming that the Seamens' Friend Society was too sectarian and too

33

concerned with preaching. No progress was made with Finch's ideas, but at least the seeds were being placed for what was to evolve in Liverpool.

The Liverpool Sailors' Home was built in 1844 and was able to accommodate seafarers. The Liverpool Seamen's Friend Society made their first move in this direction in 1881. Seamen who were arriving in Liverpool were at a serious disadvantage through not having a place ashore to which they could resort at odd times without having to fight the many temptations which befell the stranded seaman. So, a room was obtained in the Mariners' Parade and this was used as a free sitting room and reading room for seamen. It was known as the Forecastle, open all day until late at night. It proved a great haven for the men.

The biggest step forward for this Society was when a wealthy Liverpool merchant, the Right Honourable Samuel Smith, M.P., erected and furnished a building as a memorial to mark the death of his eighteen year old son, J. Gordon Smith. The Gordon Smith Institute was a beautiful building and still exists. It was built in 1900.

The Gordon Smith Institute

Soon after the outbreak of the first World War the Institute was extended. Eighty beds were installed and were much in demand by the seamen stranded in Liverpool. A public house, the Lighthouse, which adjoined the Gordon Smith Institute was bought and a further extension was created in 1925. This enabled two hundred men to be accommodated each night ... a bed, a private cabin or a hammock in the dormitory. The only condition of entry was sight of the individual's discharge book.

The Institute was quickly adopted by Liverpool and was greatly supported. On Tuesday, Thursday and Saturday of each week an entertainment of some sort was provided, mainly by amateur dramatic societies and concert parties. At the end of the twentieth century, I still meet ladies who recall the work they undertook at the Gordon Smith Institute. One dear friend, Peggy Tholen, recalls a childhood visit to the Gordon Smith Institute.

> "In my best dress, I danced and sang. They all clapped and at the end to my surprise I was handed a half-crown coin. That was great. I gave it to my mother!"

Memories live on.

The Ladies Canteen Committee supplied the best of food at the minimum of cost and organised clothing and other needs for the 'down and out'. No man joined his ship without the necessary clothing.

Whilst the Bethels had disappeared, the caring continued. The ladies visited the men in hospitals and the agents looked after the prison at Walton. They handled the Ocean Library for the British Sailors' Society in London and, for example, placed 5,657 library boxes aboard ships in Liverpool in 1952. The care of this Library system was eventually taken over by the Mersey Mission to Seamen and I found that, although it involved much work, we chaplains were more than welcomed aboard the ships with books in our hands.

After the second World War, the accommodation was modernised into 82 private rooms and a dormitory for 77 men. In 1948. a new annexe was opened on the other side of the road and was called Sefton House. A plaque was unveiled by the Duchess of Gloucester in the April in memory of Helena Maryk, Countess of Sefton, who was her aunt.

No account of the Gordon Smith Institute can be complete without the name of Stan Sherrington. Stan's story really starts on the 17th February, 1957. He was very much involved with the Bank Hall Mission in Liverpool and thought that he would work eventually in Nigeria as a missionary. The 17th February changed all that! A seaman called Tom Applewhite arrived at the Mission and asked , "What time does the service start?" Tom stayed on for supper and Stan took him back to the ship, *Mankato Victory*. That was when Stan realised that there was no need to go overseas to the Mission field, it was right here on his doorstep. And that was the beginning of a ministry to seafarers which has lasted to the present day.

Stan Sherrington used to preach in the Gordon Smith Institute when John Yates, in his middle nineties, was the Missioner there. It was good training for a young man. Stan told me that a Merchant Navy Officers' Christian Association was formed in 1910 by Captain Carre, who wrote religious books, *Through Stormy Sea, There go the Ships,* etc. This Association spread to many parts of the world. Gavin McGregor, who carried on the work, was asked, "What about the lower deck?" This was sufficent for the Association to be renamed the Merchant Navy Christian Fellowship. Stan retires next year, although we all suspect that he will continue his work aboard the ships.

With the decline in the numbers of ships and the demand for higher standards of accommodation, the Gordon Smith Institute went into liquidation in mid seventies and the Liverpool Seamen's Friend Society ceased its operation.

When I arrived in Liverpool in 1961, the Gordon Smith Institute was still fulfilling a role in caring for the seafarer. The Superintendent was Norman Williams and he was a source of knowledge and sound advice as I set about learning my new trade. Norman was succeeded by Charles Mougne, whose wife, Marjorie, was librarian at Kingston House in the College of the Sea library. They were like 'family' to me. Charles, now 85 years of age, had just returned from a six week European tour when we last spoke to each other!

The Gordon Smith Institute was an imposing building, much loved by so many people who had worked as voluntary helpers over many years. However, in the early seventies it no longer attracted the serving seafarer, in spite of great efforts to up-grade the property. No longer was it bustling with activity. The quality of life aboard ships had much improved, the expectations of the seamen ashore were much higher and this made the end of the Gordon Smith Institute inevitable. Lady Sefton House was taken over to care for students and in 1975 the Institute was closed.

So many people found safety, material support and spiritual comfort that the name of this famous Liverpool charity will remain firmly in the history of seafaring around the world. There is much more to caring for the seafarer than a knitting circle, a sock repair service and hot pot dinners, but the Gordon Smith had met even these needs. My real memories are of the dedication of the staff and the kindness shown to any seafarer in trouble.

Above all, the Society had remained loyal to its original aims to the end ... to promote 'the present comfort and future happiness of seamen and their families and of other persons connected with shipping'.

The Man who walked the shores of Galilee understood. 'Anything you did for one of my brothers here, however humble, you did for me.'

4.

The Liverpool Sailors' Home

The boarding house masters were off in a trice,
They shouted and promised us all that was nice.
Then one fat old crimp he got cotton on me:
He said I was foolish to follow the sea.
And it's ho-ro-ho, bullies ho!
The Liverpool girls have got us in tow.

A number of moves were made in Liverpool to found a hostel where, for a moderate charge, the seaman could be sure of receiving honest treatment. A group of shipowners, merchants and inhabitants held a meeting on the 25th February, 1837, in the Underwriters' Committee-room but the provisonal committee formed in the December lapsed when the Corporation and Dock Trustees declined assistance. A reformed committee acquired subscriptions for £1,800 by the 14th April, 1841, but it was not until 10th May, 1844, when the Council allocated land, that the plan could proceed.

A Public Meeting was held in the Town Hall on the 18th October, 1844 and the following advertisement appeared in the newspapers of the day.

'Borough of Liverpool

Pursuant to a requisition from the Provisional Committee appointed to make arrangements for the establishment of a Sailors' Home, Registry and Savings Bank for Seamen, I do hereby convene a

Public Meeting to be holden in the Sessions House, Chapel Street, on Friday, 25th October, at 1 o'clock in the afternoon, for the purpose of founding so desirable an object.

Town Hall   Thomas Sands.
18th October, 1844   Mayor.'

A Committee was appointed of merchants and shipowners and within a short period the sum of £13,660 was collected. The Corporation had offered a site for the new building but meanwhile in February 1845, rooms were taken in Stanley Buildings, Bath Street, for the purpose of a Seamen's Savings Bank, the shipping and discharging of crews, and a Sailors' Character Registry. This was a positive and well considered step to care for the seafarer. The influence was to spread beyond Liverpool.

The shipping business of the port was conducted wholly at the Bath Street rooms and was so efficient that the then existing Government passed their Shipping Bill of 1850 on the Sailors' Home system and to this day the shipping and discharge of crews are carried on with very slight alterations, on the same principles. It was an excellent start for this Society.

The Sailors' Home

By the standards of the mid-twentieth century, the Sailors' Home in Canning Place, whilst outwardly attractive, was considered by many to resemble a prison, complete with galleries and landings. For the seafarer of the mid-nineteenth century, it must have seemed like a palace and was well received.

The Architect was John Cunningham and the foundation stone was laid in July 1846. The object was to provide good, inexpensive accommodation for the seafarers, who were enduring inferior lodging houses and grog shops.

'In the streets and alleys of dockland there was no dearth of places where 'Seamen's Lodging House' was painted boldly on to a cracked dirt-grained fanlight and where at an exorbitant charge the sailor would be fed and bedded - after a fashion. The majority of lodging houses were, however, poor establishments, from some of which the shell-back was lucky to escape with his life, let alone with his money belt.'

(Evening Express 14 May, 1954)

'If to some the interior of the Home appears like a prison, this was not Cunningham's concept. He modelled it on ship's quarters with cabins ranged around five storeys of galleries in the internal rhomboidal court. The columns and balustrades of the galleries are powerfully moulded in cast iron using nautical themes like turned rope, twisted dolphins, and mermaids. The cast-gates were his 'chef d'oevre' in iron, a splendid casting of maritime buntings, trumpets and ship's wheels, surrounded by the crowned insignia of the legendary Liver bird, which were all handled with tremendous virtuosity.'

(Sailors' Home, typescript, University of Liverpool. 1962.)

To comprehend the importance of the Liverpool Sailors' Home, it is vital to put it into the context of a 'boom town' situation.

The Napoleonic Wars were over in 1815 and in the next twenty years, eight new docks were built. Roads, canals, railways, warehouses, offices, all demanded a large growth in the population and little thought was given for the comfort of the poor, the ignorant and the sick. Far too many families lived in cellars. Life for the workers was full of squalor and misery.

Dr. W.H. Duncan, the first medical officer of health for Liverpool, in fact for any English town, stated that in 1844 there were 6,294 cellars with 20,168 inhabitants. His report painted the picture.

'The cellars are ten to twelve feet square; generally flagged - but frequently having only bare earth for a floor and sometimes less than six feet in height. There is frequently no window, so that light and air can gain access to the cellars only by the door, the top of which is often not higher than the level of the street. In such cellars ventilation is out of the question. They are, of course, dark, and through the defective drainage, generally very damp. There is sometimes a back cellar, used as a sleeping apartment, having no direct communication with the external atmosphere, and deriving its scanty supply of light and air solely from the first apartment.'

John Newlands, the first Borough Engineer appointed in the country, presented a paper in 1858, entitled Liverpool Past and Present, in Relation to Sanitary Operations. His description of the housing conditions makes sad reading.

'An ordinary street house, with fair accommodation, originally, has had its lobby converted into a common passage, leading to the backyard. This passage is, of course, roofed over, and is in fact a tunnel from which the back room of the original house, now converted into a separate dwelling, has its entrance. The backyard has been filled with new houses in such a manner as to leave only a continuation of the narrow passage for access, and from this little area of three feet wide, these houses receive the whole of their light and air. The passage has sometimes right-angled branches of the same size and is generally terminated by the ashpit, common to all the miserable dwellings, with its liquid filth oozing through the walls, and its pestiferous gases flowing into the windows of the last two houses. This system introduced in converting one house into numerous dwellings, was imitated in the erection of new buildings.'

In the 1844 Domestic Mission Annual Report is this sentence:

'... the town appears never to have had the advantage of being planned at all; and the thirst of gain, operated at a time when the philosophy of public health was so little understood, has crowded our river banks with those ill-sewered and ill-ventilated mazes of buildings, which occupy the greater part of the lower section of the town, and in the local spirit of which there is so much that is prolific of evil.'

In an Annual Report produced by the City Mission in 1846 is a descriptive paragraph.

'When autumn passed away with its fever, winter came with its famine. Large families housed, we had almost said kennelled, in small damp cellars, with nothing but rags to cover them by day, and often nothing but a little straw to lie down upon at night; living sometimes upon one meal in twenty-four hours.'

'The Rhomboidal Court'

'Turned ropes'

There were cholera outbreaks in Liverpool in 1832, 1834, 1848-49 and in 1854. Consumption was rife and life expectancy was low. The population explosion was out of control, especially when the Irish potato crop failed in 1845.

It is against this background that the wonder of the Liverpool Sailors' Home must be placed. The population of Liverpool in 1841 was estimated at 222,954. But of more importance is the estimate of over 4,000 ships entering the river in that year and that gives us some comprehension of the need for accommodation on shore for the seafarers. For those men, the Home truly was a palace.

One of the sources of information during this period is the publication started in 1860 by Hugh Shimmin. It was called The Porcupine, a satirical weekly journal, with many observations about the suffering of people in Liverpool. Shimmin was a free-lance journalist who wrote articles about the low life of Liverpool for the Liverpool Mercury. These articles were reproduced as a book entitled Liverpool Life. The weekly journal, The Porcupine, continued until Shimmin's death in 1879.

It was in 1860 that the interior of the Sailors' Home was destroyed by a fire, probably started by one of the inmates. However, it must have been quickly restored and this allows Shimmin the opportunity to produce an article dated May 31, 1862. The title is 'Jack Ashore'.

'The reopening of the Sailors' Home the other day, together with the speeches delivered upon that occasion, showed what sort of interest those who ought to know 'Jack' took in his welfare when ashore. It is very hard to imagine how anyone in Liverpool can be indifferent to the well-being and well-doing of sailors, seeing how much commerce has had to do in making the town.

'It has been shown in these pages what provision the law makes for the protection of the sailor as well as the shipowner, in the matter of getting a crew off to sea; and it is much to be regretted by many of Jack's real friends that the Shipping Act is not enforced as efficiently as it might be, in order to protect Jack on his return home. Some go as far as to say that the law is almost inoperative, and that, in consequence, Jack is left to the tender mercies of the wicked, and everyone knows how amiable these are. Hence it is that a certain class of boarding-housekeepers and slop-sellers or outfitters are enabled to prey upon the silly good-nature and generosity of Jack. Not only do they live by him, or on him, but some of them realise handsome fortunes by the systematic plundering of England's most brave and gallant sons.

'Jack's arrival home is most anxiously looked for by this class of 'friends'. It is well known that several slop-sellers and boarding-housekeepers have boat's crews waiting in the river for the purpose of boarding inward-bound vessels, and enticing the crews to the houses of their employers ashore. How lucrative this business is may be judged of from the fact that these boatmen, or 'runners' dressed as boatmen, receive as much as thirty shillings a week, and have opportunities of increasing this by the tricks which they practise. It is not an unusual thing for these men, on boarding a vessel, to pass themselves off as 'riggers' willing to work the ship in; and they generally manage to take some drink aboard, with which the sailors are primed, in order that they may more readily fall a prey to the snare of the runner. Very great anxiety is generally manifested by sailors to get on shore as soon as ever they are in sight of port; and they will frequently, under the influence of drink with which they have been supplied, agree to give five or ten shillings to one of the 'riggers' to take their place and work the ship into dock. This is the aim of the 'runner', because if he can obtain a substitute for Jack, he hooks the fish, and has him completely in his power. Away goes Jack ashore, with the friend who has been so kind to him, and he is led off to the boarding-housekeeper; and here the 'runner's' business for the present ends.'

The simple sailor is made welcome and introduced to an outfitter who supplies a fresh rig-out. The plot then continues.

'Jack has had one or two women 'planted' on him. These harpies take him in tow. They are well instructed in their duties, and before many hours elapse Jack is soundly 'drugged' and stripped of his new clothes.'

The whole scene is then repeated when the friendly house-keeper supplies a fresh rig, until Jack eventually finds all his money has gone and he has to find another ship.

'It was to protect the sailors from the rapacity of the land-sharks and secure for them moral and social advantages, which the disreputable boarding-houses set at nought or despised, that the Sailors' Home was established. But the gross misrepresentations which are set on foot - (by those interested in the demoralisation of sailors) - with reference to the arrangements of the Sailors' Home, have had an influence in preventing this Institution from being as useful as it otherwise might have been. The deceit and lying regularly practised by runners from slop-shops and low boarding-housekeepers would be unaccountable, were it not that their motives are so clearly seen. But the friends of the Sailors' Home have both faith and patience, and these must tell in the long run.'

An American, called Herman Melville, visited Liverpool in 1839. He travelled as a cabin-boy. In his autobiographical novel, entitled 'Redburn', he describes his impressions of the port.

'The floating chapel recalls to mind the 'Old Church', well known to the seamen of many generations who have visited Liverpool. It stands very near the docks, a venerable mass of brown stone, and by the town's people is called the Church of St. Nicholas. I believe it is the best preserved piece of antiquity in all Liverpool.

'Before the town rose to any importance, it was the only place of worship on that side of the Mersey; and under the adjoining Parish of Walton was a chapel-of-ease; though from the straight-backed pews, there could have been but little comfort taken in it.

'In old times, there stood in front of the church, a statue of St. Nicholas, the patron of mariners; to which all pious sailors made offerings, to induce his saintship to grant them short and properous voyages. In the tower is a fine chime of bells.... Thirty or forty years ago, these bells were rung upon the arrival of every Liverpool ship from a foreign voyage. How forcibly does this illustrate the increase of the commerce of the town! Were the same custom now observed, the bells would seldom have a chance to cease.

'In the evening, especially when the sailors are gathered in great numbers, these streets present a most singular spectacle, the entire population of the vicinity being seemingly turned into them. Hand-organs, fiddles and cymbals, plied by strolling musicians, mix well with the songs of the seamen, the babble of women and children, and the groaning and whining of the beggar. From the various boarding houses, each distinguished by gilded emblems outside - an anchor, a crown, a ship, a windlass or a dolphin - proceeds the noise of revelry and dancing; and from the open casements lean young girls and old women, chattering and laughing with the crowds in the middle of the street. Every moment strange greetings are exchanged between old sailors who chance to stumble upon a shipmate, last seen in Calcutta or Savannah: and the invariable courtesy that takes place upon these occasions, is to go to the spirit vault, and drink each other's health.

' ... of all the seaports in the world, Liverpool, perhaps, abounds in all the variety of land-sharks, land-rats and other vermin, which makes the hapless mariner their prey. In the shape of land-lords, bar-keepers, clothiers, crimps and boarding-house loungers, the land-sharks devour him, limb by limb: while the land-rats and mice constantly nibble at his purse.

'Other perils he runs, also, far worse; from the denizens of notorious Corinthian haunts in the vicinity of the docks, which in depravity are not to be matched by anything this side of the pit that is bottomless. And yet, sailors love this Liverpool; and upon long voyages to distant parts of the globe, will be continually dilating on its charms and attractions, and extolling it above all other seaports in the world. For in Liverpool they find their Paradise - not the well known street of that name - and one of them told me that he would be content to lie in Prince's Dock till he hove up anchor for the world to come.'

Baines's 'Directory of Liverpool' (1830) gives us another picture of the port.

'Liverpool was the sailors' town. Dockside pubs were everywhere. The sound of boisterous revelling and powerful sea shanties was heard from tavern doorways as the sailors spent their few days' leave and their hard earned money on beer, women and song. Prostitutes roamed the streets and solicited the mariners for custom - the sailor could choose from brash Liverpudlian whores, fat and buxom floosies to green-eyed Irish lasses, petite dark haired Chinese street walkers and dashing exotic eastern maidens, all prepared to sell him their favours at the right price. The brothels stood alongside the beer houses on the dockside roads.'

In 1863 public houses multiplied so alarmingly that the Secretary was instructed to make every effort to oppose the grant of further licences, but by 1877 forty-six public houses were within a radius of 200 yards of the Liverpool Sailors' Home.

In the middle of all this, the Sailors' Home must have stood out like a lighthouse for the seafarer who was in deep trouble. Of interest is the fact that, when the first meeting was called to establish the Home in 1844, the Charter included the desire to open a Registry and Savings Bank for Seamen. The Liverpool Seamens' Friend Society already had created a Registry of Seamen, which was a great success and undoubtedly the Trustees of the new Sailors' Home saw the need to extend the idea further. It was an excellent way of keeping the seafarers out of the hands of the crimp and ensuring a safe berth for the next voyage.

The thinking behind the need to establish a Savings Bank arose out of another trap which awaited the unwary and gullible sailor. There were many schemes created to extract the monies from the body-belts.

Porcupine seems to have latched on to one particular scheme and in the summer of 1867 Shimmin makes his case. He points out that Friendly Societies were formed in order to help the members of a work-group in cases of sickness and death and to help the next of kin. The articles in Porcupine spell out the problems for the seaman.

'The roving lives they lead, the uncertainty of the ports they return to, the short time they are on shore, the general character of Jack when on shore, are all obstacles to the formation of such societies ... there is no class more deserving.'

There had been attempts to find an answer to the problem of assisting the seafarer to safeguard his monies. The Montreal Ocean Steamship Company's Mutual Benefit Society was established in 1863. It seemed to have much success. In its four years, it had honestly met claims for sickness and death. The Society in 1867 reported £1,200 in hand.

The West India and Pacific Company established a Benefit Club. The only expense was the salary for an assistant secretary. The shipping company expected all the sea-going and shore-based staff to be members. However, there was a case of one seaman who refused to pay the annual subscription of five shillings to this Company and, because it was a condition of employment, he took the Company to court. The Board of Trade had to uphold his objection because such a payment was not legally in the articles of employment, but regretted that they had no choice in the matter. The Porcupine adds its own spice to the case.

'When gentlemen are obliged to waste valuable time in police court, and are exposed to the insinuation that their benevolence proceeds from selfish and greedy motives, we cannot wonder if they are somewhat shy in taking trouble on behalf of seamen.'

May 4th,1867.

The Porcupine expands on the Montreal Ocean Steamship Company Mutual Benefit Society.

'The Company supply medical attendance; the only expense incurred in the management is stationery and a small salary for the assistant secretary, who is paid at the rate of two shillings per annum for every member who is in benefit, this salary not to exceed £100. Each member must pay one shilling and thereafter four pence per week while he continues in service ... deducted from his wages. During illness he will receive 13 shillings per week for the first twelve weeks, 9 shillings per week for the next four weeks, 5 shillings per week for four weeks more and then his claim for allowance will cease. In the event of death ... the entitlement is £10.'

In the September, The Porcupine comes to the defence of the seafarer under the headline, 'Keeping Watch for the Life of Poor Jack.'

Never did The Porcupine feel such pity for Jack than when he happened to read 'a certain document issued by a society, professing to have founded itself for Jack's exclusive benefit and protection.' It was the First Annual Report of the Liverpool Seamen's Mutual Friendly Society.

During their first twelve months it seems that the institution was flourishing. It had elected a president, a treasurer, a secretary and a committee. The Porcupine cannot contain itself any longer.

> '... proposes to call into question the value of the institution which is described in the astonishing compound of vulgarity, bad grammar and brazen impudence which lies before him in the shape of a report.'

He then goes on to add a few details.

The Society had obtained £1,555.3s.6d in the past year and a balance of £841.12s.11d. remained in hand. Therefore £713.10s.6d. must have been spent. Then came the question ... how much went to the seafarers? Salaries took up £363.15s.!!! Printing £81. Badges £51.14s.6d. £29.16s.7d for the funerals of seven deceased members!!! After much mathematical discussion, he concludes that not more then £60 went to the seafarer. His article then became remarkably vitriolic.

Just a few weeks later a letter is printed in The Porcupine.

'Friendly Societies.

Mr. Porcupine, Sir.

I read with surprise your recent article upon a Friendly Society of Sailors, and I have looked out pretty sharply for some kind of answer from the persons who manage the concern, but as yet I am disappointed.

Now, sir, if the Society which you noticed is conducted honestly and prudently, the required returns will before now have been forwarded to Mr. Tidd Pratt. (The registrar of Friendly Societies.) If they have not been sent, I for one shall be disposed to think your strictures were thoroughly deserved.

I am, etc.,

CANDOUR.'

Here was a problem for all seafarers and there were numerous examples of such societies taking advantage of the seamen. Obviously, there was great need to protect the seamen from such unscrupulous activities. The Sailors' Home Savings Bank had been created to achieve just that.

The Report printed by the Sailors' Home in 1877 is worthy of notice as it points to the success of the Main Home and the Branch North Home movement. There was much concern in the Port about the decline of professional seamen.

'So far as the boarders in the Home are a criterion, the conduct of seamen is certainly improved of late years, and the earnest hope is that this improvement may be progressive. The men are more ready to listen to good counsel, to believe in our interest in them, and to join in religious services. Drinking to excess, though still much too prevalent, is on the decrease, and delirium tremens, once sadly frequent, is now scarcely ever witnessed.

'The Committee hail with lively satisfaction the planting, in the midst of the ordinary public houses which unhappily surround the Home, of two British Workman Public Houses, in which no intoxicating liquors are sold, but where other drinks and substantial food are supplied, and in which sailors and others can sit and smoke and enjoy themselves in perfect safety as to mind, body and pocket.

'The Committee of the Mersey Mission to Seamen have also opened a comfortable and commodious Reading Room in the immediate neighbourhood, where the Sailor can read the newspapers and periodicals, waiting until the time comes for him to sign articles, or be paid off.

'Seamen complain that they have experienced great difficulty in reaching the Home of late; this, no doubt, arises partly from the fact that as during the last three months of the year, comparatively few vessels have arrived, mainly owing to the prevalence of easterly winds, boarding-house masters have plied their calling with unusual earnestness, even to the extent, in some instances, of offering Sailors two days' board for nothing. And the further fact that fewer vessels have docked in the docks contiguous to the Home has also operated against men reaching the Institution.

'A youth has been appointed to the Post-office department, solely in order to make it as useful as possible to Seamen generally. The result of this is that the friends of seamen, as well as the seamen themselves, have readily made full use of this arrangement for their benefit.

'The Sunday Services have been well attended, and the sailor has never before, it is thought, shewn such an earnest spirit of religious inquiry. Considerable numbers have availed themselves of the Mersey Mission Services, and of the Bethel Union Services in the immediate neighbourhood, and there have been many instances which encourage the thought that more than usual good has been done during the past twelve months.'

The Mercantile Marine Service Association (M.M.S.A) produced an article about the Home in its February, 1884, Reporter. The account gives a good summary of the work.

Apparently, the year 1883 had proved to be the busiest ever because of 'peril and disaster on the sea, as is evidenced by the fact that over 600 sailors who had suffered shipwreck were admitted into the Homes'. The financial position of the Home had much improved and it was noted that £42,093 had passed through the cashier's hands at the main Sailors' Home. This money had been deposited by the seamen and was drawn upon as needed or sent on to their families by the Home. This enabled the Home to act as a bank for the sailors and this was much appreciated,

Mr. Ernest Inman was the guest speaker at the Annual General Meeting and he spoke at length about the apprenticeship system which was in decline and the general lack of well qualified British seamen.

The M.M.S.A. had written on this matter in 1876.

'Competent seamen are needed for the Merchant Service and Royal Naval Reserve; therefore they must be trained. The compulsory apprenticeship system is abolished, and cannot well be restored, and existing supplies of boys in ships and training schools are inadequate.'

There followed a plea for financial support for the training ship, *Indefatigable.*

The Annual report continued.

'The year 1883 was one of pleasant progress, so far as the inmates and work of the Home were concerned. In the parent Home 8,073 seamen were received, in the Branch Home 1,881, making a total of 9,954; being an increase, when compared with 1882, of 404. Of this number 263 were apprentices, 3,031 were old friends, who many times have returned to enjoy the comforts and privileges of the Home.

'The health of the inmates was good; there were, however, two sudden deaths, one of apoplexy and the other of diarrhoea, both accelerated by strong drink.

'The entertainment and instruction of the sailor by means of concerts, lectures, and temperance meetings, and also by billiard and bagatelle tables and draught-boards, and also by use of a good piano by those who understand music (and they are surprisingly many) were gratefully acknowledged by many inmates.

'Inconvenience and much annoyance was experienced by the crowds of crimps and runners who still press around the sailor upon leaving the ship on arrival at the dock quay, and who accompany him all the way to the Institution, very often seducing him into public-houses by the way, so that he becomes an easy prey to their fleecing wiles. The annoyance, also, is seriously felt at the doorways of both Homes, and your Committee venture to suggest that such a state of things ought not to be allowed to exist on any plea of the liberty of the subject. In the river, vessels on arrival are protected by the River Police, so that seamen do land sober, which was far from the case some few years ago.

'A small room was set apart early in November as a Temperance Club room, and a Society was formed, entitled 'The Liverpool Sailors' Homes Temperance Society,' with the result that almost every day sailors join it; and when leaving for sea some were selected to take charge of Roll Books and Cards, to induce others to join them as Members of the Society. From these already, and from others who were helped to a more hopeful life, very pleasing letters have been received.

'The Post Office in the general hall was instrumental in placing early news from home in the hands of seamen, residing both within and without the Institution, to a large and increasing extent.

'Allotment money was collected, and transmitted, free of charge, to parents and other relatives. Parents and friends were corresponded with in reference to their sea-going relatives, and much needed information was given, and thankfully received.

'Lieutenant Garnock, R.N.R., Superintendent, and the other official gentlemen of the Mercantile Marine Offices, were, as usual, very kind in aiding your Officers in the transference of money per the free money order system, and in every other helpful way.

'The Medical Gentlemen having charge of the Dispensary report that it continues to be availed of by seamen of all nationalities; that 832 new patients applied for treatment, whilst 2,463 total attendances had been recorded. Several severe cases were sent to the Lock Wards of the Royal Infirmary, where they were readily admitted.

'Mr. James Gill, Head Master of the Nautical School, states that the School maintains its good attendance and efficiency, and continues to do useful work, both in preparing candidates for the Examinations, and in extending the knowledge of General Navigation.'

At the turn of the century, much improvement was undertaken, including the installation of electric light! The stone work required refurbishing and the officers' quarters were refurnished. The Great War - 1914 - 1918 - brought much activity. 34,553 seamen registered at the Home, of whom 8,080 were shipwrecked or distressed mainly as the result of enemy submarine warfare.

The General Strike of 1926 produced a shortage of coal and almost brought the shipping industry to a halt and this vastly increased the demand for accommodation by seamen. The Shipping Federation Ltd. became tenants in part of the home in 1927 and this meant that all seafarers had to make use of the building. The depression years proved hard on the seamen and many, regardless of their rank and training, were pleased to accept any berth in any ship. The Sailors' Home, the Gordon Smith Institute and the Mersey Mission to Seamen were all sited within a hundred yards of each other ... they all did their utmost to bring relief to the men in need.

The Second World War suddenly meant that the seafarer was needed by the country! The Home was again stretched to its limits as it afforded immediate succour to some 20,000 survivors, prisoners of war as well as distressed British seamen who landed in Liverpool.

Much money was expended after the war to improve the building, carry out overdue repairs and this included the installation of central heating! 140 men were living in the Sailors' Home at any time.

There is no need to detail the immense contribution to the welfare of the seafarer by the Liverpool Sailors' Home over so many decades. However, after more than a century of caring, the inevitable was to happen.

When I came to Merseyside in 1961, it was obvious that the whole atmosphere was changing and that the Home would not be able to cope with the more sophisticated demands of the modern sailor. The cabins were too spartan and the atmosphere too clinical. Many men still used the accommodation, but numbers were dwindling. Every Tuesday morning I used to spend an hour in the Home, talking to the residents and the staff. The men who stayed there were mainly old and 'on the beach'. I found them fascinating with their nautical tales of times past and embroidered memories.

One of my great joys was to meet the young lads from *Indefatigable* on the Menai Straits who were sent to the Home to be measured for their seafaring rigs by the cheerful Bill Hobbs. It was a great opportunity for me to talk to them as they prepared to serve their apprenticeships in *Indefatigable* before going off to sea at the age of sixteen. There was no greater joy for me than conducting a Padre's Hour for them in Anglesey and then share in their pride at the passing out parades and on their open days.

" May your ship come home
Laden with Treasure Rich
and Rare."

SAILORS' HOME

LIVERPOOL

'XMAS DAY, 1935.

No-one could have guessed the magnitude of the changes in the nautical world which we all had to face at the tail end of the twentieth century. I count myself fortunate to have glimpsed the former glories.

The closure of the Home and its demolition removed from Merseyside not just a remarkable building, but the memories of a Liverpool of a past age. In 1969 the Seamen's Canteen was closed and in July of that year the residents were evacuated and the aged and infirm moved into 'The Ash'. In May 1970, the office of the Liverpool Sailors' Home, the *Indefatigable* and The Shipwrecked Mariners' Society was moved to Oriel Chambers in Water Street. The purchase of The Ash in Aigburth Vale provided a viable Home for the infirm seamen.

The Ash was a happy place and I payed weekly calls to meet old friends and, in particular, to chat with the Warden, Captain Frank Parker and his

MENU

Soups

Ox Tail   Julienne

Releves

Roast Turkey and Sausage

Bread Sauce

Joints

Roast Sirloin of Beef

Roast Pork   Apple Sauce

Sweets

Xmas Pudding   Mince Pies

Blanc Mange   Jellies

Dessert

Coffee

Here's Health and Peace, and
Length of days,
And Happiness for ever.

The Season's Greetings

A HAPPY CHRISTMAS

Enjoyment and Good Cheer,
And everything worth having
Throughout the NEW YEAR.

wife, Nora. The Ash was closed in December 1975 and most of the seamen were found excellent accommodation elsewhere. The Parker's retired to Mariners' Park in Wallasey.

However, it was not the end of the work. The trustees in 1976 formed themselves into the Liverpool Sailors' Home Trust and this enables them today to foster the care of the modern seafarer and support the organisations still active aboard the ships and amongst the retired Liverpool seafarers and their families in their homes. This care will certainly continue into the twenty-first century. We have travelled a long way since 1844, but the demands of the sea upon the seafarer do not diminish and there is still the need to care.

The work of the Liverpool Sailors' Home Trust will continue.

5.
Around the Sailors' Home

A smart Yankee packet
lies out in the bay
A-waitin' a fair wind to get under way
With all her sailors so sick and so sore,
They've drunk all their whisky and can't get no more
Singing roo-o-o-ol, roll bullies roll,
Them Liverpool judies have got us in tow!

Stan Hugill, Shanties from the Seven Seas

One of my great joys was to play my part as the padre in the Albert Dock aboard many a sailing ship, when Stan sang his shanties with people from the seven seas. Most dressed in traditional sea-going outfits, complete with 'squeeze-boxes and guitars'. It was all very romantic and very nautical and loved by us all. Nostalgia gilds the lilies. The reality of life one hundred years before was vastly different.

Today the area around the Sailors' Home is almost 'up-market' ... the site of the old Home is derelict, but the 1876 Mersey Mission building still stands and is now the Headquarters of the Anglican Diocese. Opposite is the Gordon Smith Institute which had a face-lift and become a centre for a legal firm. Nearby is a modern hotel and the offices of Radio Merseyside. One hundred and twenty-five years ago the picture was somewhat different. Such was the interest in that area that The Porcupine ran a series of articles entitled: 'Around the Sailors' Home'. The year was 1875.

Monstrous iniquity was used as a

> 'mild description of the dark doings which take place almost daily
> on the south side of the Sailors' Home. A bandits' revel may be

compared as a Sunday afternoon in the park to it. Black harlotry, outlawed thieving, and brazen blasphemy are there in all the glory of sunlight'.

Apparently at that time around the Sailors' Home there were always plenty of police in evidence, but that was all that they appeared to achieve. The law was not enforced. We read that there was one case which actually came to court. No surprise was expressed when it was dismissed by the judge as unbelievable. A blind eye was turned on the 'goings-on' and little effort made to clean the area of its all too obvious vices.

> *Oh, I'll not forget the day*
> *When I first met Maggie May,*
> *She was strolling up and down old Canning Place*
> *In a full-sized crinoline*
> *Like a frigate of the line,*
> *As she saw I was a sailor she gave chase.*

'Look at that woman in a gay bonnet and exceedingly strong coloured plaid shawl fastened over her shoulder with a brooch as large as an ordinary sized tea-saucer. She seems a well-to-do person, and is well 'got up', as the saying goes; but how anxious she looks. That man over the way, who is working his passage through the throng in the arcade, has just left her. He appears to be as anxious as she is, and much more determined. Who is he looking for? What does he want there? He is not a sailor; his pull-down cap, his monkey jacket, muffler and all cannot hide that fact. Ah! he has got him. Certain of it; for look at the change which has taken place in the expression of the woman's features. See how blandly she smiles; she is quite a good-looking creature now ... just the sort of woman to make a man comfortable.

'Presently we see them all in a crowd before a smiling barman ordering "glasses round", not forgetting the "drop of rum; I am so cold." The anxious gentleman with the pull-down cap and muffler is alongside and is prepared to be Jack's guardian angel. The 'girls' in the bar seem to understand whose prize Jack is and keep clear.'

The scene is set and the plot continues.

'Two of the girls are having an argument as to how often Bill has called at their house, and they refer to Bill, who is one of Jack's mates, to settle the dispute. As time goes on and the drink operates, one of the mates begins to take exception to Muffler with the pull-down cap. He has seen, or fancies he has seen, at any rate he says he has seen enough. He asserts that, during the time that Jack has been paying for the drinks, Muffler has regularly taken up the change and put it in his own pocket. Someone from behind, by way of impressing the truth of the remark on him to whom it is addressed, smacks Jack's mate's face.

'Of course there is a deal of shouting, swearing, and scuffling, and other ruffianly conduct, and the barman refuses to serve any more drink. Several 'Mufflers' take up Jack's mate's cause, foremost of whom is the one who 'smashed' him, and they get him outside and plaster him up, and for their kindness Jack takes them into another house to treat them, where he meets a tender and affectionate creature who declares she would spoil the face of him if she only knew who had injured the dear good fellow. Jack's heart is touched by the interest this painted harlot takes in him, and, as he sees no other way out of the net he has fallen into, he is led by her to a cab which he has given one of the Mufflers a half-crown for fetching. If you should meet that sailor early next morning, and without his coat, looking for a policeman, you may put him down as having been robbed.'

So the story ends and The Porcupine continues with half a page of homely thought or as Shimmin puts it ... 'A word of moralising and a little explanation may here be not out of place.' A month later another article appears with another story. The scene is again 'Around the Sailors' Home'.

'We are at the end of a street facing Canning Place. We had better not go too far up the street, as there is danger which even a town-councillor would not like to face. At the corner are some four or five loafers. They are arranging something, for they are busily engaged in conversation, and they never talk about nothing. Presently one of them exclaims, in a rather louder key than that in which the general conversation has been conducted, "Here he is. Let you and me go, Joe." And off Joe and he go.

'About half-way across the street they meet with a sailor, whom they accost with, "Hallo, Jack, how are you getting on?" ... at the same time one of them shakes Jack by the hand in a hearty and sailor-like fashion. Jack, however, does not seem to see it at first, and hesitates, saying something about not knowing them.

"What", exclaims Joe, coming to his companions assistance, "not know us! Why, didn't you come home in the Scuttle and Sinker along with Captain Givitum?"

'Of course, Jack did come home in the vessel named, and he cannot deny that the name of the captain is correct also; but he does not, even yet, see what all that has to do with the individuals who are addressing him.

"Well, I suppose you're going to stand a drain for old pals, aren't you?", puts in Joe's companion. "It'll not be the first go we've had together, and I hope it won't be the last."

'At this appeal, Jack, though inwardly wishing he had not met with the men, suffers himself to be led into a public-house, which he no sooner enters than he is confronted by three others who know him, and they are so elated at having met with him that they instantly signify their cordial feeling towards him by expressing a determination to have a 'pint' at his expense. He regrets now that he did not try and shake them off when in the street. He sees what they are, knows what they are and what they want; but, although he is within a few yards of the Home which professes to protect his interests, he is as powerless to help himself as though he were in the heart of a forest. He knows, as many others have known and have expressed themselves, that the first false step he takes, those five bull-dogs will be upon him, and will rob and half-murder him. He thinks of the money which is in his pocket, and thinks, too, even while he is drinking in that apparently reckless manner, of how he had to toil and suffer on the voyage.

'Whilst they are thus drinking, a shoeblack enters, and after looking round at Jack's companions for the 'item', requests permission to clean his boots. "No", is Jack's reply; but, at a signal from one of the five, the boy falls down upon his knees and commences to polish away, and, having finished, stands quietly by as mute as though he were merely awaiting the course of events. The 'pluck' for which Jack has been drinking gradually comes upon him, and he at last expresses his determination to 'go', to which no opposition whatever is offered. All drink up, and prepare to go also.

'When in the street, Jack begins to feel himself a little shaky, and steadies himself for a moment on the arm of one of the wolves. Now is the boy's time. He has not been paid for cleaning Jack's boots; so, standing right in the sailor's way, he cries, in well-practised, piteous whine, "Aren't yer goin' to pay me, sir?" Jack, already too full up with drink and vexation, pushes the boy away, whereupon the latter sets up a cry which is especially attributed to a certain nationality, and brings down upon the sailor the howls and curses of all the 'pocket-knives' and 'orange-baskets' and shoe-blacks about. Of course, the friends take Jack's part, and make a clean sweep of the howlers, but at the same time they remind Jack that he has not paid the boy. All this only tends to increase the sailor's rage, and he now gives vent to his feelings in words which, to say the least, are by far more forcible than polite, even to loafers. At last, in sheer desperation, he throws a coin into the street.

'Huddled and jostled into a dark street, Jack finds the drink has taken a certain power of limb from him. He feels himself 'going' in a manner which he now regrets but has not the power to stay. Now is the time. He is robbed, and, if he offer any resistance, beaten.

'Gone! Tomorrow he will have to 'look for a ship', and go away without having one day's enjoyment of his previous earnings.

'We have a Sailors' Home, how is it that a man is not safe outside his own door? The way to save the carcass from being torn is to drive the wolves away. But will they do it?'

> *I paid off at the Home*
> *From a voyage to Sierra Leone*
> *And two pound ten a month was all my pay.*
> *When I drew my cash I grinned,*
> *But very soon got skinned*
> *By a dirty robbing bitch called Maggie May.*

The next article is fairly aimed at the Missions in the City; their work is questioned and advice is firmly given. An obvious statement is made about Annual General Meetings of the Missions.

' ... we hear more good things on those occasions as a man is mostly better acquainted with the good he thinks he does than that which he has actually accomplished.'

At the Mersey Mission to Seamen's A.G.M., in April, 1875, the Bishop of Chester stated

'the society was doing what it could to shelter and protect the sailor from the evil influences by which he was beset.' The Porcupine describes this as 'bosh!' Mr. Balfour, the Honorary Secretary of the Mersey Mission, is then urged to face facts and 'tell the magistrates that they are to blame for the evils which exist.'

'Around the Sailors' Home there are many 'great shames' - some greater than others, but most of them great. The pretty glazed door 'which half open doth stand' is so inviting to the thirsty soul, and the bright polished glasses seem 'courting your hand' at every turn. As if this were not enough, the many fairy forms - some of them obese and frowsy which hover around and about render the temptation even more attractive. These lightly-clad and coarsely bedizened creatures are good customers at the grog temples.

'One of the girls, who has been most loving and endearing in her caresses, suddenly leaves the room for 'a minute'. The minute becomes more than sixty seconds. Jack's hands wander to his pockets. 'Cleaned out' he terms it; a definition by the way, which instantly causes his brother-sailors' hands to wander also.'

There is up-roar in the bar and the land-lord calls up his 'loafers' to land Jack a 'quiet one or two' in the street.

'When the police arrive on the scene Jack is bleeding and his face punched to a jelly. The girls are gone, and so are the loafers, and all that remains to be done is either to make Jack 'move on' or lock him up. The whole affair is very simple; any raw recruit can do it - if he be strong enough. If not, six officers can carry him.'

'Now, this is the sort of thing which the Mersey Mission to Seamen should find time to look at. It is quite evident there is little or nothing to be expected of magistrates until they are forced into action. Let the Society do this, and it will gain the gratitude and the support of every honest man.'

The next article discusses the 'runner or tout or crimp', which is described as a cross between a 'leech' and 'loafer'. The 'tout' is the shark who catches Jack with ease and it is more difficult for Jack to escape the 'tout' than to 'get a ship without a discharge'.

'At the Home, at the docks, on board ship, on the pierhead, in the 'shames', in the streets, everywhere where Jack is, the 'tout' is also. Now you may see in him a youth, gaily dressed, heavily bejewelled, and highly scented, the very picture of the professional pickpocket; again he is there the marked descendant of that money-making, money-loving race, 'vanting Shack to buy a vatch, sheap as dirt, shelp me gootnesh'. Over the way he is instantly transformed into the stout, burly, pilot-clothed sailor putting Jack up to the 'ropes' and showing him how, by taking friendly advice, he may make a 'good thing of it'. It may be as well to let the reader see one or two of these 'Good things'.

'We are under the lamps by the south-east corner of the Home. The man who is leaning on the iron stoop before us has all the appearance of a man on business bent. He seems to be counting and recounting every link in that plated Albert chain which he is continually passing from one hand to the other. He might stay there all day without attracting any special notice ... but he is off now across the road to tell that old woman with the needle-cases and purses to go away and leave the man when she is told. And so the old woman does go away and leaves the man to him; for the old woman has been watching the man for him. So he talks to the

man and expatiates on the nuisance of having so many street-
vendors about his heels, and the man seems glad to have escaped
from them, and asks his deliverer to have a drink, which he does,
and while doing so Jack asks what time it is. Now, Jack has plenty
of money but no watch, so his friend tells him he should have one,
as nothing is so respectable-looking as a watch; and, when he sees
his remark makes Jack's face brighten up, he 'stands' Jack a drink,
just to show he is not one of those loafing fellows such as are so
numerous about at the time.

'Jack begins to think himself a lucky fellow, and there is almost a
'tussle' about who pays for the next drink. Jack says it is his turn,
but his friend is above that sort of thing.

'Jack never thought there was so much goodness in a Liverpool
man, and he grows so warmly attached to his new friend that he
calls on him for a song, but his friend never sings in public-houses,
he only sings at home or in church. He intends, he says, that Jack
shall dine with him today, and he will sing after dinner. But there
is something now that troubles Jack a great deal more than all his
money. He has heard of a watch, but he has not seen it. Now he
wants to see it, and he says so; and, to gratify Jack, his friend takes
him to a friend's house where he knows they will be safe.

'On arriving at the friend's 'house', Jack has just eyesight enough
left to observe that it is attached to a shop, and that clothes as well
as jewellery are displayed in the window. There is a very nice sort
of man in the shop, who is very civil, and to whom Jack is introduced
as 'a friend of mine whom I have prevailed upon to dine with us'.
A decanter of rum is placed upon the table, and a glass filled for
Jack's especial gratification, whilst his friend deliberately and in a
business-like manner exhibits the watch which Jack was so anxious
about, but had quite forgotten. It is described as a 'gold centre
seconds', and is offered for six pounds - no one else should have it
under ten; but Jack's friend has taken to him, and is determined he
shall have it. Through a kind of film which has come over his eyes
since he drank the rum, Jack pulls out all the money he is possessed
of, and tells his friend to 'take it out of that', which the friend duly
does, and, having carefully counted the remainder, hands it back
to Jack, with a remark that it is as well for him he has fallen into
good hands. In a muddling state now, he exclaims, "It's like an
anchor without a cable; there, let's have a chain", and out his money
comes once more. The chain is supplied and fixed for him in a

very short time, and, after another 'go' or two at the decanter, Jack settles down on the couch. Forgetting all, and shutting out all the wickedness of the world, he sleeps and snores heavily. We will look in on him ere he wakes.'

The readers of The Porcupine had to wait a fortnight before the next episode in the story of our Jack was resumed. The inevitable has happened!

'Jack is in a far different train of mind when we look in on him again to what he was when we left him. He is sober now, and in a hot, feverish state which precluded all possibility of calmness. His hand shakes, and his blood-shot eyes tell of the fire which is in his head. He wonders where he is at first. His friend has looked in upon him many times whilst he was sleeping, and he is here with him now. Jack keeps muttering about being some sort of a 'fool', and says something about being 'in for it this time, at any rate.' He looks through the corner of his eye at his friend, who is quietly looking over the 'Shipping News'. He hardly knows how to 'open the ball', as he is quite in a muddle as to where he is, even with his friend's explanation. He draws the money from his pocket and counts it; then he puts it back again, only to be taken out and counted . once more. He plays with his watch-chain, and then he rubs his head again.'

The story rather slowly unravels. Apparently Jack always goes to the same boarding-house where he is given a 'rig-out'; this enables him to go to the Sailors' Home and acquire his next ship. If he does not honour this debt to the boarding-house keeper, he fears he will be 'smashed'. However, his new friend assures him that he will protect him. Meantime, the boarding-house keeper gathers his forces.

'Finding Jack did not return in fair time, Mr. Blank, the boarding-house keeper, sets out in search of him. The 'usual places' were duly visited, the girls questioned, and the old women taken to task. And so Jack is traced to the 'shame'. With this clue the rest is easy; it is that Grapper that has got hold of him.'

Jack realises the dangers.

'He has the best of living, for which he pays the highest price; and, as a natural consequence, his money soon runs short. When he can turn his pockets inside out without dropping anything on the floor, Jack thinks of a ship.'

Having bled Jack dry, Grapper decides that it is time for him to be shipped out and got rid of and Mr. Blank is to be diverted.

'Jack is wanted at the Home at last. The rival armies are there this day. Grapper is the victor, Mr. Blank's men are nowhere. Jack is taken in a cab, and once in the Home they dare not follow him. Once Jack is shipped and in possession of his advance note, he begins to feel the sort of man he was at first. He will have a bit of a 'spree' before he goes away. Grapper cannot allow him to go and make a fool of himself, and perhaps get half-murdered. He wants his note cashed, but Grapper is not going to give him money for it. Oh dear no! There is everything Jack wants in his shop. Once Grapper gets hold of the note, Jack is at his mercy. He will have to go on board tomorrow.'

The note pays for the new outfit, but what about the four days 'board and lodge' at the 'shame'? The watch and chain must be left as an earnest that on his return, Jack pays his debts! When he tells his mates his story, they laugh at him and recite similar tales. They assure him that he will never see his watch again.

'And Jack himself laughs after a time to think what a fool he has been, and vows if he ever goes back to Liverpool he will make it all square with Mr. Blank, the boarding-house keeper, as he is not such a bad sort after all.'

> *In the morning when I woke*
> *I found that I was broke*
> *No shoes, no shirt, no trousers could I find.*
> *When I asked her where they were*
> *She said, 'Oh, my dear sir,*
> *'They're down in Lewis's pawnshop, Number Nine.'*

The scene at the dockside is described.

'The vessel is hauled out of dock, men jump ashore and jump aboard, ropes are thrown out here and hauled in there, a great deal of "Let go!" and "All right!" and "Aye, aye, sir!" and the tug steams up and they are off.'

The Porcupine asserts that the police should not 'do more than three months' about the Sailors' Home, as it was too easy for them to be corrupted and take no action. "How many grog shops did Moody and Sankey succeed in closing?" It is a story of prostitution and robbery and in all ten articles, which appear in the weekly magazine, the sailor is outwitted and defrauded with professional ease.

Any port was popular for the sailor, but Liverpool had a special magnetism. The waterfronts about the world were notoriously dangerous places ... Liverpool was no different. The ballad of Maggie May probably started in the forecastle of the sailing ships and found its way into the music-halls. She was undoubtedly Irish and according to the story was deported to Australia to Botany Bay, an Australian penal settlement. There are many versions of the song as it was adapted by the seafarer.

Come all ye sailors bold
And when my tale is told
I'm sure you'll all have cause to pity me.
For I was a goddamn fool
In the port of Liverpool
When I met up with a girl called Maggie May.

Oooh, dirty Maggie May
They have taken you away
And you'll never walk down Lime Street
any more, any more,
For you robbed full many a sailor
And also a couple of whalers
And now you're doing time in Bot'ny Bay, oooh!

The area around the Sailors' Home was the parade ground for the Maggie Mays of Liverpool. No wonder after some months at sea in an ill-founded ship with poor food and ever-wet clothing, Paradise Street to a Liverpool Jack appeared to be just that!

6.
The Mersey Mission to Seamen

We're homeward bound to Liverpool town:
Goodbye, fare ye well! Goodbye, fare ye well!
We'll stamp at the capstan and heave it around,
Hoorah, my lads, we're homeward bound!

Following his 'Cruise on the Mersey', W.H.G. Kingston called the first committee meeting for the Mission on Monday 24th November, 1856. The Rector of Liverpool, Dr. Campbell, took the chair at that first meeting, but the first permanent chairman was Mr. Christopher Bushell and he was succeeded by his son, also Christopher Bushell. The Bushell family was to serve the Mission for 96 years.

The Minutes for 1858 are not very exciting. It was not a very good birth.

'Income in Donations   £122.11s.
Subscriptions   £113.8s.
Total   £235.19s
Expenses   £237.11s.7d.

'In 1859 the subscriptions and donations not having met the necessary increased disbursements, support this year has unhappily been required from the London Society. This pecuniary obligation the Committee are most anxious to obtain the means to discharge.'

The first appointed Chaplain had been the Reverend Bellamy; his Christian name is not recorded. He commenced his ministry in 1858, but nothing is known about him. Whilst this was not a very successful start for the Mersey Mission to Seamen, the organisation was to prove itself to be a viable and enduring Society, devoted to the care of the seafarer.

The objects of the Mission were clearly defined from the beginning and have been little changed in a century and a half.

'To promote and minister to the spiritual, moral and temporal welfare of Merchant Seamen by means of :

> The provision of Institutes for seamen.
> Religious Services in the Mission and on Shipboard.
> The visitation of Ships, Hospitals and Homes.
> The circulation of the Bible.

> Arrangements for the comfort and support of seamen in need, and any other acts which may be considered of benefit to them.'

That is the essence of the Charter and the present work of the Mersey Mission to Seamen can still be judged by it.

In 1859, the Reverend Edward Thring was made the Superintendent Chaplain. The work in Liverpool was already well founded by other organisations. The two Floating Chapels, the *William* and the *Tees* were operating in the docks; the Reverend William Maynard worked in the *Tees* and the Liverpool Seamen's Friend Society looked after the *William*. The Liverpool Sailors' Home had proved to be a natural centre for the seafarer, although it was to be gutted by fire in 1860. This was the scene when Thring was appointed.

It was soon realised that the Chaplain's work was to be mainly aboard ships, in the river and in dock, and also in the boarding houses on the dockside. Much work was also needed amongst the thousands of emigrants, waiting for passage in Liverpool, all ambitious for a new life in the 'new world' of America. In his Journal, Thring records: 'Visited eleven vessels during the day. Could have had nearly as many again had we sails in our boat, rowing is such a loss of time.' He was to get his sails in due time!

The next year's Report stated that sixty thousand sailors passed through the port annually. Thring talks about visiting the canal boats in Ellesmere Port:

'It is something astounding to see the ignorance they manifest in the most simple things; they appear to live more resembling the animals. They do not let their children live afloat with them more than 5 or 7 years, as they are forced to live in one cabin; and as one poor mother said, "It won't do". They are not only dirty but filthy; their cabins are not only small, but absolutely noisome ... I pitied them from my heart.'

Thring writes about his time with the Hoylake fishermen.

'Most narrowly they looked at us as we pursued our visit from boat to boat, supposing us to be Custom House men; though our flag, which was the Society's ensign flying aloft, puzzled them still more.'

Off Runcorn, Thring was called ashore by some stone quarrymen at Weston Point.

'I could not refuse. They were very attentive indeed. As the cold wind whistled around the stone blocks it was really a picture to see those fine fellows throwing their jackets round their shoulders to shelter them from the sharp wind, and giving themselves such a decided posture, as if to say, we intend to hear you out.'

A.R.B. Robinson has written about Thring in a book entitled 'Chaplain on the Mersey 1859 - 67.' Thring's journals are full of information.

'In 1859 Thring was begged by the first mate of the *Queen of the East* to press for the appointment of river police to deal with the problem of crimping. "I refer to the practice of lodging house keepers boarding the ships as they come into the river," Thring explained, "and seducing the poor simple sailor by offering him spirit with all kinds of drugs in it in order to stupefy him, and then taking him on shore with his pockets full of money and robbing him. As the first mate said: "The cargo is not safe, nor the sailors. There is not a more dreadful body of men than these crimps; it must be law to stop them coming aboard at all."

'So the Missioner set to work to secure the co-operation of the captain, mate and pilot of every ship in the river and docks. It was an enormous undertaking, but he received ready support. Ship's officers told him that sailors with accumulated pay of £20 to £50 were found in debt a week later. One example quoted was of a man who lost £22 and all his clothes. And some crimps 'are so impudent as to bring fallen girls on board to entice the sailors.'

'It is remarkable to read in Thring's journals how captains and crews of ocean-going vessels, accustomed to every peril of the deep, seemed almost defenceless against crimps coming aboard.

It sounds as if some of the crews were bribed in advance to help the crimps, though Thring does not say so. And although the mate of an American ship said "You English should do what our captains do - send a slug into those confounded river torments", another witness said that things were just as bad in New York. There, crimps would come on board and demand advance payment from the sailors. In one instance, when such payment was refused, 109 crimps attacked the men in the forecastle with iron hooks, and 'a furious scene was witnessed.'

'The next Annual Report of the Missions to Seamen noted that 'Through the exertions of our Chaplain, energetically supported as he has been, a severe blow has been dealt to the crimping system. The protection which the law gives to the sailor has been enforced, and, at signals agreed upon, the police are ready instantly to proceed to any vessel in the river'. This was somewhat wishful thinking, as the 1863 Report, three years later, said that river police were still being sought. However, it was at about that time that a Royal Navy officer took Thring to watch a Dublin steam boat enter dock full of emigrants, 'to see what the crimps would do'; and on that occasion the crimps politely offered proper clothing and lodging for a few days until the ship was ready to sail, all for the price of eight shillings.

'The fact was that, with or without the police, the fight against crimping was under way, a matter for which the captain of a fine vessel bound for Australia expressed his hearty gratitude in 1860. "No trouble now in coming into the Mersey", he told Thring. "No longer pested by those lazy fellows." And on the *Westmoreland,* Captain Dean said "Now, Sir, it is some pleasure to drop anchor in the Mersey. One crimp came to me and I just said 'Shall I take the number of your boat, or hoist the signal?' That was enough: he was off Yes, 'twas a good effort, that."

'Thring still issued warnings. 'Held a service on the *C..... H..... S.....* , a homeward-bound ship', he wrote in 1860. 'Strongly warned the sailors of temptations awaiting them on shore, and gave them cards for very respectable boarding-houses.'

'It seemed to bear fruit. In 1861 he met the purser of a ship he had previously visited for a Sunday Service. The purser related that on the pay day after that service, 110 out of the 150 crew were in a perfectly sober state, saying that they intended to practise the advice the missionary gave them. "Such a thing, Sir, I have never seen all the time I have been at sea." And, indeed, the 110 sailors bought clothes, and invested the rest of their money - "and in a few days" the purser said, "I saw them about the docks and town more like a body of gentlemen than poor sailors."

'Not surprisingly, the crimps took their revenge on the Missioner. Thring wrote in 1862: 'I came to the vessel, *J.....*, arriving in port. The captain had ordered no crimps to be allowed on board, but some had got into the forecastle. They had not had time to begin drugging people. I went to the men there and asked them to choose between the boarding-houses and the Sailors' Home.' Apparently they all chose the Home. Thring went ashore and ordered a cart from the Home to collect the sailors' belongings from the Pier Head when the ship docked there. By that time, however, 'a large concourse of crimps, runners, tailors and outfitters were assembled at the Pier Head. Many attempted to board the ship, but the police turned them away.' They objected strongly to the Chaplain being allowed on board the ship again if they were not, and 'they poured their abuse upon me as long as I was in their sight.' As the sailors left the ship with Thring, the crimps continued to curse him, and tried to steal the sailors' boxes as they were put on the cart. Thring called the police, but even then, he said, did not dare leave his sailors in case the crimps enticed them away. 'The smell of spirits is like magic upon them and away they go.' Of the 22 who had volunteered for the Home he got 17 safely there.'

Thring was quite clear that the issue was between himself and the crimps. A week later, 'having received intelligence of a ship from Bombay, I rose at 4.30, and at 6 a.m. was on the water, rowing against the tide for two hours to reach the ship at 8 a.m.' Presumably he went aboard and sailed into port on the ship. 'No sooner had we touched the Pier Head than nearly forty crimps sprang on board and began soliciting for their houses.' On that occasion seven out of the thirty two crew were persuaded not to go. The captain of the vessel declared "he had never been so impudently treated", and that the police were no help.

"The crimps may as well take my ship", he said. "They have the fore part, and the next, I suppose, will be my cabin. There never was a quieter crew, and now look at that man, as drunk as he can be, taking off his clothes."

'The sailors are asking loudly for the Sailors' Home', wrote Thring in 1862, 'and are indignant at the exposure they are subjected to from women so constantly standing round the Sailors' Home.' Not a complaint frequently met among sailors! And, yet, many seamen at that time do seem to have been genuinely harassed. In 1863, 'at the mouth of the river, the *E*..... was in a state of confusion. The crimps had enticed two men, and they had jumped overboard to get ashore, and one was drowned. Will not these repeated instances open the eyes of the authorities of Liverpool to give us river police? The *J... L...*, just in from China, was full of crimps. But on the *D....* the captain appreciated the success of the Mission so much 'that he insisted on such an excellent effort being toasted with a glass of gin.' "I was not unwilling," said Thring, "to accept a cup of coffee in its place."

The 1864 Report of the Mission said that 'a River Police is to be established.' The 1865 Report went further.

'They have a river police, but they have taken another step. They invited about 300 of the boarding house keepers to a tea party in Hope Hall, and they promised their co-operation.'

Hope springs eternal. But Thring was realist enough to write in 1865,

'On the *W....* the sailors' appearance was wretched, their language dreadful, and yet a mixture of kindness through it all. A crew of 20 men ruined, at least for some time, by the crimps! With one voice they wished me well, but would prefer rum to the Gospel.'

Thring was to leave Liverpool in 1867 for work in South America. He was a remarkable man. He found his way to the Chincha islands, a barren place where the guano was shipped to England. It was a filthy place to work. The labourers were Peruvian Indians, Chinese, convicts and Easter Islanders. The deposits of bird lime were handled aboard the ships in temperatures above a hundred degrees. After this time in Peru, he went to Uruguay. On his return to Liverpool he served a curacy at St. George's Church, Everton (1874 - 75).

Thring's successor was John Hetherington. The affairs of the Mission could not have been in great heart as a portion of the salary had to come from London. However, it was felt that a chaplain should be appointed by the Mission to operate from the Liverpool Sailors' Home and the Reverend Adam Ford from St. Aidan's College in Birkenhead was given the task. Thring had shown how invaluable the Home was to the seafarer. In 1874, the Mission rented a room in the Sailors' Home. Up to this time all the work had been on the river and in the docks and it was decided to employ a River Chaplain and a Shore Chaplain. This was not to be a successful venture and in 1877 Hetherington was asked to resign after ten years of honest endeavour! It was a hard verdict on his ministry.

The new man, the Reverend Tom Patrick, proved to be a winner and served in Liverpool for twelve years (1878 - 89). His duties included two services

71

each Sunday in the Sailors' Home. The Home was a natural focal point in Liverpool for all seafarers and the link with the Mission was strong and effective.

As the Liverpool Seamen's Friend Society had established Bethels, so the Mersey Mission opened Mission Rooms to be used by the Scripture Readers as bases and places of Worship. In addition, a coffee room was created at the Mission Room in Price Street for the use of Captains and Officers.

An assistant chaplain was appointed to serve in the Training Ship, *Indefatigable,* and to take Services in the South Sailors' Home. It was accepted that the Mersey Mission would supply and fund these chaplains. At this time (1879) the Mariners' Church (*The Tees*), which was lying in Birkenhead Dock, was taken over by the Mission.

The desire to be free of the control of the Parent Society in London was put forward in 1874. The next year the Bishop of Manchester agreed that his Diocese would support the Mersey Mission, but in 1879 it was agreed that the Dioceses of Liverpool and Chester would become the catchment area for the Mission. Manchester was to establish its own Chaplaincy under the guidance of Missions to Seamen, London ... this work continued for a hundred years and closed during my time in Liverpool.

We cannot help but be surprised that at the Social Science Congress, at St. George's Hall, October 6th, 1876, one of the subjects under consideration was 'Divine Services on Board Merchant Ships'. A Captain Hatfield stated that this matter was often 'pooh-poohed and scoffed at', and then made his points forcibly. He ended with these words:

> "A little book is issued under the patronage of the Mersey Mission to Seamen; I think it is one of the best little books that could be put into the hands of our seamen. It contains some nice hymns, sermons, and part of the service of our Common Prayer Book; I think it is a most excellent thing, and should be encouraged."

Perhaps I should not have been so surprised to read this, because in the 1960's I was asked by two major shipping companies to produce a similar booklet.

The expansion continued. A room was acquired in Canada Dock (1878), also in 1880 at Ellesmere Port, Bootle and in the North Sailors' Home. A separate Branch of the Mission was created in Birkenhead. The Mission in Runcorn was renovated. An 'iron room' was planned (completed in 1885) in Ellesmere Port for the Boatmen and the Flatmen and a Missioner was appointed. In 1883 a new site was purchased for Price Street. Most important of all was the new Central Institute in Hanover Street, opened the 10th December, 1884, by Mr. Ralph Brocklebank. Speeches were delivered by the Bishop, Mr. Balfour, Mr. T.H. Ismay, Sir Thomas Brocklebank and Mr. James Beazely. (This fine building was to become Church House, the head-quarters for the Diocese of Liverpool, in 1956.)

The Mission Committee was composed of men of great stature and influence on Merseyside. In 1885 R.H. Lundie wrote a Memoir on Alexander Balfour. Balfour was the Honorary Secretary of the Mission from its inception in 1856 until his death at the age of 89 in 1886. He defrayed the entire cost of the Mission Room at the north end and also paid the salary of one of the agents. Balfour recorded in his note-book, whilst travelling to Valparaiso on the *S.S.Panama,* the following thoughts.

'On board the *Panama* there are 32 sailors, firemen and stokers, of whom only three possessed Bibles - I distributed among them 28 copies of the scriptures - as a memento of our voyage.

'In the evening ... went and spoke to the men in the forecastle ... counselled them to trust in the love of God who has given His Son to die for us individually.'

Balfour with the aid of Ralph Brocklebank established a Seamen's Orphanage and a Home for apprentices and junior officers. Together they also instigated the Liverpool Committee for Enquiry into Conditions of Merchant Seamen.

'...that sailors' employment might be made more regular, their temptations to drink reduced, their families provided for in case of death...'

With men like Alexander Balfour it is no surprise that the Mersey Mission had become a force in the port and that the people of Liverpool gave it ready support.

In the Mersey Mission Report of 1888 is the following statement:

'The Sailors' Home and the Mersey Mission Institute are in the heart of an enormous migratory sea-going population and we can do little but wonder at the change which has come over this locality within the last few years.'

Much had happened during the ministry of the Reverend Tom Patrick, the first in the Mission to be called the Chaplain Superintendent. He retired in 1889 after eleven years on the Mersey.

Next came the Reverend Charles Maxwell Woosnam ... a man of strong character, he continued to keep the Mission on the map. Above all, he attracted remarkable men to work alongside him.

The Reverend Alan Williams joined the staff with particular responsibility for *Indefatigable*. There were five training ships on the Mersey at this

The Central Institute, now Church House

time. As they played a firm part in the story of 'Mersey Mariners' they each deserve chapters to themselves.

The Reverend Alan Williams was to go on to work in South Africa. He went there because of ill-health! He had resigned from Liverpool in 1896 and until the London Parent Society agreed to take over the work in Cape Town, the Mersey Mission Flag was to be flown there. He quickly extended the work to East London. When the Boer War started, Williams was there to welcome the troops under the Liverpool Flag!

Perhaps the best known chaplain appointed by Woosnam was the Reverend James Fell, who came to work in Liverpool in 1890. His name was to become a legend. For three years he had been at Sunderland and West Hartlepool under the London Society. Three years after coming to Liverpool, Fell asked that he might be sent to San Francisco. His work in Liverpool must have opened his eyes to the plight of the British seafarers in that city. In 1893 an agreement was made with the Mission in London and Fell departed.

Almost immediately he opened a Mission. The upper floors of a three-storey building at 33, Stuart Street near the Market were rented and opened on 3rd June, and there the Flying Angel well known to Mariners throughout the world proved a welcoming beacon to the British in particular and to all other seafarers. Ninety per cent of all seamen in that port were British. On arrival at the port most crews were paid off and found their way on shore as best they could. Obviously they proved to be easy targets. Fell's initial task was to deal with the crimps and tales are told of chases through the streets and much opposition. Probably all that was needed was to co-ordinate the authorities and appeal to the public conscience. Fell was the man to do just that.

There certainly had been a major problem in San Francisco. An article, which appeared in 1893 in the Mercantile Marine Service Association's Review gave some details.

'British shipowners were being intimidated by the crimps and boarding masters and an American Association of Shipowners was formed 'to meet and combat the evil'. That Association attempted to co-ordinate its activities with the English Federation. The Americans complained: although British Shipmasters in the port of San Francisco were eager to avail themselves of the advantages afforded by the influence of the Association while it held a coign of vantage, yet that their timidity and supineness when their power was assailed and vital points seemed to be at issue, proved a real

Group taken in 1895 at the start of Lambert's ministry in Liverpool.
Top row: Mr. Rose, Mr. Hendrickson, Mr. Thomas Williams, Mr. Green,
Archdeacon Woosnam, Rev. S. Lambert, Rev. H. O'Rorke, Mr. Howard,
Rev. H.J. Dawson.
Middle row: Miss Morgan, Mrs. Williams, Mrs. Woosnam, Mr. C. Bushell,
Mrs. Lambert, Mrs. Horan, Mr. Forbes
Bottom Row: Rev. H.E. Elwell, Mr. Hutton, Rev. Alan Williams, Mr. W.
Shaw, Rev. C.T. Horan.

weakness to the cause and was actually the prime element of temporary defeat. The terms of the Association were eagerly accepted and upon the first difficulty arising in their minds as to procuring a crew they ratted and went over to the enemy.'

There certainly was a problem in San Francisco in procuring new crews for the return voyage of British ships and it was freely admitted that the 'blood money' was paid to cover the cost of procuration and that it was often extortionate. Fell's main contribution was to provide lodgings and supply the crews, in this way by-passing the crimps. It was dangerous work. He was successful.

Fell was to remain for six years and the Mission was to spread across the United States. He returned home to work in the Lake District and his achievements went unnoticed. All that is left today is a plaque in the present Mersey Mission Chapel at Colonsay House in Crosby.

Woosnam retired from Liverpool, having been appointed the Archdeacon of Macclesfield, and was succeeded by the Reverend Edgar Lambert. He remained in Liverpool for sixteen years (1895 - 1911).

The Mersey Mission was busy with connections with London, San Francisco, South Africa and the Training Ships on the Mersey. Under Lambert there were six chaplains, seven lay readers, five Institute Keepers, two Launchmen, who were working from seven Mission Churches and Institutes. It was big business.

Work was also undertaken along the Leeds - Liverpool Canal at Crabtree, near Burscough. A mission was established in the hay-loft of the shop at Crabtree Lane. The Reader in charge was Mr. Hendricksen. Very quickly this was found to be inadequate and a corrugated-iron building, known as St. Andrew's Mission, was erected in New Lane in 1905. It is still in use as a daughter church of Burscough. During my three decades on the waterfront, the Mission staff were always asked to preach at the Harvest Festival Evensong. The small building was ever over-flowing and never was the hymn, *Eternal Father,* better sung.

Next in line was the Reverend D.W. Dobson (1911 - 1922). Almost immediately an Institute was built in Birkenhead and this was followed by a new Institute in Garston. The First World War was a challenge for the Mission. A Seafaring Boys' Home was established, the Central Institute in Hanover Street was extended. Dobson had eleven assistant clergy. It was a busy time.

Dobson resigned in 1921 and became the Rector of Heswall in Wirral. His successor was Lord Thurlow, who with Harry O'Rorke had joined Fell in San Francisco and then in Valparaiso. Thurlow had also run the

Mission at Portland in Oregon. O'Rorke, who had worked with the Mission in Liverpool, was to take over from Fell and had also taken with him as an assistant another Liverpool chaplain, the Reverend A.B.L. Karney. Karney was to work eventually on the East Coast of South America and was based in Buenos Aires. Later he became the Bishop of Johannesburg for ten years and then returned as Bishop of Southampton.

Lord Thurlow was in Liverpool for eight years (1922 - 1930). They were not the easiest of years. Shipping was laid-up, and ship-building almost stopped. It was the time of the general strike, hunger marches and world depression. Thurlow faced a period of retrenchment. The Institute in Hanover Street was no longer viable, but the work continued.

The Reverend John Reginald Weller (1931 - 1934) realised that the Gordon Smith Institute and the Sailors' Home provided more than enough accommodation for the seamen and restructured the Mission in Hanover Street as a Club for Junior Officers and Apprentices. Many men who officered the Merchant ships during the second world war were grateful for this innovation. Weller, however, soon departed to become the Bishop of the Falkland Islands.

The ministry of the Reverend George William Evans proved vital to the continuance of the Mersey Mission (1935 - 1956). He faced changing problems. After fifty years usage, the iron building on the Shropshire Canal at Ellesmere Port was closed and in the following year (1935) a new institute was opened in Garston. A Shipboard Libraries' Service was inaugurated in 1935. The Mission launch, *Good Cheer III*, was given up and the work aboard ships was operated from the docks. World War Two was to transform the activities of the Mission.

Liverpool suddenly became the 'front line'. Ship visiting became a priority and the Mission was the main distribution centre for all woollen comforts, libraries, etc., for the Merchant Navy and the mine sweepers. First Aid instruction had originated in the Mission in 1896 and was carried on during the war by Dr. Murray Cairns. Boys were sent to the Mission in preparation for their first voyages and there was close liaison with the Gravesend Sea School and the *T.S.Exmouth*. A Home was established at 20 Princes Avenue for these boys ... sadly many were not to return from the war. A Social Club was opened in 5 Ranelagh Street (opposite Central Station) with accommodation for 35 boys. A Club was established at 31 Princes Avenue. Above all, Merchant Navy House for officers of the Merchant Navy was opened in 1941. This was an excellent contribution and there were to be five extensions ... 1 Percy Street in 1941, 4 Canning Street in 1942, 6 Canning Street in 1944 and 1950 and the New Wing in 1947. In charge was Miss Bridger. She had been a Cape Horner ... having voyaged around the Horn under sail ... and she ruled the young officers with little difficulty.

Liverpool in the mid-thirties

Sadly in the early sixties she was killed in a coach accident whilst on holiday in South Africa. She is still remembered.

Underlying all this work was the daily contact and care of hundreds of thousands of seafarers. This was the real work of the Mission and is still fondly talked of today.

The post-war demand was a mixture of the desire to revert to a previous time and the desire for change. The explosion of clubs for the 'hostilities only' men was over and that activity was removed. Whilst Merchant Navy House continued, other places had to be closed. Ellesmere Port was finished. The Seamen's Club at Strand, Bootle was closed. The Club and Chapel at Runcorn, where the narrow and flat boatmen and their families had been cared for, was obsolete. The property was sold. As after the First World War, it was time for retrenchment.

The Indian seafarers had been the concern of the Mission since the turn of the century. A Club had been opened for them in Birkenhead in 1901. In 1941 a similar place was opened in 11 Paradise Street in Liverpool; this was replaced in 1948 by a Club on Derby Road in Bootle for Indian and Pakistani seamen. Many hundreds of men came off their ships each night to enjoy films in their own language and culture. The days of the Lascars walking the streets of Liverpool with blankets on their backs were well over and the Clubs met the new needs of these men.

Plimsoll House, 1 Gambier Terrace, over-looking the Cathedral and very near to Merchant Navy House, was taken over by the Ministry of Labour during the war as a residential club for seafarers. It was opened in June 1942 by Ernest Bevin, who at that time was Minister of Labour and National Service. In 1946 the responsibility for seamen's welfare was transferred from that Ministry and the Government decided that the welfare of seamen should be the concern of the industry and, after negotiations with the National Maritime Board and the voluntary societies, the Merchant Navy Welfare Board was constituted and commenced operations in March 1948. That Board asked the Mersey Mission to act as trustees of Plimsol House. It was a fine house, in a fine situation and provided accomodation for 55 men. But the following year, July 1949, the Merchant Navy Welfare Board took over the management with a long term lease.

Plimsoll House was a fine building with spacious rooms. In 1949 the cost of a single room was 7s., including bed and breakfast, and a double room was 6s. Luncheon was provided at a cost of 2s. 3d., and high tea was 1s. 9d.

In 1956 the Mission took a great step. The Institute in Hanover Street was sold to the Diocese of Liverpool for use as Church House and it was decided to build a new headquarters in James Street.

This was well conceived and at the time was the right building in the right place. The Merchant Navy Establishment (the Pool) was to open new premises across the road on Mann Island in the November of that year and this ensured that most seamen would have to report there in order to have a berth aboard ship. The Mission erected a hut on the other side of the road whilst the new Mission was being built. The new building was to be called Kingston House in honour of the founder W.H.G. Kingston in 1856. A fresh start was being made just one hundred years later.

Kingston House was opened by the Duke of Edinburgh in 1957. Canon Evans had retired and the new Chaplain Superintendent was the Reverend Noel Thomas, who had served the Missions to Seamen in Santos and Southampton.

However, all was not well. The dramatic changes in expectations and the conditions of service for the seafarer had not been fully understood. Kingston House was a fine four storey building on the corner of James Street, but was not well used by the visiting seamen. It had been designed on the pre-war thinking of the division of officers and men. The seamen were confined to the ground floor canteen with concrete tables and little comfort. There were no activities organised to attract the men off their ships. Meanwhile, Atlantic House in Hardman Street was bustling with dances every night, with well designed lounge bars, a first class restaurant and all the comforts required by the modern seafarer. Kingston House was failing.

At the end of 1961 the Reverend Noel Thomas resigned and even though I had arrived to work as an Assistant Chaplain a mere nine months previously and had not expected that I would remain more than two years, I was asked to become the Chaplain Superintendent. Little did I realise that I would remain in charge until 1989, apart from a short spell back in a parish. The committee and the Bishop of Liverpool obviously felt that I had been in Liverpool long enough to assess the problems and that I knew what had to be done. Kingston House had to be made to work.

'Officers Only' signs were all removed, together with the concrete tables. Old furniture was replaced, lights and carpets and cheerful curtains arrived, a new bar was built ... all men were welcome regardless of rank, colour, creed or nationality. A dance band was engaged, local girls became my Flying Angels and we slowly began to bring life into the new Kingston House. Hard work was fun.

My most important task was to visit the ships in the docks. Each morning we turned to what we called the 'maternity section' of the Journal of Commerce, 'Ships Expected Shortly'! With two assistant chaplains and two or three students, we were aboard each vessel on its day of arrival.

There were about one hundred and fifty vessels in dock at any time. Suddenly there was much to do. Friendships were to be established which have lasted to the present day.

Liverpool was on the threshold of the music explosion that shook the world. Beatlemania was upon us. Happily I was able to engage four members of the Liverpool Police Band to play in our third floor ballroom every night and everyone wanted part of the fabulous new sound that had put Liverpool on the map. We all rocked and rolled and twisted. Kingston House was full as we averaged over five hundred seafarers passing through the swing doors every day. Kingston House was bubbling.

Our Chapel of the Good Shepherd attracted over twenty seamen every night of the week for a family service and it was obvious that the majority of seafarers were happy to 'pop-in' for a quiet moment or two. With over one hundred and fifty girls it was no surprise that some of them asked that we prepare them for confirmation. Boy met girl and I officiated at many a marriage.

Lunchtime was busy as eight waitresses served in the restaurant from noon 'til two. A three-course meal was served for half-a-crown. There was not a shipping office in which I did not have a friend to contact and sort out any problem. I no longer felt isolated, but belonged to a large family. Every board room of every shipping company was open to me. With so many seafarers every day using Kingston House, suddenly it all became big business and eventually we were to employ fifty-five staff members, apart from the chaplaincy team.

The College of the Sea and the Seafarer's Education Service had a library on the same floor as the Chapel and my study. Men came to borrow the text books for their marine examinations and this opened the Liverpool Nautical Colleges to me. Marjorie Mougne and her successor, Elizabeth Edwards, were in charge of the library and were known all over the world. Each year we displayed a national art exhibition of seafarers' work. The standard was remarkable. Many men studied for 'O levels' and 'A levels' and my task was to be the invigilator. Numbers of seamen were to start their training as officers as a result of all our endeavours.

Many cadets aged sixteen were sent to us for interviews before making their first trip to sea and this also established lasting friendships. I always wrote to their parents and this simple courtesy was well received. Then there were Padre's Sessions in the Merchant Navy Establishment for men off to sea for the first time as firemen. These were fairly tough characters, but as nervous as anyone else as they prepared for a life at sea. The young men from the training establishments *Indefatigable* and *Conway* were all given the same treatment. The Mersey Mission was playing a vital role in the care of seafarers.

Every month there was a meeting of the Port Welfare Committee. The members came from all the organisations concerned with the well-being of the seafarer, together with the Port Police, the Port Health Authority and the representatives of the Unions and the Ship Owners. It was an excellent clearing house for ideas and information. In the early sixties the chairman was Ronnie Swaine, a director of Alfred Holt Shipping Company. The year was 1963 and he asked me directly whether we were prepared to complete the building of Kingston House. The answer was obvious.

We planned a ten storey hotel with sixty-two bedrooms, a dining room with a bar, staff rooms and offices for the staff. The total cost was about two hundred thousand pounds. We sold our Officers Club, Merchant Navy House, to the Merchant Navy Welfare Board and within two years or so the new project was clear of all debt. With our fifty-five staff members, a large number of voluntary helpers, a four storey Club and a ten storey Hotel, the Mersey Mission to Seamen was ideally placed to meet the needs of men from every corner of the port. Life was very busy. It was to be a decade of frenetic activity in Liverpool. Everyone wanted to become involved. Hindsight tells us that it can never ever be like that again.

The work of the Padre opens every door and friends are made for life. The great joy of this ministry is the meeting of people and the remarkable stories which are then quietly unfolded. This happened when asked to conduct the funeral of the aunt of a friend, David Backhouse. His aunt, Ethel Gertrude Caldwell, died at the age of 91 and ten years previously she had attached a note to an old painting. It told the story.

'Henry Buchanan: my great grandfather was born in Demerara in 1815. He was educated at Whitfield House Academy, Roby, near Liverpool by Messrs. Baron Brothers, in Classical Literature, Commercial Education, Mathematics, Navigation, Geography and use of the Globes.

'He was Mate of the ship *Mendora* and he sailed from Liverpool to Australia in 1857. He was a gold digger in New Zealand in · 1870 and was also a cabinet maker, and owned property in Queen's Place, Rock Ferry and other property.

'He married Mary Jane Roby and had a daughter Maria Emilia, who married Walter Woolley, and they were my grand-parents. Henry Buchanan's father was George Buchanan, born 15 June 1782. He was a sugar merchant of Demerara and Landed Proprietor. He returned to Demerara in 1828. He died in Finnich Malice, Drymen, Scotland, 1832.'

This was a perfect example of a chance meeting and a conversation spanning two centuries.

In 1974 I left the Mission to become the Vicar of Rainhill as I felt that my contribution was completed. Five years later to my immense surprise I was back in harness. Three chaplains had come and gone and the affairs of the Mission were in need of a man with experience. I was to remain for a further ten years until I retired in 1989.

That last decade which I spent in the Mission was dramatic. The port was changing speedily. The South Docks were closed, together with much of the North Docks. The shipping was centred around the Royal Seaforth complex. The nature of the vessels changed. The very large container vessels were able to turn around in twelve hours. Crew numbers of over one hundred disappeared as the new vessels were manned by no more than eighteen seafarers. The same volume of trade was handled by just one tenth of the number of ships. Twenty thousand dockers had their ranks reduced, not without a struggle, to around five hundred. Shipping offices disappeared, together with most of the major company names. The British merchant fleet was fast disappearing All this had a direct influence on the Mission and on every other organisation. It needed a clear head and an even clearer vision of the purpose of the Mission in order to survive. Above all, it needed a Committee with the courage and wisdom to ensure that the Mission was to survive.

In the early eighties, we closed Kingston House, the Merchant Navy Welfare Board removed their presence at Merchant Navy House and our Roman Catholic friends sold Atlantic House. The Sailors' Home and the Gordon Smith Institute had already closed their premises. The day of the 'big club' was over It was very painful, but was the only way to meet the changes that rushed upon us. The British seafarer was no longer to be needed in any great numbers. We had to adapt or disappear. It was not without pain.

The Apostleship of the Sea centralised all their activity at their Stella Maris complex in the Strand at Bootle, almost to the same spot where they had started at the beginning of the century. It was hard to accept that the great days of Atlantic House in Hardman Street were over and that it would not ever be needed again. Atlantic House had become a legend and we both had enjoyed a healthy rivalry.

Whilst for a short time we were joined by the British Sailors' Society on the ground floor only of Kingston House, it was an experiment that was not to last. We sold Kingston House and we were reduced to a welfare officer, the company secretary and myself. Ship visiting continued as well as the care of the seafarer in his home. For a year my wife and I were housed in a retirement bungalow in the Wallasey Mariners' Park. At least

Colonsay House by Jill Dagnell

we were able to maintain the primary function of the Mission .... to visit the seafarer aboard his ship. Then everything fell into place as we acquired Colonsay House at the edge of the Royal Seaforth Dock system.

It was quickly realised that almost by chance we again had the right building in the right place. A vast amount of restructuring was needed, special licences sought, a new staff appointed. Above all it was the right size for the numbers of seafarers available and very quickly we were established.

Very little could be achieved without the financial aid and encouragement of those who support the work of such Societies as the Mersey Mission to Seamen. The Liverpool Sailors' Home Trust, King George's Fund for Sailors, the International Transport Workers' Federation, The Merchant Navy Welfare Board, NUMAST, The Shipwrecked Mariner's Society, etc., and many other individuals and organisations, all play a major role in the caring for the seafarer on Merseyside. We would not survive without this help so willingly given.

We all realised that it was essential to work together and an excellent example was a sport's week, held under the guidance of the Norwegian Government Seamen's Welfare Service. The Swedish and Norwegian Chaplains, the British Sailors' Society's Padre and the Mersey Mission's team all worked together. We in the Mersey Mission continued to handle the distribution of grants on behalf of the Shipwrecked Mariners' Society and visited about a dozen homes each week. A new way of life was discovered as we learned to visit ships which might dock at midnight and sail away at noon the next day. More and more our concern was for men of the Third World and for seafarers aboard vessels under arrest. Often I was able to liken our problems to those faced by my predecessors in the last century! There was never any doubt that the Mersey Mission was as necessary as ever.

The parishioners of Christchurch became great supporters as along with the local clergy we re-established ourselves as a 'going concern'. It really was a fresh start in Colonsay House.

Even the Dock Company vacated their sumptuous Pier Head Building and re-established themselves almost alongside Colonsay House. This was a real indication that we were all in the right place to meet the demands of the twenty-first century.

I retired in 1989 and was succeeded by Canon Ken Peters. Ken had worked with me as a student and also as an assistant Chaplain, before transferring to the Missions to Seamen. He had spent seven years in Kobe in Japan and achieved great improvements there, notably financing and building a new club. For this achievement he was made an Honorary Canon of Kobe Cathedral. Ken was to remain on Merseyside for five years before being

Chaplain Roy Paul continues the care for all who travel on the highway of the seas.

recalled to work with the Missions to Seamen in London as the Chaplain responsible for legal rights of the seafarer world-wide.

As we reprint this book I continue my retirement and my love affair with the Mersey Mission to Seafarers and the sea. The future is fascinating. Roy Paul is the first non-ordained chaplain and he carries the responsibility of the Mission into this new millennium.

As the millennium begins, a major evaluation of the work of all the Seafarers Missions on Merseyside is being carried out in the hope that the ecumenical work which has gone on in the past can be formulated into a closer working together and may be the development of an international Seafarers Centre.

The modern port of Liverpool is here to stay. Ports of the Mersey continue to grow and the needs of seafarers are perhaps as great if not greater than in times past . The Mersey Mission to Seafarers will continue its care for all who travel on the highway of the seas.

7.
The Apostleship of the Sea

'....... we rely particularly on the organisation of the Apostleship of the Sea in order that in collaboration with the other organisations of sailors, it will, opportunely but courageously, by its active presence in international life, make the voice of the Christian conscience heard on the great problems of seafarers, and the maritime world.'

Pope Paul VI.

The story for Liverpool starts with Father F.O. Blundell, O.S.B., who was a Benedictine monk at Fort Augustus Abbey. From there he used to visit the Fleet at Invergordon. In 1908 Dom Odo Blundell celebrated the first Roman Catholic Mass on board a Royal Navy ship since the Reformation in 1688. All this was at Lamlash on the Isle of Arran. The ship was the *Temeraire.* During this time Father Blundell became a great friend of Admiral Jellicoe and was accepted in the Fleet. Father Blundell was the man who was to leave his mark on Liverpool.

At the outbreak of the First World War, Blundell went to Scapa and lived aboard the Hospital Ships in harbour. He was given permission to visit all the R.N. ships and to minister to the Roman Catholics aboard. This was a big step forward.

Roman Catholic priests were naturally taken into the Royal Navy in 1914, but remained as civilians. They were called Officiating Chaplains. It was not until the 2nd August, 1918 that an Order in Council enabled those serving to become Acting Chaplains with temporary commissions. Another order in Council in October 1922 allowed the title Temporary Chaplain to be used. In fact it was not until a further Order in November 1943 that the Roman Catholic Chaplains achieved parity with the Chaplains of the Established Church. This had taken sixty-seven years! The Roman Catholic Bishops in England had asked the Admiralty in 1876 that their chaplains be afforded the same footing as those of the Church of England. It had been a prolonged battle.

Catholic Chaplains had first worked in the Royal Navy in 1856, as the result of negotiations between Cardinal Wiseman and the Admiralty. However, by 1915 there were some thirty Chaplains, ashore and afloat. It is hard to believe at the tail end of the twentieth century that it was not until the latter half of the eighteenth century that Catholic seamen could join the Royal Navy without giving up the practice of their religion.

Father Blundell joined the Grand Fleet and served in *H.M.S.Collingwood.* At the Battle of Jutland, Blundell gave the general absolution for the men of the warship *H.M.S. Defence* as she was sinking. Finally, in 1918, he was invalided out, but continued to work with the Fleet until 1920.

The next vital step in our story was when Archbishop Whiteside invited Father Blundell to draw up a statement of the spiritual wants of Catholic seamen aboard the merchant ships in Liverpool. As a result, in 1922, Blundell was appointed to superintend the Altar Cases on board the Passenger Steamers sailing from Merseyside. Then, in 1923, Blundell was chosen to be the Chaplain to the newly formed Apostleship of the Sea in Liverpool.

To go back to the beginning again, whilst Blundell is firmly associated with Liverpool, there were many efforts being made by the Catholic Church around the world to care for the seafarer. A booklet produced by the Apostleship of the Sea tells the story.

'In 1890, for instance, a letter written by the Very Reverend Canon Archibald Douglas appeared in the English 'Messenger of the Sacred Heart' appealing desperately for attention to be given to the problems of Catholic seafarers. The letter was not without effect and the various seamen's institutes set up under Catholic auspices in London, Montreal, Sydney, New York, Philadelphia, New Orleans, Belfast and other ports may well have had their initiative from this appeal. Shortly after this, in 1894, a movement began in France called Societe des Ouvres de Mer. This was directed mainly towards fishermen but it was a big scale operation which, besides establishing shore bases, sent hospital ships and Chaplains out with the great North Atlantic fishing fleets.

'The name 'Apostleship of the Sea' actually came into being about this time when in 1896 a special sailors' branch of the Apostleship of Prayer was formed and given the new name. This early Apostleship of the Sea has really no part in the history of the present organisation which bears the name for it was little more than an association of Catholic seafarers united in prayer. Actual welfare work for Catholic seafarers in this country was being undertaken almost exclusively by the St. Vincent de Paul Society.

'Just after the turn of the century, it is obvious that serious thought was being given to the need for a really international organisation to deal with the requirements of a community, the seafaring community, which was itself more international than anything else on earth. So in 1910 the Reverend Dr.Poll of Osnabruck, Germany, after establishing a Catholic Seamen's Club in Naples, asked and received the blessing of the Holy See for a scheme to link up all existing Catholic Seamen's Institutes. Without being aware of what was going on in Naples, Dr.W.H. Atherton of the Montreal Catholic Sailors' Club was busy working out a similar scheme. Neither of these schemes saw fruition but they were straws in the wind ... indications of the mind at that time.

'Although credit for the beginnings of the present world-wide Apostleship of the Sea organisation must be given to a group of enthusiasts, one member of that group must be singled out for special mention, firstly because of having helped to form the new constitutions in 1920, it was he who took them to Rome in 1922 and received for them the approval and blessing of Pope Pius XI and secondly ... he has written a good deal on the subject of the Apostleship of the Sea. He is Peter Anson, then 'Brother Richard', an Oblate of the Benedictines of Caldey. When these first constitutions were presented on Brother Richard's behalf to the Holy Father, the resulting letter of approval, signed by the then Papal Secretary of State, Papal Cardinal Gasperri, was prophetic in its assertion that the enterprise would spread along the sea-coasts of both hemispheres. At that time, Peter Anson was the Honorary Organising Secretary of the new Apostleship of the Sea and the Most Reverend A. Mackintosh, Archbishop of Glasgow, was shortly to become President. From then onwards, international organising was carried on from the headquarters in Glasgow until March 1928 when, in conjunction with the Society of St. Vincent de Paul, the 'Council of the Apostleship of the Sea' was formed for the further co-ordination of the services of Catholic organisations engaged in work for seafarers. From this evolved the APOSTOLATUS MARIS INTERNATIONALE CONCILIUM which, with Arthur Gannon as the new Organising Secretary, became familiarly known as A.M.I.C., and was recognised eventually throughout the world and sponsored development of the Catholic Sea Apostolate right up to the historic year of 1952 when, through the instrument of the Papal Constitution 'Exsul Familia', the Apostleship of the Sea ceased to be a Society helping in the work of the church but became a part of the pastoral structure of the Church itself.'

Peter Anson, who played such a large part in the early days, tells us that he called his own little boat Stella Maris ... Star of the Sea ... after the tender which carried passengers from Tenby to Caldey Island. It was a small step to call each home of the Apostleship of the Sea ... Stella Maris.

In his book 'Harbour Head ... Maritime Memories', Peter Anson describes a visit to Merseyside.

'As to Liverpool, I cannot say that I got a warm welcome when I first visited Merseyside towards the end of the last War. Apart from Father Walter Hothersall at St. Alban's, Atholl Street, few of the many priests to whom I spoke about the needs of Catholic seafarers appeared to consider that any special provision was necessary. They explained that practically all the seamen whose ships traded from Liverpool had their homes in or near the city, and that they could always get to Mass and the Sacraments if they chose to do so. The older priests reminded me that a small Club for Seamen had been opened in Derby Road, Bootle, as far back as 1893, and the fact that it did not survive more than a few years was sufficient proof that there was no real need for any Catholic Club, Home or Institute in Liverpool. Some of them recalled that about twenty years previously Archbishop Whiteside had appointed a priest to take charge of the seafarers. All sorts of difficulties in the way of starting any kind of Apostolate were put before me, and nobody appeared to be the least bit optimistic that it would ever succeed if tried again. So 'a-walking down Paradise Street' (like the sailor in the shanty 'Blow the Man Down') I met many another sailor. But out on the Mersey there were no more packets flying the Black Bull flag or 'spanking-full-rigger,' 'bound away, bound away where the wild waters flow.' Times had changed; ships and seamen too. Yet, so far as I could make out, there was need for a sea apostolate.'

Peter Anson's vision of such work was to be amply fulfilled in Liverpool.

Mention must be made of Miss Scott-Murray who since 1890 sent parcels of Catholic reading matter to sailors. Along with Miss Margaret Stewart she took over the Apostleship of Prayer. It was to flourish. In 1894 it was decided to form a Seamen's Branch of the Apostleship of Prayer and it was called the Apostleship of the Sea. The Benedictines of Caldey with Peter Anson took this work over from 1917 to 1924.

This was the international background when Father Odo Blundell O.S.B. was appointed in 1923 to be the first Port Chaplain in Liverpool. As with so many other organisations, the original Catholic Sailors' Club started in the Sailors' Home in Canning Place with just two rooms. The probable date was 1924. This first centre of the Apostleship of the Sea in Liverpool was opened formally in 1924 by Admiral Earl Jellicoe. It was a good start and the Apostleship of the Sea, or Stella Maris ... Star of the Sea ... as it is known to most seamen, was not to look back.

Liverpool was to play a large part in the First International Congress for Catholic Seamen held in 1927 at Port-en-Bessin in Normandy. The British delegation was led by Admiral Sir Edward Charlton. Two years later another Congress was held in Boulogne with delegates from five countries. A third Congress was held in Liverpool in 1930. Here is a quotation from the report.

'Almost one hundred delegates, representing ports in fourteen countries, accepted the invitation of His Grace Dr Richard Downey, Archbishop of Liverpool, to attend the Congress and they ... many Prelates and other clergy and also a great number of local Apostleship workers and seamen ... assembled in the Concert Room of St George's Hall, Liverpool on the night of September 5th, to meet His Grace.

'Archbishop Downey, welcoming the delegates, spoke of the Congress as a Catholic gathering in every sense of the word ... catholic because it was universal in its representation and Catholic because of its Christian religious principles ...

'Let the spirit of Charity reign supreme throughout our discussions and let us have before us the single-minded purpose of the welfare of the man who goes to sea.'

Many other congresses were to follow, but this one in 1930 was to put Liverpool firmly on the international scene.

Meanwhile, the Liverpool Club in the Sailor's Home had become very popular. The records for 1927 are interesting. It was not unusual to find 40 to 50 men at dinner hour, whilst throughout the day the average was from 25 to 30. The attendance was recorded three times a day: at noon, at 4 p.m., and at 8 p.m., and shows an average daily attendance of 117, and a total for the year of 42,705. 1,130 men were given 'chits' to cover board and lodge for 2 or 3 nights.

Very important, from an international point of view, were the official Sunday services for the men of foreign Navies visiting the port, most of whom were Catholic. The summer of 1925 was special for the men of three Italian cruisers, when 600 Catholic Seamen and their Officers marched to Mass at St. Patrick's Church, attended by the Regimental Band of the Lancashire Field Artillery Corps and by City Mounted Police. They were accorded a wonderful reception all along the route. Nor was the enthusiasm any less in the following year when 700 Catholic Naval Cadets of the French Training Ship *Jeanne D'Arc* again marched along Park Lane to St. Patrick's.

The Club in the Sailors' Home eventually proved to be inadequate. Thus the decision was taken to lease a portion of the former White Star Works at the north end of the docks. The date was Christmas Day 1936. It was opened as 'Atlantic House' on Friday 19th February 1937 by the Earl of Derby.

On the ground floor was a large Reading Room, a Writing Room with tables for draughts and chess, Cloak Rooms and the Chaplain's Study. Above was the private room for officers and a very large Recreational Room, 120 feet by 40 feet. There were two billiard tables, table tennis, and a skittle alley 20 yards long. There was also space for 100 whist tables. It was also expected that there would be the occasional dance. The very first function was to welcome the crew of the *S.S.California*, 150 men including the Ship's Band. Atlantic House proved to be an immediate winner!

They held a Christmas Party for 135 men on the 8th January. It was also noted in the Annual Report that a Super Whist Drive was organised to raise funds in Reece's Cafe in town on 14 May. There were 600 players!

Father F.O. Blundell retired in 1937 after a remarkable ministry in the service of seafarers. It was fitting that Father Blundell's last official action was to say Mass on board *H.M.S. Royal Oak*. He had achieved much since that first Mass aboard the *Temeraire* in 1908 and had laid firm foundations for the work of the Apostleship in Liverpool.

His successor was Father John M. Dawson, who had spend much time and great energy working in China and had also spent part of his ministry in the U.S.A. On his return to this country, he had joined the Parish of St. Francis de Sales. Sadly his stay at Atlantic House was brief since the endeavours in China had been too much, and he had to retire through ill health.

His successor was a well known priest, Father Dennis J. Kelly, from St. Cuthbert's in Wigan. The war was to take him away from the Apostleship and in 1940, Father Kelly was in a ship which was torpedoed; he was taken aboard a German Prisoner of War vessel and left marooned on a Pacific island. He was to spend the rest of the war in Australia. During his brief two years with the Apostleship he did enough to found the hostess system and the Guildmen Apostolate of voluntary workers

At the outbreak of the Second World War, it was decided that Atlantic House in Strand Road was needed for use by the military and the Apostleship received notice to leave on the 23rd September 1939. The Club had only operated for two and a half years, but had already established itself as a viable concern in every way. Action was needed urgently.

Thanks to the Very Reverend T.B. McEvoy, O.S.B., Rector of St. Augustine's Church, who offered the Society the Recreation Rooms at Little Howard Street near the centre of Liverpool, the work was able to continue with little interruption and on the lines already established with success at Strand Road. By the close of 1939, the new Atlantic House was rapidly achieving the popularity of the previous location. It had been a whirlwind of activity.

In 1939 Father George J. Waring was appointed as Assistant to Father Kelly, who soon departed off to war. Father Waring was ordained in 1932 and started his ministry in St. Cecilia's. His appointment played an important part in the history of the Apostleship.

Whilst bombs were to scar the building, nothing was to stop the work and this was acknowledged on the 8th October, 1941, when the King visited Atlantic House. He was accompanied by Admiral Sir Percy Noble, K.C.B., C.B., C.V.O., Commander-in-Chief, Western Approaches.

The King was met by Father G.J. Waring, who presented his fellow-chaplains, Father J.J. O'Connor, Father R. Buelens (Belgian), Father H. Josko (Polish), Father T.Bede McEvoy, O.S.B., and the members of the Committee.

His Majesty inspected the Canteen, the Woollens Room, where gifts from Canada, the United States, Australia and New Zealand were displayed, and then went to the Dance Hall, where dancing was in progress. Here he found the hall packed with sailors enjoying themselves and partnered by members of the Guild of Our Lady of the Ships and W.R.N.S. A loud burst of cheering greeted the King, who smiled his pleasure at the warmth of the welcome.

The King's Christmas message that year particularly mentioned the Merchant Navy. His visit to Liverpool had struck home.

'Today is Christmas Day, the festival of home. But most of you to whom I send this message ... the officers and men of the Merchant

The King visits Atlantic House

The Duchess of Gloucester with Father Waring

Navy and Fishing Fleets ... are spending it far from your own folk. It is to them that your thoughts are turning, as you stand your watch on the bridge or at a gun-station, in engine-room, or stokehold; and they, too, you may be very sure, are thinking of you with gratitude and pride. In that, the whole nation joins, for there is not one of us on shore who does not know the extent to which the safety of our common heritage of hearth and home depends upon you. At this festival of peace in the midst of the world at war, I send you every good wish, and pray, in the old familiar words, that you and the ships in which you serve may return in safety to enjoy the blessings of the land with the fruits of your labours.'

The work flourished. The Stella Maris Recreation Centre at Birkenhead was opened in August, 1942, by His Lordship The Bishop of Shrewsbury. It had all the ingredients of Atlantic House, including a beautiful Oratory. The Birkenhead chaplain, Father McHugh, was to return to Eire in the December and was succeeded by Father John Garry. The work in Birkenhead was to carry on for some twenty years.

Once the war was over, the need for Atlantic House was as great as ever ... a home from home and a safe place when on land.

The Minister of War Transport at a meeting on 7th February 1946 stated that he was anxious that the Voluntary Societies should have an equal say with the Shipping Authorities in the matter of Seamen's Welfare. Consequently he proposed that the new Seamen's Welfare Board should consist of representatives of the Shipping Industry and the Voluntary Organisations on a fifty-fifty basis. This was the birth of the Merchant Navy Welfare Board.

The three chaplains at Atlantic House in 1946 were Father George J. Waring, Father John J. O'Connor and Father C. Kane. They were assisted by the Lay Apostolate. The Altar Case Committee looked after the needs of the altars and altar cases aboard ships. They were mainly ladies. The Legion of Mary held weekly meetings in Atlantic House. The men of the Legion of Mary visited ships with newspapers and periodicals, whilst the ladies performed hospital and family visits. The Guild of Our Lady of the Ships was concerned about the welfare of the seafarer and acted as hostesses. Upon them fell the task of providing a welcome and a home from home. Finally, the Guild of Our Lady and St. Nicholas comprised young men who served at Mass and Benediction. It all proved to be a remarkable team and great things lay ahead.

At the Annual General Meeting in 1947 Father Waring gave a progress report on the building of the new Atlantic House in Hardman Street. He announced that the main portion would be opened on June 14th 1947. It was an impressive enterprise.

It was like walking into a first class hotel with a large and comfortable lounge and an equally efficient bar. There was a restaurant with good food at reasonable prices. The ballroom was elegant and very large. Moreover, there was splendid accommodation for forty seafarers at very cheap rates. This was a new concept in caring for the seafarer.

The Oratory was beautiful. There was a mural of Our Lady of the Ships, showing the Madonna and Child, with the infant holding a small sailing ship. On the Monstrance were three galleons, interspersed by four lighthouses, a miniature life-buoy and a Rosary of amethysts with the Liverpool Coat of Arms. The Sanctuary Lamps depicted the Crosby and Bar Lightships. The Tabernacle carried two fishes and a basket of loaves to illustrate the parable of the feeding of the five thousand. The oak Altar with the crest of the Apostleship of the Sea was carved to give the impression of rippling waves. When the sliding panels dividing the Oratory and Ballroom were removed, it became a modern Church with accommodation for 350. It was a place to remember.

On the 11th June, 1947, the Atlantic House in Little Howard Street was closed. It had done its job well since those dark days in 1939.

Unfortunately, because of the illness of her mother, the Duchess of Kent was abroad and had to postpone the fixed date for opening, but a week later all was well. It poured with rain, but on the 19th July, 1947 the new Atlantic House was formally opened with huge cheering crowds around the building. Seamen from every corner of the world saw it as their home in Liverpool.

The morale of an organisation is only as good as its leadership. Father George J. Waring in 1949 moved on to be the parish priest of St. Francis of Assisi, Garston. He had been born in New Jersey in 1909 and was the nephew of Monsignor Waring of New York, who was Chaplain General to the American Forces at the outbreak of war. After a seven year curacy in Tuebrook, he had become Assistant Port Chaplain in 1939 and then the following year he succeeded Father Dennis Kelly as Senior Port Chaplain. They had been remarkable years and Father Waring was loved and respected around the world.

Father John O'Connor was the successor. Born in Eire in 1910, he had spent his first six years at Christ The King Parish in Liverpool and became an Assistant at Atlantic House in 1941. He was experienced and knew the task ahead of him.

There were two Assistant Chaplains, Father Cornelius Kane who had arrived at Atlantic House in 1946 and the latest addition to the team Father Richard Firth.

As with all organisations concerned with the seafarer, there was no discrimination of race, colour or creed. In fact, some fifty per cent of men who used Atlantic House were non-Catholics and no pressure was ever put upon them. For many men it was the only 'home' that they had.

By 1954 there were 75 bedrooms and some of the public rooms had also been extended. Commodore C. Ivan Thompson, as he was at the time, was Captain of the *R.M.S. Queen Mary* and in the January of 1954 he had appealed over the radio for financial assistance to fund the extensions. One paragraph told the real story.

'I have said conditions at sea have changed very much for the better. That is so. But do you realise what a sailor misses, however good the conditions? He is a home-loving man, yet he must spend a large part of his life away from his home, separated from his wife and children.'

In 1958 another eighteen bedrooms were added and the main lounge extended. As the National Headquarters of the Apostleship of the Sea had been transferred to Liverpool two years before, extra office accommodation was also added. In fact, Atlantic House was bulging with 94% occupation of the rooms. This was big business.

After ten years of work, Father Firth was moved back into parochial duties at St. John's, Kirkdale. His replacement was Father George Mooney, who was a specialist in Canon Law, having obtained a degree in the subject in the Gregorian University in Rome.

1960 saw the departure of Father O'Connor when he became parish priest at St. Joseph's, Wrightington. For twenty years he had guided the Apostleship with a sure hand. He had been sent to work with Father Waring for just a few weeks in 1941! The pair of them had to start Atlantic House all over again in the middle of air raids, black-out and shortage of almost everything. The seamen had come in vast numbers and many were in great need. That was when Father O'Connor had learned his trade. He went to the first Rome Congress of the Apostleship in 1950 and was a member of the National Board. Seven years later he was the National Secretary. In the field of the Church's pastoral care of seamen, Father O'Connor must be counted as one of the greatest pioneers. His twenty years made history.

Next in line was Father Francis Frayne who had worked in Atlantic House for six years. Not only was he the Senior Port Chaplain, within a few months he was appointed as National Secretary for the Apostleship of the Sea. At the same time, Father Bernard R. Boardman became an Assistant Port Chaplain. My arrival at the Mersey Mission to Seamen in Kingston

Father Frayne greets Princess Alexandra

House coincided with these appointments. We were soon to be great friends. Father Boardman and I played indifferent golf together and were able to share our enthusiasm for our work.

Father Waring came back to Atlantic House to speak to the 1964 Annual General Meeting. He reminisced with thoughts about the beginnings.

'However, going back to the work, the Apostleship of the Sea in Liverpool started in 1923 in Canning Place at the Sailors' Home and in those days they used to have a Whist Drive at Christmas to try and meet their expenditure. I understand that on one occasion the prizes were live poultry geese, and what they would have you and I believe is that they got adrift in the street and the people more or less had to chase after their own geese round Canning Place! The Apostleship moved to Strand Road in 1936 and began to develop its work very well and it was at that time that Father Dennis Kelly came and introduced into the work the idea of bringing girls to meet the sailors and to become hostesses in order to reproduce home life. What a sailor needs, he felt, is home life when he comes into port. He can't go up and speak to a strange woman; he can if she's the wrong type but if she's the right type she will have nothing to do with him. ... I went with Father Kelly in 1939 to Little Howard Street and we began to arrange dances every night. When I tell anybody I've been to a dance every night they look twice at me!'

Just twenty years after the plans were laid for the building of Atlantic House in Hardman Street, 1965 was the year when plans were made for a second club ... a Stella Maris in Bootle. The work was to start in the July for forty bed-rooms, a bar-lounge, a games room, restaurant, T.V. rooms, library, ballroom, a conference room and, of course, a chapel. The site was opposite the Strand Shopping Centre and was well placed to serve the North Docks. At that time we did not realise that within a decade all the port activity would be at the north end of the port. The new building was to be in the right place.

An important appointment was made the same year. Father William Mills was to be a shipboard chaplain. In spite of ill health, he was to spend over eight months each year at sea in such vessels as the *Empress of England*, the *Reina del Mar* and the *Nevassa* and the *Uganda,* the two old *Queens* and, of course, the *Q.E.11.* He cared for the passengers as well as the crews and in no time Father Billy Mills was known and loved by many thousands of people. We all knew Billy Mills! It must be that smile. His last trip was in 1992 aboard the *Q.E.*11 on a voyage to Halifax, Nova Scotia ... just 150 years after the first sailing from Liverpool to Halifax. I still meet him at the Canadian Pacific re-union lunches when we 'swing the lamp and tell the tale' of shared cruises and old friends.

Work on the Bootle venture was to be completed by the summer of 1968, but much preparation had to be done. The chaplains were busy. Then with the appointment of Monsignor Frayne to the International Bureau of the Apostleship of the Sea in Rome, a post which required his being away from Liverpool for about a third of the year, a good deal of extra work had to be done by Fathers Boardman and Stringfellow. Many thanks were due to Mr. Rafferty, who managed the forty permanent staff members.

In the early seventies the Royal Seaforth Dock was opened and it was becoming obvious that the seafarer was facing a new world. The ships were to turn around not in weeks or days, but in hours! With less than twenty four hours in port the basic problems of being a seafarer were magnified and aggravated. This was to be part of the challenge facing Father John White as he developed the Stella Maris at Bootle.

Father White was to become a good friend as we shared the Chaplaincy work for the Royal Naval Reserve in *H.M.S.Eaglet*. Apart from the weeks away with the Royal Navy and the odd weekend on the tenders, most Wednesday evenings we both made an appearance and spun a coin to decide who would lead the Divisional Prayers that evening!

Another exciting venture for the Apostleship was the negotiations to purchase Gateacre Grange, which had been a Private Hospital. Contracts were exchanged in March 1969 and by the September the Apostleship took possession of the fine building and grounds in Woolton. The building had to be adapted, rewired and renovated. Official permission was given to house 42 retired seafarers. Within months it was increased to 46 and the house was full and there was a waiting list. It was an instant success. I loved visiting and meeting old familiar faces.

More excitement was to follow immediately. The Chairman of the Gateacre Grange Committee presented the Apostleship with a cottage at Cemaes Bay in Anglesey. The retired men at the Grange could enjoy a holiday! To stand on the verandah which overlooks Cemaes Bay, and to see the big ships going up towards Liverpool was a thrill for the retired seafarer. This, together with all the small boats in the harbour, was to bring a genuine link with the old days.

In this way the endeavours of the Apostleship continued with Fathers Stringfellow, Brownbill, White and Mills ... a formidable team!. By 1974 the financial statements of the Apostleship suggested that all was well. The outstanding bank loan of twenty-six thousand pounds had been repaid. So the work of the Societies continued, but the port and the state of shipping was changing. A new world was emerging.

The slump in the shipping industry and the aura of economic depression was beginning to have repercussions. Jobs were not easily available for the seafarer. Men spent far longer waiting and hoping that there would be another ship for them. Crew numbers in each vessel were falling dramatically, adding to the general uncertainty about the next voyage. Time in port grew even less. All this was beginning to touch the foreign seafarer, often working under flags of convenience. Men were being employed from the poorer, undeveloped countries, and were receiving below the universal minimum wage. Too often the ships were under-manned and conditions were unsafe. Many were signing contracts for voyages of up to two years, which imposed an impossible strain upon themselves and their families. Seafarers knew that they were being exploited and they had little redress and scant protection. The need for those who cared for the seafarer was increasing.

Perhaps all these facts helped to draw the organisations closer together. A joint Sea Sunday Service was held in the Chapel of the Mersey Mission to Seamen with the Lord Mayor of Liverpool and the Lady Mayoress. Ecumenical meetings were taking place with the Mersey Mission to Seamen and the Pastors from the German, Norwegian and Swedish Churches. Without doubt at this time the most important event was the Third Triennial Conference in New York of the International Christian Maritime Association. There were one hundred and fifty-four delegates from seventeen nations and diverse Christian traditions. The theme of the conference was: 'Christ in the Maritime World: Evangelisation and Pastoral Care of the Seafarer'.

Disaster struck Atlantic House on Friday, 4th January, 1980. A raging fire, apparently due to an electrical fault, was discovered in the first floor. No-one was hurt, but in a short time the ballroom was gutted, the Chapel badly damaged and thirty bedrooms put out of commission. However, everything was eventually refurbished.

By this time, it was becoming evident to all concerned that changes would be necessary for the institutions involved with the care of the seafarer. A meeting lasting a week was held in the Stella Maris to consider the eventual way ahead. The date was in December 1981.

In June 1982 the Mersey Mission to Seamen closed its residential accommodation at Kingston House and co-operating with the British Sailors' Society, opened an International Club for Seafarers on the ground floor of its former premises. This was one of the few experiments in co-operation between Societies in Liverpool ... Padre Bob Evans and Pastor Peter McGrath were at the helm.

Six months later the Merchant Navy Welfare Board's residential hotel fell victim to the shipping decline and closed its doors.

In 1976 there had been 1,614 ships flying the Red Ensign; in 1982 there were less than 900 and the graph was firmly dropping. Change was essential for survival and to meet the new demands of the shipping industry the Societies had to change too.

Ironically when the armed conflict occurred in the South Atlantic, the action could not have been undertaken without the support of over fifty ships of the Merchant Navy. A decade later there would not be sufficient numbers of such vessels.

'A piece of Liverpool's seafaring history is to close'. So said the press report in October 1984 when it was formally announced that Atlantic House was to be put on the market and shut its doors once and for all early in the New Year. The name was not to be lost. The national headquarters of the Apostleship of the Sea was to be transferred to the Stella Maris in Bootle and the building there was to be called Atlantic House. This was only a few hundred yards from its first home in the 1930's. Atlantic House had been based in three homes. This was to be its fourth.

When the Mersey Mission to Seamen was to close Kingston House completely and relocate at Colonsay House in Crosby, and when Atlantic House was in the Strand, Bootle, these moves symbolised the changing shape of the Port of Liverpool. In a few years the Dock Company also abandoned Pier Head and built a new Headquarters in the Royal Seaforth Dock complex. The old Port of Liverpool was concentrating its shipping world some three miles from the city centre. The Voluntary Societies had led the way!

For over sixteen years Father John White, S.T.L., R.N.R., had been responsible for the Stella Maris at Bootle. At least once each week we had met on the Drill Deck of *H.M.S.Eaglet* where we both operated our chaplaincies. It really was a long standing friendship He became Parish Priest at the Sacred Heart in Liverpool and was sadly missed by the seafarers. His contribution had been immense.

Monsignor Stringfellow and Father Brownbill, at the closure of Atlantic House in Hardman Street, were to carry on the work of the Apostleship at the Stella Maris in Bootle.

Whilst all this turmoil of change was being rationalised, Gateacre Grange continued the care of the retired seafarers ... the oldest resident, Ralph Davidson, at the grand age of 96, received a heart pace-maker and a new lease of life! The Beach House at Cemaes Bay was completely refurbished thanks to a grant from the Liverpool Sailors' Home Trust. The Liverpool Sailors' Home had provided the first 'home' for the Apostleship in the early twenties of the century and the Trust continued the care by supporting the projects of the Societies. For the Apostleship it was business as usual.

However, ill-health was about to bring about another change in the affairs of the Apostleship.

Monsignor Tony Stringfellow had started as an Assistant Port Chaplain in 1964 at Atlantic House, then in the Stella Maris from 1967 - 1973, before returning to Hardman Street. In 1981 he became the National Director and in the middle of all this he was responsible for the closure of Atlantic House and had the joy of re-establishing the new activity at Bootle. It had been a formidable task, but well done. However, the stress and strain had taken its toll on his health and sadly Monsignor Stringfellow retired back into parish life in 1988 to the parish of Holy Family in Cronton, Widnes.

1989 was a great year of change for the Apostleship of the Sea in Liverpool. Father Brownbill went into semi-retirement and took up residence at Gateacre Grange. Father John Seddon took over as Port Chaplain at Stella Maris, Atlantic House. Incidentally, it was the year that I also retired from the Mersey Mission to Seamen. We had shared dramatic changes in the port and in our lives. Naturally the work continued.

At last the port was growing increasingly busy. In the year 1990 the Port News (the Journal of the Mersey Docks and Harbour Company) reported that it was: 'Best-ever profits despite UK gloom'. The profits topped £10 million in a year which saw cargo handled through the Port of Liverpool rise to a record 23 million tonnes. However, this was not to have too dramatic effect in Stella Maris as the vessels turned around often in a matter of hours. Men just did not have the time to come ashore and the Chaplain had to go to them.

Father John Seddon left the Apostleship on the 1st September, 1990, to take up a new appointment as the Youth Chaplain for the Liverpool Archdiocese. The new Port Chaplain was Father Brian Cane, who had been the parish priest of St. Benedict's, Warrington.

Sadly Mr. Theo Larsen died in February 1991. He had been the General Manager for many years in Atlantic House and in Stella Maris. He was known by seafarers around the world. Also Mr Matty Molloy died in the same month. He had been the Night Manager. Between them they had served the Apostleship for over sixty years. Without such workers the Apostleship of the Sea could not have continued its material and social care of the seafarer.

There were more changes. Father Cane was appointed to be parish priest of St. Paschal Baylon, Liverpool, in January 1992 and his place was taken by Father Patrick Harnett, S.C.J., who for many years directed the Youth Service of the Archdiocese.

The Silver Jubilee of the Stella Maris was marked with Archbishop Warlock as the principal celebrant at a Mass of Thanksgiving. It was a great occasion.

Father Patrick Harnett

Father Patrick Harnett ended his report that year with these words.

'Looking back at over seventy years of the Apostleship of the Sea's efforts in Merseyside and Stella Maris' twenty five years, we have cause to be grateful for God's blessing on our work. We note the dedication of so many benefactors, helpers and our staff in serving the needs of our visitors. With such a background of service, we can look forward with confidence in continuing to do our utmost in offering a 'home' in Merseyside to the 'strangers' who come to our shores.'

During my recent visit in July 1997 to Stella Maris in order to borrow photographs from Father Pat, I was pleased to meet a very old friend, Miss Nora Griffin. Nora started as a voluntary hostess in Hardman Street on the 14th February, 1949 and is a great source of information as she continues to be a voluntary worker.

It is right to end this chapter with a statement made by Pope Paul VI in 1966.

'The gesture of the Apostle who confronts the seafarers and breaks bread with them (Acts 27, 33 - 36) you repeat both spiritually and materially every day, during your voyages, or in the chapels and centres of the Apostleship of the Sea, in fraternal contact, in the assistance rendered when necessary, in the priestly and social work, which is accomplished both ashore and on board ships between sky and sea when the spirit of the seafarer loses its self more in nostalgia for his far-away family and opens itself more and more to friendship and confidence towards the priest. Continue then, with faith and generosity in the fulfilment of the ministry so provident and necessary. The Pope is with you. The Church launches you out on to the sea lanes, so that the message of Christ may resound to ever greater horizons, for the comfort of man, for his spiritual and religious elevation, for his conscious and living insertion into the community of the sons of God....'

The work continues.

8.
The Orphans

My love lies drowned in the windy Lowlands;
Lowlands, Lowlands, alas, my John!
My love lies drowned in the windy Lowlands ...
My lowlands a-ray.

On December 16, 1868, the first move was made to interest the people of Liverpool in the possibility of the establishment of an Institution where the orphan children of seamen would receive care. The sponsors were shipowners and merchants with a concern as how best to help the widows and families of the Merseyside men lost at sea by drowning or who had died as the result of an accident or through natural causes.

Liverpool by this time had become a major port as was described by Sir William B. Forwood in his 'Recollections of a Busy Life'.

In the 1860's the great trades of Liverpool were those carried on with America, Australia, Calcutta and the West Coast of South America. The clipper ships, belonging to James Baines and Co., Imrie and Tomlinson, McDiarmid and Greenshields and the Brocklebanks, were justly celebrated for their smartness and sea-going qualities.

'Charles MacIver ruled over the destinies of the Cunard Company
... William Inman was building up the fortunes of the Inman Line
... the Bibbys and James Moss practically controlled the
Mediterranean trade ... the Allans were forcing their way to the
front. Mr. Ismay was establishing the White Star Line, Mr. Alfred
Holt was doing pioneer work in the India trade with some small
steamers with single engines. These he sold and went into the
China trade in which he has built up a great concern. The Harrisons
were sailing ship owners but they also had a line of small steamers
trading to Charente. They afterwards started steamers to the Brazils
and Calcutta.

'Among the most active merchants of Liverpool were T. and J.
Brocklebank, Finlay Campbell and Co., Baring Brothers, Brown
Shipley and Co., Malcolmson and Co., Charles Saunders, William
Moon and Co., Ogilvy Gillanders and Co., T. and W. Earle and
Co., J.K. Gillat, J.H. Schroeder, Rankin and Gilmour ...'

There was no Welfare State and these were some of the names who found
time to help the less fortunate, the sick and the destitute. The fatherless
children and widows of seamen came top of their list.

A Public Meeting was held in the Mercantile Marine Service Association's
rooms in Water Street on 16th December, 1868. It was well attended and
a resolution was firmly passed.

'That this meeting being deeply impressed with the moral obligation
resting upon shipowners of this great port to provide for the
protection and education of the Mercantile Marine orphan children
resolves that an establishment for feeding, clothing and educating
the fatherless children of seamen be brought before the merchants,
shipowners and general public of Liverpool for support.'

Three rather long paragraphs of appeal then follow. Reference is made to
'our streets and courts and alleys full to overflowing of perishing
innocents'! Then comes a firm proposal.

'It is proposed, in the first instance, to rent a roomy house in a
suitable locality as a temporary Home. A Shipowner of this port
has promised £500 towards a Building Fund, provided nine others
will each contribute a like sum.'

These men really meant business.

Present at the meeting was Mr. James Beazley, a shipowner and a member
of the Mersey Dock Board; he had been much involved with the formation
of the Mercantile Marine Service Association in 1857, the establishment
of the school ship *Conway*, the setting up of the training ship *Indefatigable*

and of the reformation training ship *Akbar.* This was the man who was elected as chairman of the executive committee. He actually had been the gentleman who had promised the first £500.

An appeal went out on March 27, 1869, asking for general support from the public. It was not to fall on deaf ears.

'The number of seamen at sea in British merchant vessels in the year 1866 was 196,371. No fewer than 4,866 deaths were recorded during the year - 2,390 of these by drowning.

'Statistics show us that deceased married sailors leave on an average three children, and these with the widow are in the great majority of cases almost destitute, and oftentimes absolutely so.'

Monies received were sufficient to make a start. Number 128 Duke Street was a large three-storied house in its own grounds and it was available. Plans were drawn for dormitories, class rooms, kitchens and the necessary accommodation for the staff.

There was no delay. On August 9, 1869 the Liverpool Seamen's Orphan Institution came into being and the first children arrived. By the end of that year there were 60 of them in residence, 46 boys and 14 girls. Miss McGregor, the Matron, made them all welcome.

From the outset the question of providing educational facilities which would equal the standards set by local educational authorities was given priority.

Mr. Ralph Brocklebank, the first President of the Institution, addressed the subscribers at the annual meeting in 1872.

"You are aware that no children are taken in under six years of age and that they only remain until they are 14. You will thus see it is impossible to give the children what are called the higher branches of education because such branches are very rarely entered upon - such for instance as mathematics and things of that sort previous to 14 years of age.

"I wish you to bear that in mind because it is very important to show what the committee are doing in the education of the children. The stated school hours (at the Institution) are from 9 o'clock to 12 and from 2 o'clock to 4 during which time the lessons comprise scripture, writing, composition, arithmetic, reading, history, grammar, geography, mapping, and dictation and as they advance it is intended to introduce book-keeping. One hour in the evening is devoted to study.

"The children have next free-hand drawing and that will be followed by mechanical drawing which will be of great advantage inasmuch as I look forward to the period when some of the boys educated in the Institution will in all probability go to the offices of the engineers, where they will finally develop their knowledge of this branch of education.

"Many are practising the harmonium, and one of the boys who left the Institution at 14, and I am happy to say has got an excellent situation, for some time previously performed at our morning and evening services and displayed great ability.

"In arithmetic also he was the best boy in the school having advanced so far as proportion and in addition to the ordinary branches by reading, writing, etcetera he was taught to clean knives and shoes, to clean plate, to scrub a floor, to wash his own linens, to knit, to mend his own clothes and also to make bread which he could do with perfection."

By today's standards that all sounds forbidding, but 'life was real and life was earnest'. At Christmas there were toys and gifts and 'special treats' in the summer, together with magic lantern shows, entertainments, visits to pantomimes and river trips.

The Newsham Park Home

In April 1870 the Liverpool Town Council gave a gift of 7,000 square yards of land at the north east side of Newsham Park for the construction of a Seamen's Orphan Institution. The foundation stone was laid by Mr. Ralph Brocklebank and £8,000 was collected in a few months. An infirmary was also planned as three boys had died in the Duke Street Home in 1871 because of a scarletina and smallpox epidemic in Liverpool. Another addition was to be a chapel.

On January 31, 1874, 68 children left Duke Street and with an extra 46 'new' boys and girls, the Newsham Park Home was opened. Soon there were 200 children and another 62 were on the Outdoor Relief List. These outdoor youngsters were given an allowance of ten shillings each month and an annual suit of clothes 'conditional upon the production of a certificate that the child was attending a school in the district'.

The formal opening was on September 30, 1874, the ceremony being performed by the Duke of Edinburgh, the 'Sailor Prince', fourth son of Queen Victoria and the Prince Consort.

Christmas at the Orphanage

An unknown writer has left a pen-picture of a visit to the new Home. 'I turned into Newsham Park from the West Derby road, at Tue Brook. What a striking vista had the last six months accomplished! From the corner of the road leading up to Newsham House a very good view of the chapel and Orphanage is obtained. It is much to be questioned whether any public building in or about Liverpool can present such a picture of architectural beauty, combined with simplicity of character and chaste adornment.

'We enter the porch ... dimly lit by quaint little windows at the side, in which the 'bull's eyes' of the small panes produce a very pleasing effect. The spacious entrance hall, from which rises a noble staircase, is soon reached; and at each side of the door stands one of the orphan boys, with a plate to receive contributions. The large dining-hall, now used for Sunday Service was fast filling ... the boys sit upon a gallery ... the girls at one side of the room before the organ.

'At about ten minutes before eleven the boys are marched in, entering from a door by the side of the organ. They wear their Sunday suits - jackets, vests, and trousers of blue cloth (every day they wear Jack Tar suits) and the girls follow in blue merino frocks, with black cloth capes and pretty straw hats, around which is a small blue ribbon.

'The chaplain, the Reverend Drummond Anderson, in his surplice, commences the service punctually ... it is the morning service of the Church of England ... and it lasts an hour.'

The chaplain was a regular letter writer for the newspapers and must have produced many contributions to the cause. On the 22 May, 1875, he tells of a seaman returning from an African voyage. "Alas! It was not to home that he returned. It was from the ship to the Royal Infirmary they carried the poor sailor. He had to undergo a capital operation, under which he sunk and died within not many hours. Ah, me! What a coming home! The sequel is sad, very sad.

"The widow was left with three little children, the eldest under five years of age. It was her mother's cellar I found her in. She gave what she could - a shelter. And the bereaved woman tried to do her best. She undertook hard work in a rice-mill; hardly, I think, fit for a woman to win the precious bread for her little ones. But she never lifted her head, and some days ago she died of a broken heart. What an episode in the strange, eventful life of man! The sailor brought home to die under such tragic circumstances; the widow struggling for a while to keep her head above the waters, and then struggling no more. You may be sure the Seamen's Orphanage Institution is doing the best it can for the forlorn children."

Another picture emerges when on one day in the July of 1875, it was reported that 150 boys from *Indefatigable,* under the charge of Captain Groom and his officers, paid a visit to the Orphanage. They were trying to create a link between the two establishments so that a boy might move to the ship and then proceed to sea. The venture was a great success. I suspect that the *Indefatigable* boys were pleased to be away from their 'home'. The weather was apparently appalling, but the *Indefatigable* Band played 'joyful tunes' and there was ample food. All this was followed by 'a romp in the school-yard and the boys departed amid the ringing cheers of the Orphanage boys and girls.'

From its inception it was realised that the activities of the Orphanage could not be confined to a building. Over the years this aspect was to increase to the extent that the number of children helped was to far exceed the number of children in the orphanage. However, if the Institution had relied upon public subscription, it would not have survived for long. The founders continued their generosity, legacies began to flow and the revenue from the boxes aboard the liners on the Atlantic trade ever increased. It was the generosity of the president, Mr. Ralph Brocklebank, which defrayed the entire cost of a sanatorium in 1879.

Queen Victoria with the Duke of Connaught and Princess Beatrice visited the Orphanage on May 12, 1886. The Queen became a patron and enhanced the standing of the Institution in the country.

From 1892 the boys' school was placed on the list of Public Elementary Schools and was in receipt of a Government grant. Six years later the girls' school was included. The Inspectors were much impressed by the standards they found at the schools. However, this did not alter the arrangement under which, under the auspices of the Diocese of Liverpool, the children were examined each year in religious knowledge; in addition the girls continued to be examined in needlework and knitting. A carpentry shop and a shoemakers' had also been built.

At the turn of the century there were 321 children in the orphanage and 508 were receiving out-door relief. The total year's expenditure was £3,106 and the total income for the year was £5,422. The new age was marked by the building of a swimming pool.

The first World War increased the need. In 1916, 292 children lived in and 654 were helped in their homes. By 1918, 265 lived in and 773 lived out.

LIVERPOOL SEAMEN'S ORPHANAGE.

Patrons: HIS MAJESTY THE KING.   HON. SIR ALFRED WILLS.

Dietary Scale 3 meals a day.   Supply strictly limited.

Number of Children, 320.   Receives from Public annually £14,000.

Matron   Mrs. POSTANCE.

	BREAKFAST 7.15 TO 8 A.M.	DINNER 12 TO 12.30.	TEA 5.45 P.M.
SUNDAY	1 thick slice of dry Bread, 1 mug of Cocoa.	Stewed Beef and Cabbage. Rice pudding.	1 thick slice of Bread and Jam.
MONDAY	Porridge with one mug of milk between 2 children	Corned Beef and Potatoes or 1 plate of Rice & Prunes.	1 thick slice Bread and Treacle, 1 mug of Cocoa.
TUESDAY	Bread and Milk.	Lentil Soup.	1 thick slice Bread & Dripping, 1 mug milk & water.
WEDNESDAY	AS SUNDAY.	Suet Pudding & Treacle, (1 helping).	AS TUESDAY.
THURSDAY	AS MONDAY.	Fish and Potatoes or Beans & Stew.	AS TUESDAY.
FRIDAY	AS SUNDAY.	Cold meat & Potatoes, or Beans & Stew.	AS TUESDAY.
SATURDAY	AS SUNDAY.	Pea Soup, Bread and Cheese.	Bread & Treacle, Milk & Water.

A SMALL PIECE OF BREAD ALLOWED FOR BOYS' SUPPER.

The Dining Hall

The major event in 1921 was a visit by Her Majesty the Queen and Princess Mary. As a direct result His Majesty the King bestowed the title 'Royal' on the Institution and also granted it a Royal Charter of Incorporation.

The work was to continue unhindered with the development of a Domestic Science Room for the girls and an Arts and Crafts room in which the boys were taught handicrafts and the girls dressmaking. Further schemes included a workshop with benches and tools for the boys and a Science Room where chemistry, physics and biology were taught. These were dramatic advances, but the clouds were gathering. War was again imminent.

An excellent picture of life at Newsham Park has been described by George Bennet, who at present is the Secretary of the Royal Liverpool Seamen's Orphanage Old Scholars' Society. His book 'With No Regrets' tells of his eight years in the orphanage starting one sunny afternoon in August 1937. He was aged seven.

'With my younger brother Tom ... I was assigned to the infants' section where we spent that first afternoon being issued with school clothes, bedding, and the hundred and one other oddments necessary for our comfort.

'Life in the infants was carefree and exciting, although the days were short, and by 6.30 each night we were in the land of Nod. Unfortunately, my stay here was all too short. Inside two months I was transferred to the 'big boys', where I was stunned by the strict discipline which reigned - no talking during meals, boots spick and span and clothes spotless for morning parade, a deadly silence in the dormitories, and clothes tied in a neat bundle at the foot of the bed each night for inspection.

'During that first year I have vague recollections of a miserable existence, being knocked from pillar to post by masters and seniors alike, and having little time to call my own. I was a member of the famous Drill Squad, which comprised all juniors and new boys. For one hour, six days a week, we drilled and marched until we were perfect, and then we marched and drilled again.

'But a year or so of this rough life hardened me until I became accustomed to the harsh discipline and the unusual customs, many of which seemed needless to me. During the summer months home-work was for a while cast aside and we spent several evenings a week in our indoor swimming baths under the eye of the stern Mr. Jones. Mr. Jones' method of teaching us the noble art of water-craft was as brutal as it was original. Two reliable swimmers were placed in the shallow end of the bath while two others took a victim by the arms and legs and unceremoniously tossed him into the yawning depths.'

The start of the War dramatically altered the lives of all the young people. George Bennett wrote that he was to leave 'behind the harsh ways of the old school and ahead lay what was to become a period filled with a new way of life and untold adventure.'

The immediate task was to ensure the safety of the children. There was an urgent need to take precautions against air-raids and to plan the evacuation of the school. Happily a solution was at hand. Mr. E.B. Royden, a member of the executive committee, and Mrs Royden placed at the disposal of the orphanage their own home and grounds at Hill Bark, Frankby in Wirral. Before the outbreak of war, huts were built in the grounds and all the essential facilities were installed. 'Operation Evacuation' was successfully carried out on the 11th of September, 1939.

Life at first was not to be easy. 'One small building, a draughty, unheated garage, served as a recreation room for over a hundred of us, boys and girls. Here, during dark winter evenings we amused ourselves as best we could with chess and draughts, dominoes, ludo, snakes and ladders, cards and Chinese chequers. Groups huddled together for warmth, but unfortunately an imaginary line across the room divided the two sexes!

'Our dining room was a tumble down shack, so small that it housed only half the school, and two sittings were therefore necessary for each meal. A gloomy mice-ridden hay-loft above the garage was improvised as a dormitory, straw mattresses being laid on the floor for our special benefit. This dilapidated loft had no windows; the only light penetrated through a small entrance-way. By day it was dim, cheerless, by night a very morgue, with swinging hurricane lamps casting fantastic shadows among the rafters.'

Eventually the problems were overcome and the early privations were put into perspective by the resilience of youth. The daily routine continued and, in spite of staff being called up for the services, the education syllabus was maintained.

In 1941 there were 18 children who had lost their parents through the bombing of their homes and more than 100 whose fathers had been killed by enemy action. A new scheme allowed children up to sixteen and who had found employment to stay in the Home. This enabled them to continue their education. This development was to have a profound effect upon the future administration of the Institution.

George Bennett was to leave Hill Bark on June 19, 1945. His memories were mixed and vivid.

'My happiest school days were undoubtedly those of my last two years spent in Standard VIa, which being the highest grade, contained only a handful of boys. We used the masters' library as a classroom, this being the only suitable accommodation available. Mr. Barker was our class teacher, but he had so many other commitments that often instructions for our daily work were left on the blackboard to be tackled in his absence.' They wrote and performed their own sketches for their make-shift stage - 'The Tuck Shop' (a Billy Bunter tale), 'Sweeney Todd the Barber', and snatches from 'Oliver Twist'. He ends the memoirs with a nostalgic sigh as the hard times were forgotten.

'And in after days I sometimes sigh and wish to be transported back to Hill Bark for one brief spell. To feel again the exhilarating sensation of trotting on to the field before a football match; to water my plump marrows, pausing betimes to nibble at an unripened radish; to revel in hazardous escapades through the forbidden woods in search of birds' nests, blackberries, chestnuts, acorns, in fact anything edible or worth bartering; or to enjoy the fresh country air and the tang of autumn leaves. Ah! to relive those halcyon hours!'

One of my trusted friends, Jonathan, was at Hill Bark from 1941 to 1947. At a recent chance meeting I asked for an immediate impression of his childhood there.

"I couldn't understand why I was separated from my sister ... it made no sense!"

Obviously the memory was still hurtful. Jonathan was five and his sister was a year older. The tragedy was that their mother died in the July of 1941 and the father was lost in the October aboard a Blue Funnel ship. We chatted.

"It was a Spartan place, although I loved the countryside and the feeling of space about me. We lived in huts with tubular beds and no real comfort. Between the huts were huge, six feet high, mounds of coke for the furnaces Part of the fun was searching for toads and newts in the stream. Don't forget that I was only five at the time. We seemed to walk everywhere, but best of all was Thurstaston Hills and the Common. It was a long walk from Frankby to the open air pool at West Kirby. I learned to swim by jumping in and getting on with it ... the first time I cut my feet on the muck at the bottom. You never forget that! On Sundays we all marched in three's to the Church with the beat of a drum, boys in front and the girls behind. Mr. Royden sat in a four wheeled carriage and just one boy and one girl were allowed to sit behind whilst Mr. Cornish held the reins. That was quite a memory. Then there was breakfast! Mondays, Wednesdays and Fridays we ate 'pobs' ... that's what we called bread and milk. Cornflakes appeared on Thursdays, but I cannot recall the rest, except that the main meals were generally soups ... endless soup! Saturday was the great day when the tuck shop opened and the youngest received a penny and the older one's were given sixpence. In the evening we sat in the hall on benches, boys one side and girls on the other, and watched a silent film."

Jonathan was to attend Riversdale College and trained as a ship's engineer, sponsored by Brocklebank. He was there for two years before spending eighteen months sailing 'deep sea' and then he qualified after a further year in college in Glasgow. Eventually, he 'swallowed the anchor' and was ordained in 1971 into the Anglican ministry and now by chance is my local Vicar!

In 1946 it was decided to return to Newsham Park and it was hoped to achieve this in 1948. However there had been great changes in the state's legislation in the post-war years. Designed to assist people in need these new measures included Family Allowances, Health and Medical services, including free school meals, and many other financial benefits, all of which was hoped to ease the problems of families in reduced circumstances. The need for children to leave their homes was vastly reduced. By 1948 there were just 65 boys and 55 girls. New legislation was to reduce the numbers to 69. The plans to rebuild Newsham Park to house 400 children were not needed.

At the annual meeting held on July 25, 1949, it was decided to close and two days later this was effected. The date was Wednesday, July 27, 1949. The orphanage had been in existence for 80 years, first at Duke Street and since 1874 at Newsham Park. The huts and equipment at Frankby were sold by auction and Newsham Park was sold in 1951 to the Ministry of Health and was reconstructed as a hospital.

Many of the children, at the request of the mothers, continued in other boarding schools. This cost was carried by the Institution. The care of the children of deceased Merchant Navy seamen was to continue. Some children went to the Royal Merchant Navy School at Bearwood or to the Sailors' Children's Society at Hull or to the Liverpool Blue Coat School.

A new pattern was evolving. It became obvious that there was a constant flow of requests for advice and help. There was a special place for the Institution in helping to resolve the fears and anxieties of widows of seafarers suddenly confronted with the task of bringing up families, often without the financial resources to do so. This was firmly in line with the intentions of the founders. Above all, the Orphanage had always stressed the importance of education.

When I arrived in Liverpool, I quickly came alongside the Secretary, E.J.G. Walford-Headen. His successors were to be Bill Edwards, Glyn Roberts and Les Dodd. The Institution operated from an office in Oriel Chambers, Water Street, Liverpool. Recently the address is Unit 3a Ground Floor, Tower Building, 22 Water Street, L3 1AB and the new Secretary is Linda Smith.

Death at sea was still all too common and my task was invariably to break the news to the families. Then a telephone call was all that was needed for the Institution to 'adopt' the family. If an arrangement had been made by the parents for the children to go on to boarding or fee-paying schools, that wish was and still is honoured. Children are supported into their University careers and wise counsel is always available. In many instances the Committee is looked upon as 'in loco parentis'.

One of my great joys to the present day, even in retirement, is to attend the annual general meeting in Liverpool Town Hall. There it is a great joy to meet the committee and the staff and to appreciate the work still well done. Always I read the long list of 'Achievements gained in Further Education by a number of our Beneficiaries during the current Academic Year'. It is always impressive. The 'high spot' is never the platform performers, but the young men and women who tell their story ... truly the Royal Liverpool Seamen's Orphan Institution needs no better publicity!

Life at sea and social conditions ashore have certainly changed and improved beyond recognition, but death through illness or aboard ship still leaves the widow with a fatherless family.

The original brief in December 1868 was 'to feed, clothe and educate the fatherless children of seafaring men'. I have been well placed over the last four decades to observe this remarkable Society ... and it has never failed. Throughout the changing years, those today who are responsible for the Institution have kept faith with the founders.

The work deservedly continues.

9.
Runcorn and Widnes and Garston

I must down to the seas again, for the call of the running tide
Is a wild call and a clear call that may not be denied.
                                                            John Masefield

The efforts by the various religious denominations to provide spiritual
and welfare amenities for seamen and watermen seems to have begun
about 1830 in Runcorn. When the ecclesiastical Parish of Holy Trinity
was formed from All Saints in 1840, the Anglican Mariners' Mission
Church was already there in Irwell Lane. This had been built for the
town's watermen by the Earl of Ellesmere in 1831.

In the first thirty years of the last century, Sunday working on the canals
and on the river became common practice because of the growth in traffic.
Sabbath working was necessary because the consequences of not taking
advantage of the Sunday tides could mean a congestion of shipping at the
docks and in the shipping channels. It was held that there was little religious
feeling among the seamen and flatmen and it was said that they were 'of
a low and debased standard'. However, by 1840 there was nationwide
pressure on canal and railway companies to end Sunday working. At a
'very numerous and respectable public meeting' which was held in
Runcorn in 1839 the following resolution was carried:

'That this meeting, deeply feeling the importance of the due
observance of the Lord's Day, as connected with the glory of God

and the good of man, beg most earnestly, to solicit the proprietors of the several navigations in the Parish of Runcorn, as well as the different companies trading upon the same, to make such arrangements as may secure to the flatmen and boatmen the privilege of the day of rest. That the sailing of packets is equally offensive to Almighty God and injurious to the morals of the community, causing disorder, confusion and gross irregularities on the day set apart for divine worship and the performance of other duties enjoined by our holy religion.'

(The Chester Courant 25th May, 1839)

As a result of this new attitude to Sunday observance, the Trustees of the River Weaver Navigation Company in 1841 built a church at Weston Point for their employees and their families. It was called Christ Church. The Trustees were generous for they built a vicarage, paid the vicar's stipend and also made allowances to the church cleaners and choristers. A school was provided for the boatmen's children and a house was built for the schoolmaster whose salary was also paid by the Trustees. This was a remarkable and immediate response to public feeling.

This church at Weston Point has a fine octagonal spire and the plan is in the form of a cross. When the church was newly-built it stood on a small headland which jutted into the Mersey. By 1894 the Manchester Ship Canal had replaced the river on one side of the church, whilst the Weaver Navigation Canal formed another boundary. Two inlets between these canals left Christ Church on an island so there is some justification in the claim that the church is the only one still in use on an uninhabited island in Britain.

The parish registers of Christ Church, Weston Point, record its nautical connections. The entries include such occupations as boatman (narrow boat man), waterman (river flat man), and pilot. It is said that during the evening service in winter months of later years the Church blinds had to be drawn in order that the church lights should not be mistaken for that of the nearby lighthouse.

The pressure, which some congregations had brought to bear on the canal companies, had its desired effect, for, on the 12th August, 1839

'great joy was expressed by the Reverend John Davies and the Holy Trinity congregation' in Runcorn when the Weaver Trustees ended Sunday working and 'granted the boatmen the Sabbath to its fullest extent'.

(Diary of Richard Lea. 'What was Runcorn like in 1838?')

One of the earliest Welsh religious centres on Merseyside was the Welsh Chapel in Back King Street, Runcorn, as it was established in 1829. The

Welsh community in the town grew quickly during the first three decades of the century as seamen, dock workers and quarry men from Wales settled in Runcorn.

The minister at the Welsh Chapel was the Reverend John Jones and in two letters published by him in 'Y Drysorfa' (The Treasury) in 1843 he reviews six years of his ministry from 1837 to 1843. (Evans, H, Hanes Methodistiaeth Lerpwl, Cyfol II, 1932 p72) Mr Jones said that his 'congregation numbered fifty to sixty of Runcorn people alone and seamen, sometimes more than eighty of them, swelled the congregation on occasions.'

Before 1826, sailors from Wales were given credit for beginning a religious movement among Welsh people in Runcorn when they held prayer meetings aboard a barge in 'chapel basin'. The Duke of Bridgewater's Trust contributed £10 per annum towards the cost of the venture but nothing more is known of its subsequent history. A Welsh Chapel was built in Rutland Street in 1856 and in its early days the congregation received support from Canon Barclay, the Vicar of Runcorn.

The Welsh community in Runcorn was considerable. According to customs officials half of the 4,418 ships to visit the port in 1865 were Welsh vessels and the essay prize at the Welsh Eisteddfod held in Caerleon in 1866 was the gift of Welshmen living in Runcorn. The first recorded formal Methodist Chapel meeting in Widnes occurred in 1863 and here again the initiative came from Welsh seamen.

(Eames. Ships and Seamen of Anglesey, Anglesey Antiquarian Society 1973 p377)

The Bridgewater Trustees encouraged church missionary activity at their docks and in the late 1840's they provided a floating church. The church seems to have been adapted from an old barge. Originally it had been moored at the Locks, later to be moved down the line of the old locks to a new berth near the river. Services on board the strange craft appear to have been well attended. Canon John Barclay, writing in 1864, stated that the average attendance for the 129 services held during the previous year was ninety, which must have meant near capacity congregations for the barge church.

The minister in the floating church for the first years of the mission's existence was the Reverend E.D. Garven, M.A., and the Bridgewater Trust Mission, of which the church was the nucleus, eventually included a Sunday school and a day school for the children of the boat people.

Canon Barclay, in a report, gives a remarkable picture of the work achieved in the Floating Church.

'During the year 1865, 4,418 vessels visited the port of Runcorn and about 20,000 canal and river boats. The total services in the Floating Church was 158, which were attended by 14,584 persons, viz. 4,320 at Sunday morning service, 8,170 at Sunday evening and 2,094 at weekday services.'

In addition to providing the floating church, the Trustees paid part of Mr. Garven's stipend of £110 per annum and they also gave financial support to the day school. When in 1866 the timbers of the barge church were found to be rotten, the Trustees provided a building to serve as St. Peter's Mission Church and the first service was held in December of that year. This was to be the room in which the famous William Shaw was to start 'with the addition of a horse-drivers' kitchen'.

When trade was flourishing in the 1860's, Sunday working on the river and on the canals became the rule once more and the committee of the Mersey Mission to Seamen approached the Earl of Ellesmere of the Bridgewater Trust, drawing his attention to this undesirable practice. It stirred up a hornets' nest.

(Warrington Guardian (Supplement) 26th Feb, 1870).

A reply to the Mersey Mission's protestations was received in February 1870 from the Bridgewater agent who stated the company's regulations on Sunday sailings. He pointed out that vessels leaving Liverpool on Saturday, when tides occurred between 4.00 p.m. and 10.00 p.m., were to proceed to Lymm where they were to remain between 5.00 a.m. and 6.00 p.m. on Sunday, and then go forward to reach their destinations in Manchester in time for business on Monday morning. Vessels sailing from Liverpool after 10.00 p.m. on Saturday:

'... were to remain at Runcorn until 6.00 p.m. on the Sunday, and then go forward, except those laden with cotton or other competitive traffic, (in which case the Liverpool station will issue a speed note to each flat) when they must proceed to their destinations without stopping.'

The committee of the Mersey Mission got little satisfaction from this as the Trustees were not prepared to stop much of their Sunday traffic. Times had changed. The reply concluded with the vague statement that: 'All vessels will be required to tie up between 6.00 a.m. and 6.00 p.m. on a Sunday except those laden with down goods and such as may be from Liverpool carrying speed notes.' In fact, nothing was to be the same again.

The transfer of the Bridgewater undertaking from the Trustees to a limited company in 1872 seriously curtailed the missionary work in the docks and it brought about the end of the Mission Church. The directors of the new company discontinued the payment of the minister's stipend and they refused to make any contributions whatsoever towards the maintenance of the floating church and the day school.

The Mission attempted to carry on after the Trustee's contribution had ceased, but eventually services were discontinued and the establishment was closed. The Mission's activities for the temporal welfare of seamen and boatmen's families in times of hardship also came to an end. The date was 1872.

However, the cessation of Church missionary work at the Bridgewater docks was not of long duration, for it is known that a lay preacher was working among the flatmen and their families about 1873, but nothing is known of his activities.

It was not until 1875 that the Committee of the Mersey Mission to Seamen founded a Seamen's Mission headquarters in the town. The man they appointed to establish the new headquarters was Mr. William Shaw. He arrived in the town without detailed instructions or money to begin his life's work among the town's seamen and their dependants. It was an inspired appointment. Mr. Shaw was still actively engaged in serving the maritime community nearly fifty years later when he was over eighty years of age.

The new Missioner made his headquarters in the old mission building, which had not been used since the Floating Church Mission had closed. This old St. Peter's Mission Room, Bottom Locks, became the centre of William Shaw's ministry. One report was to state that Shaw's best work was

'... in the drivers' kitchen, where he used to address the class of people who most needed his services. On one occasion there were 75 people present. The open-air services at the docks, on board the vessels, and at the Top Locks have been the means of doing much good.'

Shaw was born on the 16th September, 1841 in the small town of Upton-on-Severn in Worcestershire. He spent his youth on a canal boat, then became a seaman and sailed to Spain in a ship which traded there. Later he joined an emigrant vessel and went to Auckland in New Zealand. Next he visited China, in particular Shanghai. At the age of 18 he entered the Royal Navy, and the brig he served in was commissioned to survey the China Seas. She cruised for some months and then returned home. Next he volunteered to serve in *H.M.S. Pioneer*, and soon sailed to Melbourne, Sydney, Brisbane and Capetown. After eleven years he returned at last to England.

On leaving the Navy in 1863, Shaw went to Liverpool, where he joined the River Police Force. He remained in that work for ten years. During that time, on 12th July, 1872, he was presented with the Liverpool Humane Society's certificate for gallantry saving the life of a comrade. There was another occasion when he had the misfortune to be in a boat which capsized and all hands were drowned with the exception of himself. He considered

The River Police Force   William Shaw

that the Lord had permitted his life to be saved and he turned to the church. Shaw became involved with St. Bede's Church and with St. James in Toxteth. The Vicar undertook his training for the ministry as a missioner. In Liverpool he married a Manx lady and she was to become 'the chief nurse and mother' of the Mission Church and Institute in Runcorn.

So Missioner Shaw started his work at the old St. Peter's Mission Room and his early reports illustrate his devotion to his work. With the assistance of four boys and three girls, Missioner Shaw visited boatmen and seamen in their homes and on flats and ships. In one year his visits totalled 7,447. There were thirty-three Band of Hope and Temperance meetings and seventeen open air meetings conducted aboard ships and at the docks.

In order to counteract the attractions of the many public houses, Mr. Shaw provided a bowling green, a skittle alley and a recreation field for the seamen, as well as a recreation and reading room. This man was no ordinary Missioner and was probably regarded with some suspicion by the clergy of the day!

He was even instrumental in providing a seamen's grave in the town cemetery for those who died locally but who came from all parts of the world. Apparently, he was affronted by the practice of burying sailors in unconsecrated ground, because there was no money to defray the burial costs. Runcorn had many public houses and so many seafarers fell into the docks because of drink that he formed a Grappling Corps ... volunteers armed with ropes and grappling hooks ... to retrieve the bodies. At the time of Missioner Shaw's retirement in 1921 forty-seven seamen had been buried in the grave. The stone commemorates seamen from Dublin, Anglesey, New Brunswick, Bordeaux, Norway and the United States.

Shaw was one of the instigators of the Victoria Memorial Hospital (known locally as the Cottage Hospital). His wife, Mary, had taken many sick seamen home to be nursed. With a family of six girls and six boys there could not have been much room!

Throughout the period from about 1877 to 1910 the local press frequently reported on the Mersey Mission to Seamen's attempts to relieve distress during periods of unemployment, or during times when work on the canals was stopped because of ice. Typical of the reports is the following from the Warrington Guardian of 17th December, 1879.

'During the four days the soup kitchen connected with the Mersey Mission to Seamen has been open, no less than 468 meals have been given away. Mr. Shaw having announced that a free meal would be given away on Sunday morning, there was a large muster and 128 children were regaled with tea and buns. Should the thaw continue the soup kitchen will cease its operation after this day.'

127

The Shaw Family

The Mersey Mission to Seamen at Runcorn continued to be a tranquil haven for seamen and the indomitable Missioner, William Shaw, was tireless in his relief work among the destitute families of boatmen and flatmen.

Shaw had built a Mission Church in Station Road in 1891 and in the first Annual Report it was noted that there were 898 narrow boats registered at Runcorn, and 1,857 sea-going vessels and river craft visited the port. His influence was felt beyond Runcorn, for in 1880 he had helped to establish a Mersey Mission base at Ellesmere Port. The new church in Runcorn could accommodate 250 people and included a Sunday School for the children of the watermen. The total cost was £1,460.

His wife provided him with active support in this charitable work, and for thirty-seven years she gave practical help to many needy individuals among the boat people. Mary died in 1913 and a stained glass window in the Mission Church was dedicated to her memory.

After forty-six years of incomparable altruism, Mr. Shaw retired in 1921. He was buried in Runcorn Cemetry on 4th June, 1926. For Runcorn it must have seemed like the end of an era and hardly possible that a man of such similar great standing could be found to replace him.

However, his successor, Samuel Towers, proved to be a Missioner of equal ability and generosity, and he soon won a reputation for unselfishness that equalled that of 'Captain' Shaw. Although Mr. Towers was to serve the Mission for many years, the Station Road Church was universally referred to as 'Shaw's Mission'.

Few ships came to Runcorn after the war and in 1946 the Mersey Mission to Seamen's building was closed and its work was taken over by St. Michael's Church in Greenway Road, the Parish in which the Mission was situated. The building in Station Road was sold to the Cheshire Education Committee in 1956. It was demolished in the early 1970's to make way for a new road.

When I started work in Liverpool in 1961, it was always a pleasure to visit Runcorn. The vessels were small, but the welcome aboard was ever cordial. At the time it seemed correct to do little more than make the occasional ship visit in order to meet the men aboard.

However, in the middle of 1970, another effort was made to establish Mission work in Runcorn. The Apostleship of the Sea in Manchester, under the guidance of Father Keagan, placed a porta-cabin on the dock estate. It was an ecumenical effort, supported by the Apostleship of the Sea in Birkenhead, the British Sailors' Society, the Missions to Seamen in Salford and the Mersey Mission to Seamen.

The temporary building included a lounge, bar and recreation room. It was manned each night and the international telephone system proved to be popular, but sadly it was not very well used by the seafarers, who had become accustomed to visit the local hostelries or to remain aboard their vessels. We had moved into a different era and the needs of the seafarer had changed. After about five years, it was the unanimous decision of all the participants that the experiment be terminated, and the cabin was moved to an East Coast port. The Mersey Mission reverted to occasional ship visiting and responding to emergencies.

The Missions to Seamen in Salford had closed in the seventies and the Missioner was withdrawn. In no time, the Apostleship of the Sea was also to cease operating in Salford and in Birkenhead.

We in the Mersey Mission still continue to this day to visit the half dozen vessels which use the port of Runcorn. Pastor Peter McGrath of the British Sailors' Society also continues to 'do the rounds'. Runcorn is not forgotten.

Conditions aboard ships are vastly improved from the days of Missioner Shaw and the need for a shore facility does not exist. The Mersey Mission's only contact on the Bridgewater Canal was when I was asked to conduct the occasional Rally Weekend Service for the 'fun-users' of the canal. Canal boats 'ain't what they used to be'!

Remarkably, even today it is still possible to mention the name of Shaw to elicit a knowledgeable response. In this way, I came across Shaw's great grand-daughter, Mrs Jean Popperwell. She was happily able to provide much material. I had merely asked about the name Shaw at the counter of the Runcorn Public Library when a gentleman called Ken Hillidge overheard my request.

"I'm distantly related", he said. "But his great-grand daughter lives up the road!"

In no time I was drinking coffee and chatting about the great William Shaw. Seventy years had passed but his memory was still alive.

Shaw and his fellow workers would have been very aware of the activities across the river at Widnes and they would undoubtedly have been involved in the work there.

The turning point in the story of Widnes was the early 1830's. In 1833, the St. Helens to Runcorn Gap Railway Company was opened. Widnes was the natural outlet for St. Helens' industrial life. Also in 1833, the Sankey Navigation Canal was extended from Fiddlers Ferry and terminated in Spike Island. At Spike Island, a new dock was built with railway sidings to transfer the coal on to the flat-bottomed sailing barges. This was the first railway dock in the world and it was opened in July 1833. By 1850 the chemical industry was also in full production.

Since the 12th century there had been a ferry between Runcorn and Widnes. Before Shaw's day it had been 'Tuppence per person per trip'. This was not cheap and it was not an easy trip. At low tide the river had two streams, each one close to the shore. The passenger from Runcorn took the first boat, then the wet sands had to be crossed by foot, before the final trip to the West Bank of Widnes. A walk-way over the railway bridge, built in 1868, almost ended the ferry traffic and the Transporter Bridge (1905 to 1961) finished it completely.

Problems soon arose in Widnes because access to the docks was not easy due to the lack of water in the river and also because of the increase in volume in trade. The Parish of St. Mary's was well placed to handle the trade, but only if the dock was to be extended. Another solution had to be found. The answer was to be Garston.

The St Helens Railway Company decided to extend their lines to Garston and a dock was opened there on the 21st June, 1853. There were two entry gates each 50 feet wide. In 1870 a new line was opened to Wigan which linked the St Helens line. This increased the trade and led to another dock being opened in Garston in 1875.

All this activity enabled coal to be exported and by the end of the century some 50% of the coal trade on the Mersey went through Garston. The little port was busy.

The Mersey Mission to Seamen built a Mission in Garston in 1912. Incidentally, the Mission also opened a new Institute in Birkenhead in the same year. However, thanks to the generosity of Miss Jessie Singlehurst, who provided the entire monies, the Garston Mission became known as the Singlehurst Institute. After the first World War, this Institute was divided into a Chapel for the Parish of Garston and a recreation centre for the Mission's care of seafarers. However, in 1936 the property in St. Mary's Road had become obsolete and it was replaced in the same year by another Mission, a new building at the entrance to the docks.

The Mission which Shaw had helped to be established in Ellesmere Port was closed about the same time. The minutes recount the story.

'It is exactly fifty years since a signal act of generosity on the part of the Shropshire Union Canal Co. made possible an extension of the ministry of service of the Mersey Mission to sailors, floatmen and flatmen. An iron building to serve as a shore-going Institute and club was offered to us by the Company. For all except the first nineteen years of the time it has been under the faithful ministry of Mr. A.T. Baguley. Now, however, under the changed conditions of the post-war years the commitment is no longer justifiable.'

At the end of September (1935) the Institute was returned to the donor and the Lay Reader gave up his charge for a well-earned retirement.

It was during my years that we finally closed all the remaining stations around the port. The Mersey Mission to Seamen has a proud history of caring for the seafarer. We had reached as far as Crabtree, near Burscough, in the north, to Garston and Runcorn in the South. Ellesmere Port and Birkenhead also had their properties. Including the two clubs for the subcontinent of India and the various Boys' Clubs, the Mission had extended into over a dozen enterprises on Merseyside. This shows the great strength of the Mersey Mission to Seamen and also of all the caring Societies... quick to respond to a need, but having the courage to withdraw when that need diminishes.

10.
Poor Jack

With all her poor sailors all sick and all sore:
To me, way hey, ohio!
They'd drunk all their lime juice, and couldn't get more,
A long time ago.

To understand the need for caring it is necessary to recall the conditions of service of 'Poor Jack'. Whilst life ashore was hard and depressingly grim in the last century, the danger for the men aboard the ships was not just restricted to the sea-worthiness of the vessels. There was much ignorance of the causes of diseases and this was particularly true of the dreaded scurvy.

Scurvy was recognised by

'swollen limbs, with dark discoloured blotches caused by haemorrhages under the skin, and foul mouths, with swollen, ulcerated and bleeding gums, but milder forms of the disease would have attracted little attention because, apart from a loose tooth or two or occasional bleeding from the gums, there were no obvious symptoms.'

('The Englishman's Food'. Drummond and Wilbraham page 161)

Naturally the symptoms were much more common at sea and were attributed to 'sea air, sea salt and salted meat and fish.' In 1593 Sir Richard Hawkins set sail to the South Seas in the *Daintie*, provisioning in Plymouth with 'Beefe, Porke, Bisket and Sider.' Just past the Canaries, scurvy appeared and Hawkins noted the 'lasinesse' of the sufferers just before the onset of the disease. He blamed the sea air and ordered the decks to be washed with vinegar and that tar should be burned. Finally they reached Santos with much relief. Actually Hawkins was aware of the properties of 'sowre Oranges and Lemons', but sadly did not see them as vital for good health. (Ibid page 166)

The first English expedition to the East Indies sailed under the command of Master James Lancaster on behalf of the newly formed East India Company. Four ships left Woolwich on February 13th, 1600, and after a slow voyage crossed the Tropic of Capricorn on July 24th, 'August began with ... very many of our men ... fallen sick of the Scurvey in all our ships, but one ship, the Commander's, had surprising few cases.' '... he brought to sea with him certaine Bottles of the juice of Limons, which hee gave to each one, as long as it would last, three spoonfuls every morning fasting.' Impressed by the experiences of these first two voyages the East India Company arranged for a supply of lemon-water for all its ships.

'The third voyage, commanded by William Keeling, set out in 1607 and returned in May 1610. With the help of lemon-water and occasional supplies of fresh fruit they kept free of scurvy.'

(Ibid pages 167ff)

However, little notice seemed to have been taken of all this. Probably a sub-acute form of scurvy was common on land and the sufferings of the seafarers would be seen to be peculiar to sea-going. With hindsight the lessons were there to be understood.

The food in the Royal Navy was deplorable.

'Scurvy was a grim spectre feared by the commander of every ship undertaking a long voyage. During the Seven Years' War (1756 - 1763) 185,000 men were raised for sea service, of whom no less than 130,000 died from disease. One doctor held that two thirds of this number may be safely charged to the account of diseases which take their rise from putrification.'

(G.Anson 1748. 'A Voyage round the World' 1740-1744.)

'In 1795 after endless discussions and, let it be noted, nearly two hundred years after Captain Lancaster had proved its value on the long voyage to the Indies, the Admiralty decided on the recommendation of Sir Gilbert Blaine and Dr. Blair to adopt lemon-juice as the principal anti-scorbutic. The allowance was fixed at one ounce, together with an ounce and a half of sugar, and the ration was usually issued after the sixth week at sea. The result was dramatic. In 1760 there had been 1,754 cases of scurvy in the Naval Hospital at Haslar; in 1806 there was one.'

(Drummond and Wilbraham, page 320)

One might assume that the problem of scurvy had been solved by the start of the 19th Century and many long voyages were completed with no recurrence of the disease, but the Mercantile Marine was slow to reform itself. It was not until the Merchant Shipping Act of 1854 that it was decreed that lime-juice or lemon-juice must form part of a ship's discipline. Hence the term 'limers' or 'limeys' was invented. It was later to be discovered that the lemon was three times as effective as the lime.

The editor of The Porcupine in the editions of 1st and 8th June, 1867 makes an interesting statement.

'Dreadnought, the London Seamen's Hospital, has given some recent details about the incidence of scurvy aboard ships. In 1865, there were 102 cases in which they were involved ... that is a twenty per cent increase over 1864. Of the ships involved, 31 came from Liverpool.'

'... that cases from that port are twice as many as from Glasgow and Greenock taken together and nearly double that of London vessels ...'

'Samples of lime juice taken off ships in Liverpool proved that out of every ten samples, only one was of value!'

'... every shipowner knows well that in Calcutta, Callao, San Francisco, Quebec and many other ports sailors are usually shipped in a state of drunken stupor and that the enormous advance on account of wages, as well as a handsome fee per head which the captain pays before the drunken hump of humanity is parted with, goes into the pocket of the crimp.'

'It is also noted that scurvy occurred in men who had shipped abroad. It is the highest in the ports where desertion and crimping are most rife.'

We can assume that in spite of the 1854 Merchant Shipping Act, there was no desire to implement the ruling on lime and lemon juices. Again it would not be unusual to find scurvy in a milder form when men had deserted and had an irregular diet. It was no surprise when it was discovered that the disease was widespread in Ireland in 1845 after the potato crops had failed.

A letter written to the Editor of the Liverpool Critic by 'Jack Caustic' on 2nd December, 1876 is well worth reading. No editor would accept so many words these days ... our attention span must have decreased dramatically. Here it is unexpurgated. The title is 'How Sailors Are Fed'

'During my stay on shore I have heard landsmen, poor as well as affluent, curse their destiny, and complain - the former of the sameness and hardness of fare to which they are fated - the latter to want of appetite to relish their food with gusto. This has occurred so often that it has excited my warmest sympathy, and sailors being proverbially generous in relieving those in distress, has induced me to offer a remark or two by way of advice, the adoption of which will materially tend to mitigate some of the evils to which these complainants are subjected.

'In the first place then, touching the sameness and hardness of the fare. As a substitute I can do no better than offer them that provided for the seamen aboard the barque *Sterling* of Liverpool.

'Variety is what they want, and variety is what this would supply; not Sambo's variety, who, on his wedding day, said; 'We hab dipperent wariety, for we hab boiled piece ob pork, roast piece ob pork, pig's cheek, and anodder piece ob pork'. The *'Sterling'* variety consists not only in the various kinds of edibles, such as flour, pease, salt, beef, fat pork etc., but also in the number of made up dishes, dishes that would puzzle Mrs. Glasse, or even the great Soyer himself to concoct; dishes whose names to seamen are as familiar as household words, such as cracker-hash, sea-pie, dog's-body, dandy-funk, the long-famed and ne'er to be despised duff, a mass of flour, slush and water, and boiled into what is termed 'Natice Clagger', and last, though not least, 'sop', an excellent dish, a veritable luxury - a dish as famed as the fabulous one in which pearls were dissolved - a dish that would excite the gastronomic powers of an obese, over-fed, and dyspeptic alderman after a civic feast; in short, a dish fit for old Epicurus himself.

'This renowned dish is so worthy of mention that I cannot refrain from giving the receipt for its preparation. It is invariably made by steeping hard tack or sailor's biscuits in water, and with the addition of a little slush or grease is baked in an oven. The slush or grease is of the same quality as that used for the lubrication of the axles of cart wheels, ship's masts, etc. The biscuits must also be of such tenacity, hardness, and consistence as to elicit from seamen the well-merited name of Pantiles. They, moreover, must be perforated by myriads of small unctuous creepers, as a necessary adjunct to the fatty matter.

'Beside the above perfection of the Marine Cuisine, there is the gubbins or menaolius from the dog-basket, the sailor's cornucopia, a conglomerated mass of such things as scraps of ham, pieces of half eaten pancakes, the rind of bread, preserved potatoes, and other heterogeneous matter, forming in all the Olla Podrida of the

Spaniard, the Gallemaufry of the several districts of Warwickshire, and the Wiampanoa of the Indian.

'But by far the greatest inducement I can offer is the tea and coffee. Gunpowder and Mocha have both been surpassed by the mixture meted out to us on board the *Sterling*. They are both of such excellent quality that but an extremely small quantity is issued daily to each man; stimulating in its properties, and guileless of but little in the shape of sugar or molasses, it possesses the extraordinary property of acting as an emetic if taken copiously. But the best recommendation it possesses is its transparency, for a tea-spoon would be clearly visible at five fathoms of this mixture. It is, therefore, incumbent on me to propose that a medal of honour be awarded to the ship's cook for the invention of these rare beverages. In addition we have other dishes too tedious to enumerate here, such as 'strike-me-blind', or 'swamp seed', etc., but I forbear, as the names would be perfectly unintelligible to landsmen.

'Appetite, the loss of which is greatly to be deplored, can easily be regained aboard, for the owner, Captain K. has with admirable forethought and benevolence, supplied his vessel with an apparatus (i.e. a pump) placed abaft the mainmast, a real appetiser, the manipulation of which every second hour throughout the twenty-four will work a complete cure.

'The medical faculty have also unanimously decided the above apparatus to be the best anti-scorbutic extant. Should any however, be troubled with a surfeit (a very rare occurrence aboard a British ship) of nausea or the like, a trudge up to the mast-head in a heavy head sea would make him emit all superfluous matter.

'To crown all, the captain, with characteristic prudence and forethought, deeply interesting himself in the comfort and welfare of his seamen, has strenuously opposed and strictly forbidden the use of the oil-lamp in the forecastle, the glare being highly injurious to the retina of the eye, and had advocated in lieu thereof the use of the British Marine Slush Lamp. British par excellence, the invention being purely British, for during one-and-thirty years' experience of a sea life I have never seen, heard, or read of any vessel under any other flag attempting the use of this celebrated lamp.

'My pen is too feeble, and my words too inefficient to do full justice to the component parts of this great acquisition to our comfort. But imagine an old tin plate, slung with wire similar to the weighing bowl of a pair of scales, on which is placed an old tin pot razed down for a burner. This burner is filled with salt, slush, or grease, an extract from your own salt beef, in lieu of oil, paraffin or petroleum. The wick is composed of tarred rope-yarns fastened to a piece of sharp-pointed stick, which is thrust into half a raw potato; thus completed, the lamp is ready for lighting. This extremely ornamental chandelier, swinging with the motion of the ship, acts the reverse of the lights over a billiard table, for it concentrates its rays and throws them on the ceiling, leaving the lower parts (in fact all places below the level of the light), in what the Scotch call a gloaming. Reading, writing, or mending is completely out of the question, for the light emanating from a single lucifer match would pale that of this extraordinary illuminator.

'Now I invite landsmen, rich and poor, little and great, one and all of those who are discontented with their lot, to join the *Sterling* on an experimental trip, and witness the comfort and luxury which are provided for seamen, when I guarantee that they will renounce all the tame pleasures of the land for those of the sea.'

That sums up the sea life of 'Poor Jack'. The Editor covers himself with the explanation ... 'Our readers will understand that the name of the vessel in this letter is fictitious'.

Charles Dickens in The Uncommercial Traveller (1860) writes a chapter entitled 'Poor Mercantile Jack'. He paints a miserable picture.

'Come along, Mercantile Jack! Ill lodged, ill fed, ill used, hocussed, entrapped, anticipated, cleaned out. Come along, Poor Mercantile Jack, and be tempest-tossed til you are drowned!'

Then Dickens shows his concern as the policemen tour the dockside, looking for trouble.

'Sharpeye opened several doors of traps that were set for Jack, but Jack did not happen to be in any of them. They were all such miserable places that really, Jack, if I were you, I would give them a wider berth. In every trap somebody was sitting over a fire, waiting for Jack. Now, it was a crouching old woman, like the picture of the Norwood Gipsy in the old sixpenny dream-books; now, it was a crimp of the male sex, in a checked shirt and without a coat, reading a newspaper; now, it was a man crimp and a woman crimp, who always introduced themselves as united in holy matrimony; now, it was Jack's delight, his (un)lovely Nan; but they were all waiting for Jack, and were all frightfully disappointed to see us.

"Who have you got up-stairs here?" says Sharpeye generally. (In the Move-on tone.)

"Nobody, surr; sure not a blessed sowl." (Irish feminine reply.)

"What do you mean by nobody? Didn't I hear a woman's step go up-stairs when my hand was on the latch?"

"Ah! sure, thin, you're right, surr, I forgot her. 'Tis on'y Betsy White, surr. Ah! you know Betsy, surr. Come down, Betsy darlin', and say the gintlemin."

'Generally, Betsy looks over the banisters (the steep staircase is in the room) with a forcible expression in her protesting face of an intention to compensate herself for the present trial by grinding Jack finer than usual when he does come. Generally, Sharpeye turns to Mr. Superintendent, and says, as if the subjects of his remarks were wax-work:

"One of the worst, sir, this house is. This woman has been indicted three times. This man's a regular bad one likewise. His real name is Pegg. Gives himself out as Waterhouse."

No wonder Dickens thought of a seafarer as Poor Mercantile Jack!

When W.H.G. Kingston came to Liverpool in 1856 for his important weekend, during which he founded the Mersey Mission to Seamen, he had made time to visit the ships on the river. In his booklet, A Cruise on the Mersey, he included this account which well illustrates the lot of Poor Jack.

'We pulled for the *Boanerges*, a large ship of 1350 tons, lying off the west end of the town. A strong wind and tide, meeting, created a sea rather trying to landsmen - indeed, so rough at times is the Mersey from this cause, that boats have considerable difficulty in boarding ships. We were received most kindly and politely by the first officer, an earnest, zealous young man. The masts and spars, as well as the hull of the ship, were in a sadly shattered condition. She had sailed some weeks before, with emigrants from Liverpool, and had twice put back dismasted, once into Cove and next into Plymouth, where she got on shore and had to land her passengers.

'He gave an account how he and the second mate went aloft in the gale, with axes secured to their wrists, to clear the wreck of the masts, yards, and rigging from the ship, yet, though shattered spars, blocks, and ropes were falling on the deck, crowded with the affrighted passengers, not one of them was hurt.

'One seaman, a fine lad of nineteen, was holding on by the main rigging, looking after his cap, blown off his head. As the ship rolled, the rigging slackened, and he was jerked overboard into the

Georges Dock basin in 1858 showing St. Nicolas' Church

raging sea. The life-buoy was let go, and the order given to lower the life-boat. Eagerly did those on board watch him, but it was winter weather, and he was thickly clad, with heavy boots on his legs. Full of youthful strength, he boldly struck out towards the life-buoy. There was a cry of horror on board. A power greater than his was pulling him down. Ere he reached it, he threw his arms above his head, then sank for ever, to join the thousands of gallant seamen who lie buried in ocean's caves. Such is the uncertainty of the seaman's life - one moment in health and strength, on the deck of the stout ship long accustomed to the buffet with the waves; the next, struggling alone, too often in vain, on the wild billow-covered ocean.

'After she lost her masts, the ship was struck by a sea which washed fore and aft, the affrighted emigrants rushing on deck in their night-clothes, believing she was foundering - yet again, not one was injured. She had just come round from Plymouth, her crew consisting of only twenty-five men.'

The statistics in 1899 produced by the Board of Trade for the year 1897-1898 are alarming. 681 lives were lost from British vessels, but large as this total is, it compares very favourably with the annual average of 1,744 for the previous 22 years. Obviously a ship foundering with a large compliment can quickly inflate the figures. In the year 1895-96 the *Drummond Castle* was lost with an addition of 247 victims to the death roll. The year previous saw the *Kow Ling* sunk with 1,150 Chinese soldiers aboard, who, being carried on a British ship, reckoned as passengers lost. When the list for 1899 was compiled, it was to include the *Stella* and 10 steamers from the first three months. Out of the 681 lives lost under the year being reviewed, 289 were through casualties to steamers and 392 from sailing vessels. For the previous 22 years the average loss from steamers was 691, and from sailing craft 1,051.

The work and care of the different societies for the seafarer must be understood against this depressing background of ill health, poor food and deplorable conditions aboard. Sadly, even today many seafarers are still lost at sea and unbelievably even the ship-board conditions are in many cases questionable.

A simple way of illustrating the plight of the modern 'Poor Jack' is to produce details at random from the December 1996/February 1997 edition of Flying Angel News, which is the newspaper of the Missions to Seamen. Copies are always available from the Missions to Seamen, St Michael Paternoster Royal, College Hill, London EC4R 2RL.

the river Fal, Cornwall, have been repatriated, but eleven seafarers who replaced them are now suffering a similar fate.

'Almost the only visitor to both crews has been the Mission's Cornish port chaplain, the Reverend Simon Brocklehurst. He has acted as their friend and counsellor and link with their families and the international union which has been working on their case.

'To visit the ship, Mr Brocklehurst had to take a rowing boat. "I felt I was doing something that our founder John Ashley would have done", he said. "He didn't wait for the ships to come alongside but was active in reaching out to those who were isolated on ships anchored off-shore."

The story continues.

'This chaplain also visits five other vessels on the Fal ... three of these are under arrest, one is being refitted and the other is awaiting cargo. Sadly it is not unusual for many erstwhile state-run companies from the former Soviet Union and Eastern Bloc to be facing financial crises.

'Seven Indonesian and four Chinese crew members of a Korean fishing vessel, who said they had been abused and beaten since they joined the ship, managed to escape when it called at Honiara in the Solomon Islands.

'The Mission's Honiara chaplain Wilson Mapuru is now trying to arrange repatriation for the eleven seafarers because they are afraid to return to the ship.'

The new Port of Spain chaplain Colin Sampson tells a startling story of 'horrendous' conditions on board a St Vincent and Grenadines flag vessel.

'There were shortages of food, and on a number of occasions the crew said they had resorted to eating pigeons and doves to supplement their meagre rations. The total lack of fresh fruit and vegetables had resulted in serious bouts of sickness, including dysentery and malnutrition. When the chief cook asked permission to see a doctor, he was told by the master to get out of his sight.'

This situation was ultimately resolved by the International Transport Workers' Federation in London and also at a meeting in the Mission of the owner, the crew, a local ITF lawyer and the Mission chaplain.

The Secretary General of the Missions to Seamen, Canon Glyn Jones, spoke recently at a conference in London on the theme 'Achieving Safety at Sea'. "A well found ship with a well trained crew would not be a safe ship if welfare and social issues were ignored and if crew morale was at rock bottom." He went on to point out that seafarers were suffering greater isolation and working under greater pressure than ever before because of smaller crews and quicker turn-around times.

We can so easily forget the seafarer. Yet we could not survive in this country without him. Ninety-two per cent of our trade still arrives by sea. We need to care for these men.

11.
Strikes

Bound away! Bound away!
Through ice, sleet an' snow,
She's a Liverpool packet,
Oh, Lord let her go!

The Press in the last century looked upon the seaman almost as a figure of fun ... Jolly Jack Tar, Poor Jack and Honest Jack. His courage at sea was never questioned, but his folly as soon as he came ashore became a legend. Novels and television scripts today tend to portray the same attitude when they tell about the 'olden days'.

In fact, the seafarer always seems to have been exploited, at sea and on shore. Of course the seaman was really a casual labourer, as was the docker, and there were too many of them. Conditions were poor and the life was harsh. The seaman was therefore fair game. Perhaps this is why the various churches and caring societies began their work in the ports of this country and about the world. Experience tells me that 'Poor Jack' is still too often misused even today.

When I started working at the Mersey Mission to Seamen in Liverpool in the early sixties, the advance note and allotment note were still being issued. The advance note system enabled the man to have a portion of wages in order to kit himself out for the voyage. Allotment notes allowed the family to draw money whilst the man was at sea. Sadly, in the early days, a high rate of interest was sometimes charged. Again goods bought aboard the ship were well over-priced. All these deductions often left a man with very little at the end of a voyage.

The political discussions of the 1840's concerned free trade and protectionism. Seafarers cut across the argument, realising that free trade would produce greater benefits for them as more ships would use the port. The Liverpool Mercury commented on 19th March, 1841 on the advantage of free trading.

'Here is employment for thousands of shipwrights, blockmakers, riggers, joiners, ropemakers ... and all stopped - for what? ... For dear bread, dear butter, dear beef, and dear cheese'.

Free trade was certainly attractive to seamen. The Morning Chronicle of 26th August, 1850 reported that 'of the crews of American ships out of Liverpool, twelve or fourteen out of the twenty-four are Englishmen or Scotchmen'. The Liverpool seaman was content to take work aboard any available vessel. He worked as an individual with no sense of solidarity with his fellow seafarers. No wonder he could be and was exploited!

The Porcupine in May 1866 produced an article under the heading: 'The Sailor's Home and the Seamen's Strike.' It is worth recording every word, even though again it is over-long when compared to the modern tabloid handling of the news.

'Once upon a time the geese in a certain farmyard placed themselves under the protection of the fox, and with tears in his eyes Reynard vowed he would stick to his constituents to the last. He kept his word for he never left that farmyard as long as there was a feather to be seen about it.

'Very forcibly were we reminded of the geese when the other day we saw poor, thoughtless, reckless Jack strolling about town, proud of the little bit of blue ribbon stuck in his button hole, and rejoicing in the novelties of music and speech-making. Still more forcibly were we reminded of the fox when we heard that Jack's demonstration was got up under the auspices of the 'Seamen's Protective Society', alias Seamen's Advance Note Protection Society, and that the boarding-house fraternity had announced their intention to stick to him 'through thick and thin'. We have no doubt that, like the fox, the crimps will be as good as their word, and so long as Jack has a shilling in his pocket or a shirt to pawn they will manifest the most anxious attention to him and his.

'Let us not be misunderstood, however. If Jack thinks that his labour is not fairly remunerated, we do not dispute his right to take legitimate steps to obtain a fair day's pay for a fair day's work. Indeed, we should rather sympathise with him in any such movement, for we are inclined to think that he is not always as fairly paid as he might be; but, in common with all his true friends, our very sympathy induces us to look well that the movement is wisely and judiciously timed.

'The folly and infelicity of the present movement are, however, so palpable that it would be a waste of words to attempt to prove them. Most people are convinced, by painful experience, that the present is a period of great commercial depression, and that the shipping interest is bearing a full share of the burden. Freights are ruinously low - there is scarcely a trade which is not overdone with tonnage - and most ships are now being sailed at a loss to their owners. The conclusion to which these facts point is, however, unseen by Jack. He does not reason closely; indeed, he does not reason at all, but believes whatever the boarding-house crimp chooses to tell him. He thinks that he has only to 'hold out' and shipowners must pay him high wages or lose money by their vessels. How he is to hold out without a shilling in his pocket and dependent upon his advance note to pay for his board, he does not well know; but the crimp says he will see him through, and Jack thinks it is all right.

'Now, in the crimp's anxiety to have Jack well paid, we have the secret of the whole combination. We do not suppose that anyone is simple enough to believe that the discounting, outfitting, boarding-house, and brothel-keeping fraternity are actuated by an earnest desire to elevate Jack either in a pecuniary or a moral sense. For our part, we doubt not that, if a ground-shark could speak, he would express intense interest in the physical condition of the people likely to bathe in his waters, and we are quite prepared to find the land-shark as keenly alive to all that is likely to make Jack's purse plump and worth snapping at.

'We have repeatedly exposed the proceedings of the land-shark, and shown how easy he makes Jack his prey; and had we needed testimony to the fidelity of our sketches, we could not have desired better than offered to us by 'The Seamen's Protective Society'. We think the directorate of that body amply corroborates our assertion that the bulk of Jack's hard earned money finds its way into the pockets of men who live by squeezing him. Moreover, the speeches made at the meetings of this worthy society afford the public a faint glimpse of some of the evils we have from time to time endeavoured to drag to light. 'Shanghaiing' appeared to be a familiar and well-understood phrase there; and such little dodges as keeping capstans, round which country boobies are trained to pass as sham sailors, create no surprise.

'But we are not going to waste time in dwelling upon frauds which we have repeatedly exposed, and which are well known to the mercantile and nautical portions of the community.

'The root of the evil is the advance note system, and until that is abolished Jack will be in bondage to the crimp, and as long as he is in bondage to the crimp his character must deteriorate. We are often told that sailors are not what they used to be. Shipowners are constantly grumbling about the degeneracy of seamen; but, let them be true friends to their men, and they will soon have a better state of things. Let them give fair wages, and make no advances, and they will soon find Jack a better man and a better servant.

'One of the worst features in the recent organisation is the position occupied by the Sailor's Home, and we think no true friend of that institution can regard its recent appearances in public without feelings of shame and regret. But a short time since we had the head of one department flourishing in the Police Court as a discounter of notes, and now we have the head of another department speechifying at a meeting of the Protective Society, and in the 'Strawberry Gardens', of all places in the world. How far this may meet with the approval of the Board of Trade we cannot say; but we know that shipowners complain, and we think justly, that an official whose duty it is supposed is to protect their interests, as well as those of the seamen, should have acted diametrically in opposition to them. Certainly, if the Home desired to give colour to the rumours which are abroad concerning it, a better course could not have been adopted. It is broadly stated that it lends all its influence to the 'Protective Society'. It is said that when a note is presented at the Home, drawn in the form that society finds so 'unsatisfactory', every obstacle is thrown in the way of the holder of the note. It is further alleged, that the business of the Shipping-office is conducted in a peculiar way, and that when a master applies for a crew something like the following takes place:

OFFICIAL: "What wages do you give, captain?"

CAPTAIN: "Three pounds, and no advance."

OFFICIAL: (in the voice of a Stentor, so that every sailor in the room may hear him): "Oh! you won't get men for that! I am afraid you must give £4 and a month's advance!"

'It will readily be imagined that £4 has then been given. Moreover, the indisposition of the Home to move in some cases of desertion, and its alacrity in others are the subjects of much unfavourable comment. Of course, all these rumours may be exaggerated, or the circumstances may be capable of explanation; but they show the false position in which the Home is placing itself. Nothing can show the rottenness of the system which permits the Home to be a discounter of notes more than the fact that, in public estimation, it is becoming rapidly identified with the crimping interest.'

This was probably not the first, nor the last time, that any attempt to sort out problems produces culpable side effects.

The Porcupine always excelled itself and was aptly named. The problems over the advance note were dealt with by Parliament in 1881. However, it is worth observing that when the author started working in the Mersey Mission to Seamen, hardly a day passed without being asked to cash an advance note for a seafarer who had obtained a berth, but needed clothing for the voyage. As far as possible we did our best to make sure that the monies were well spent. If we had known of the Sailors' Home dilemma a century before we might have been even more circumspect!

Whilst general trade in Liverpool was in good heart in the early 1870's, it only hid the explosion of unrest that was to bring the port to a halt.

Seafarers were basically casual labour (in my time they were called unestablished). This condemned them to live on the edge of poverty. The other equally important consequence was that they could not easily be brought together as a group to fight for a living wage and better ship-board conditions. Such groups as existed were mainly sickness and burial clubs. In 1870 the atmosphere on the Liverpool waterfront was to change

Two men were at the centre of the revolt. William Simpson ran a catering business at the St. George's Landing Stage. He became famous for his support of good causes and this was promoted by the 'Simpson's Bowl'. This bowl was placed in his cocoa rooms for voluntary causes and proved to be a winner. He became the champion of the under-privileged and was very popular, but he did not advocate strikes or the organising of labour. James Samuelson was of a different calibre. He favoured the formation of trade unions for the unskilled.

Almost twenty years later the Liverpool Review of February 16th 1889, contained an article about Simpson's Bowl.

'It would be impossible to close this article without a reference to Simpson's Bowl, which in its day was universally known and which was originated by the late William Simpson, one of the most remarkable men we have had in Liverpool for many a day. It was at the time of the Indian famine that Mr. Simpson, a man of most generous impulses, determined to start a collection by means of a bowl.

'It so happened about the time the idea occurred to him that he mentioned it to his daughter, Mrs. William Cross, wife of the celebrated William Cross, the great animal dealer of Liverpool. Mrs. Cross immediately suggested that as her father was going to make a collection for the starving Indians, he should do so in a genuine Indian bowl which she happened to possess and with which she at once presented to him.

'The famous bowl, which is of polished metal, is now justly treasured by Mr. Simpson's widow and her family, and occupies a place of honour in one of their sitting rooms on the landing stage. Round its edge are inscribed the various amounts collected when the beneficent bowl was on duty: .

Indian Famine Fund	£203.1.3.
Welsh Distress Fund	£1079.19.11
Kind	£1000.0.0
Haydock Colliery Accident Fund	£585.0.0
Liverpool Distress Fund	£600.0.0
Kind	£100.0.0
Irish Distress Fund	£521.0.0
Mercane Colliery Accident Fund	£526.0.6$^{1}/_{2}$
Kind	£150.0.0'

The Liverpool Review of April 6th 1889 contained the following comment.

'The Simpson Memorial water fountain at the corner of Chapel Street, erected in 1885, is at present a positive eyesore. The bronze medallion portrait of the popular friend of the masses, with lettering underneath, is being absolutely eaten away with verdigris and this is at the spot which thousands of people pass daily and where thousands of thirsty souls, hundreds of them 'stone-broke', perhaps refresh themselves free, gratis and for nothing.'

Incidentally, the fountain still exists today at the corner of Chapel Street on the boundary of the Parish Church. Sadly, there is no water!

Simpson appealed to the chairman of the Mersey Docks and Harbour Company on behalf of the gatemen, then he met the chairman of the Cotton Brokers' Association. It was the start of troubles in the docks. This was the tail end of 1872 and it was no surprise that the seamen had begun to feel the need for industrial action.

A deputation of men from the south end, mainly off sailing ships, met with the chairman of the Shipowners' Association, but received little help apart from the surprising advice to form a union. So the Liverpool Seamen's Union was formed in May 1872. Two hundred men joined.

The Simpson Memorial

Little was achieved as in a few weeks most of those men were at sea and the Union ceased to exist. This was the first time that the seafarers in Liverpool attempted to co-ordinate their protests.

Simpson and Samuelson, who mainly worked for railwaymen and shop assistants, continued trying to champion the cause of the dock workers and the unskilled. It was all to come to a head in 1879.

Both the dockers and the seamen in the port were to strike for some three weeks. In the January of that year, it was proposed to reduce the wages of the dockers and on the 1st February, when the cut was implemented, all the men came out on both sides of the river. Including the corn porters, some 10,000 men were on strike.

At first they were disorganised, but then Simpson and Samuelson helped to pull their cause together. Wages had been not much more than 15 shillings a week for the docker and the strike reduced that to nothing. The families were suffering. Fearing trouble, the army was asked to patrol the docks.

In the second week of February, the seamen joined the strike. Simpson was asked to address a meeting. As a seaman was earning less than £3 a month, the first complaint was naturally that the wages were too low. Then they denounced the misuse of the advance note and the allotment note system. Next came the conditions aboard their ships and the cost of the ship's provisions. Finally, they objected to the casual way in which they were employed. These were all reasonable complaints.

By the second week in February, the Liverpool Mercury estimated that 35,000 men were on strike in Liverpool and Birkenhead. The Daily Post suggested that some 10,000 to 15,000 were sailors. On the 13th February, the Mercury reported that at least 60,000 were on strike, 'the largest strike that has ever occurred in any one town'. The week wore on with much discussion. It was very cold and wet and the families were starving. On the Saturday morning, the representatives met in Simpson's cafe on the landing stage. In spite of this meeting between both sides, with the Mayor of Liverpool in the chair, no real decision was taken and the workers began to despair. Simpson washed his hands over these futile discussions.

In the meantime, the seamen had again formed a union, the Liverpool Seamen's and Firemen's Bowl Union. The Mercury on the 12th reported that over 4,000 had joined immediately. Meanwhile, Simpson had been investigating the claims about the misuse of the advance note system and declared them well founded.

The employers were not idle. Men were imported from other parts of the country and in the third week of the strike, the dockers were becoming disheartened. The south end returned to normal working and soon the strike was over. On the 24th February, John Maitland, who had continued to fight for the dockers and was in consultation with Simpson, was reported in the Mercury to have placed placards around the docks.

'Under existing circumstances, I advise you to resume work at 5 o'clock this day, accepting for your labour the reduced rate of 4s. 6d. a day and 7d. an hour overtime.

February 24th, 1879   (signed) John Maitland.'

Some seamen fared much better. On the 18th February, the Mercury reported that the Secretary of their union had agreed terms with a number of the shipowners. Simpson had continued to attend these meetings. On the 27th February the Mercury said that the strike had been amicably settled.

The Daily Courier of the 12th March, 1879 stated that four resolutions were to be forwarded to the government:

1. The scale of fresh provisions and water should be increased.
2. Government inspection of provisions to be strictly enforced.

3. An independent shipping office to be established unconnected with the Sailors' Home.

4. The advance note to be a legal document to be made payable within three days.

The seamen's wage demands were certainly honoured by a few companies as a necessary living wage, but the majority of ship owners refused to co-operate. So the dockers and the seamen settled into an uneasy truce. Little had been gained.

The Courier in April 1880 reported that:

'Acting on Mr. Samuelson's advice, a meeting of the members of the union (The Union of Stevedores, Labourers and Quay Porters) will be held early next week ... and a decision will be arrived at as to the course to be adopted'. The time was ripe. The railway porters had received a 3s. a week increase, from 21s. to 24s. and this had incited the dockers into action. The port had much recovered and was busy and naturally no shipowner would wish to disturb this. As the dockers were now organised with a union, it seemed to be a good time for them to open new negotiations. The Liverpool Daily Post on 13th August, 1880 summed up the result. 'I presume that the settlement made by the arbitrators may be considered permanent; I congratulate the men on the happy termination of their difficulties'.

The seamen were not so fortunate. The strike of 1879 had achieved little for them. Wages continued to decrease; the success of the dockers did not help. By the May of 1880 there were two unions in Liverpool - out of the Liverpool Seamen's and Firemen's Bowl Union had evolved The Seamen's and Firemen's Union (Liverpool Branch) and the other union was the Amalgamated British Seamen's Protection Society. These two unions joined forces to demand a 10s. wage increase a month for all grades. The seamen went on strike until the end of the month. However, the shipowners conceded and the matter appeared to be settled for a while.

In 1880 two bills were introduced into the House of Commons ... the Merchant Seamen (Condition of Service) Bill and the Merchant Seamen (Payment of Wages, etc.) Bill.

London must have seemed a long way away from the problems of the seafarer in Liverpool. He was pulled in every direction, used as a pawn for commercial profit, and was unable to fight for his cause. The Liberal Review, which dealt with politics, society, literature and the arts, in the August of 1881 published an article with the headline - 'A Hint to Striking Sailors'.

'There is just now a sailor's strike in Liverpool, and in the neighbourhood of the Sailors' Home those who live upon sailors earnings are at present flourishing. The seamen who arrive in the port with large sums due to them as wages of long voyages are generous and give of their abundance to a fund which, in their innocence, they think is to benefit those who are poorer than they are. It would be well if Jack would be a little less benevolent and a great deal more business-like. He should enquire what becomes of all the money which is collected by those who profess to be friends of the sailors, and who are living very comfortably without apparently doing any business.

'At the present time the sailors are not well paid, we know; but they are not bettering their position by a strike. They are not organised in such a way as to be able to successfully combine. What they are doing is, generally speaking, to give their hard-earned money to crimps, adventurers, boarding-house masters, and the man-catching fraternity, who are doing extremely well, since they not only benefit by subscriptions, but at a good profit supply owners of vessels with indigent seamen, out of whom no more is to be made on shore. Some of the agitators are honest enough, perhaps; and of them we have nothing to say, except that they are not likely to serve seamen by their present course of action. But the honest agitators are few in number and we advise Jack to open his eyes.'

In due time things began to happen in London. The advance note was to be made illegal from 1st August, 1881; crimps were not to be allowed on ships; seamen were to be graded and an able-bodied seaman to be so classified would be required to have served at sea for four years; the sailors lodging houses were to be inspected and licensed by the sanitary authority. The Bills received the Royal Assent.

The two seamen's' unions were not to prove to be very effective and soon disappeared as useful organisations. In 1887, J. Havelock Wilson founded the National Amalgamated Union of Sailors and Firemen in Sunderland (NAS & FU) and, by the end of 1888, it had spread to ten ports, including Liverpool and Bootle. This union eventually was to re-emerge as the National Union of Seamen (NUS) in 1926 and Havelock Wilson to remain the Union President until he died in 1929. The Weekly Courier of 10 November, 1888 stated that the two Merseyside branches had a combined membership of 1,000. Almost immediately the seamen came out on strike. For fourteen weeks shipping was restricted and then there followed sporadic stoppages until the union was wound up by Wilson in 1894.

The Liverpool Review of January 26th, 1889 records an interview with an old sailor.

'Mingling with a crowd of seafaring men about the Sailors' Home, the Review man at last hove against a likely subject in the person of a tall, weather-beaten, but grey-headed and despondent-looking 'Jack', who, hands thrust deeply into his pockets, was walking listlessly in and out among his fellow seamen. Having made this typical 'A B' snug and comfortable in a convenient parlour, the 'seeker after truth' began on his somewhat tough and glum companion.

"Are you one of the strikers?" asked the Review man.

"Well, I am one, and I ain't. I come out, wuss luck, cos I was obliged to, with the rest of 'em."

"How long have you been going to sea?"

"Nigh on forty years. I was in McIvers' boats long afore they was called Cunarders, and have been all over the world a'most in my time."

"What do you think of the wages question and the present strike?"

"I dunno what to think. Sailors gets little enough, Lord knows, but then £4 a month afore the mast's not bad. A feller can't keep a wife and family on much less, can he, now? When I first went to sea, the wages were something like what they were before this strike, but 5 or 6 years ago they dropped us to £3 a month for seamen and £3 10s. a month for firemen. I gen'lly get 5s. a month extra in the wheelhouse, being a quartermaster. Yes, I have been bosun, too, and got better money still in that berth. I served a five years' apprenticeship and am qualified for a sailing ship or a steamboat. 'Pierhead jumpers' ain't; they wouldn't know how to begin in a sail or a line most on 'em. But they get thar, for all that."

"How long have you been walking about doing nothing on account of the strike?"

"Near six weeks."

"Was pressure brought to bear on you, to make you leave your ship?"

"Yes, and more'n me. We didn't care to get hammered; beside we thought it just likely that we would get a rise, anyway. 'Pears to me, though, that it's a losing game for us. Six weeks' hanging about is bad business."

"Have you joined the Union?"

"No, and I don't know as I mean to, either. It costs half-a-crown to join and 4d. a week. No, the members don't get anything back."

The start of the fourteen week strike was just before Christmas, when there was always a shortage of labour aboard ships. The Daily Courier on 1st January, 1889 reported that 'the shipowners as a body are not strongly opposed to the demand because the rates asked for are those now in force in Glasgow'. The request was for an extra pound a month.. The owners, especially the sailing owners, quickly complied, together with some of the steamship owners. Cunard resisted strongly. By early February 1889 the battle was between the union and the Atlantic trade owners. The Courier declared that eight companies would not comply - Cunard, Warren, Beaver, Dominion, Allan, American, Leyland and Johnson (9th February, 1889). The resistance of Cunard was to win in the end. On the 18th February the strike was called off. The owners responded by employing non-union men!

The Courier recorded on 24th May, 1889 that the Union on Merseyside had grown to over 7,000. Havelock Wilson came to Liverpool to negotiate with the owners, but failed to obtain any response. The men struck again. The owners feared the growth of trade unionism and resisted all approaches. Non-union men continued to be employed. Obviously Wilson was not going to succeed.

The Mercury noted that on the 29th June at a mass meeting Wilson admitted that he was prepared to accept arbitration. He suggested this to the Association of Shipowners. They in turn rejected such thoughts and continued to look for non-union labour. The battle was lost and by the 13th July the Union allowed their men to sign on for the old wages. After six months the Union had to admit defeat.

An article produced by the Mercantile Marine Service Association under the heading of Nautical Jottings attempted to put the strike of 1889 into perspective.

'The demand for higher wages made by the seamen and firemen of Liverpool has caused those shipowners who are not disposed to yield to the men's request some little inconvenience. Men have been imported from Glasgow and other places to complete the full number of crews on board the liners and other large steamers, but, notwithstanding, the Union men in one or two cases have gained their object, as owing to the great inconvenience and loss of time Owners have been obliged to grant the rate.'

The Union was disbanded in 1894. With no strong leadership the seamen continued to survive as best they could for the next two decades. The shipowners set up their National Shipping Federation in 1890, partially to deal with any action taken by seamen. However, a number of major companies did not subscribe to the Federation. Incidentally, one hundred years later, the NUS was to amalgamate with the railway workers in 1990 to become the Rail, Marine and Transport Union

The year 1911 produced a major crisis. The Liverpool Daily Post and the Liverpool Courier covered the events in full. Merseyside was to be in turmoil for seventy-two days as the whole transport system became embroiled, which led to a general strike. Liverpool was the centre of the turmoil and the seafarers engaged in the conflict.

Economically the country was improving, but wages had remained static. . The wage rate for the average seaman in 1911 was no more than four pounds and ten shillings a month. The demand was for an extra ten shillings a month.

There was a growing move from the workers to use their power to overcome the capitalists. Branches of the Industrial Workers of the World had been formed in most of the big towns and the leading light was Tom Mann. The first move in Liverpool was on the 31st May, 1911, on St. George's Plateau. It was organised by the newly formed Transport Workers' Federation and most of the unions of seamen, dockers, carters, tramwaymen and other dockside trades were part of it. There followed a three day conference. There were marches across the city with brass bands and banners. The Daily Post mentioned 'seamen and firemen, ships' cooks and stewards, dockers, carters, railway servants, canal workers, motormen and other workers in the transport industry'. Amongst the speakers was Havelock Wilson, the seamen's leader. A firm resolution was passed urging the full support for the two seamen's unions who 'may shortly be involved in dispute with the shipowners'. Wilson fixed, but did not reveal the date for action. The two unions were the National Amalgamated Sailors' and Firemen's Union and the National Union of Ships' Stewards, Cooks, Bakers and Butchers. This latter union had been founded in Liverpool in 1909 by Joseph Cotter, known as 'Explosive Joe'.

1911 was a blazing hot summer and Liverpool was a good choice as a centre for industrial action. A number of major shipping companies were not affiliated to the Shipping Federation. This was the employers' weak link, waiting to be exploited.

The seamen were beginning to formulate their demands. There were problems about the medical inspections when men were engaged by companies and the lack of union protection. Money was important - a request for some wages to be paid whilst in port during a voyage and, of course, a request for ten shillings a month across the board. Above all the fight centred on the need for recognition of their union.

On the 14th June, 1911, five hundred men refused to sign on for the Canadian Pacific's ship *Empress of Ireland* and the White Star's *Teutonic* and *Baltic*. Tom Mann, the chairman of the strike committee, called a dockside meeting and declared that the strike had begun. Actually, it had been planned for the following day.

Cunard, Elder Dempster, Booth's and Alfred Holt's quickly agreed to meet a deputation. These companies did not belong to the Shipping Federation. Progress was made. Alfred Holt agreed immediately, followed by Canadian Pacific, Lamport and Holt's and the White Star Line.. Actually they had arrived at only partial acceptance, but it was a promising start. Within a week the acceptance was completed and this included the union's right to negotiate.

At this juncture, a ship called *Pointer* arrived in port from Glasgow with 'black-leg' firemen aboard. The dockers refused to handle the vessel. These dockers were not in a union, but were directly employed by G. and J .Burns, the owners of the *Pointer.* The Daily Post said, 'This means that unionists and non-unionists (on whom the employers relied) are now banded together.' It was a vital move. Up to this point the Shipping Federation had dealt with strikes by using 'scab' labour, even to the extent of using a depot ship to house non-union seamen from other ports. For the first time this would not work as the seamen were united nationally. Suddenly the unions were in demand. The Daily Post said, 'Officials of the unions were kept busy all morning, taking names and issuing membership cards to stewards and cooks who were answering delegates' appeals to join the union.'

Unity was catching The dockers and the carters were supporting the seamen in their action. This was remarkable because the dockers were mainly Roman Catholic and the carters mainly Protestant. For the first time they worked together to decide which ships were to be 'blacked'.

On the 26th June the Mersey Quay and Railway Carters' Union, at St. Martin's Hall, loudly applauded Tom Mann and agreed not to handle any ship where the owners were in dispute with the seamen. The Shipping Federation of Shipowners realised by the 27th that they were fighting a losing battle. 'Strike ending', wrote the Liverpool Courier on the 28th June. It was premature. On the 28th all work stopped in the docks, 4,000 dockers walking out, followed by all the seamen and other workers. 10,000 men were out by the evening.

A new idea had been born and acted upon. The dockers realised that concerted action had won the battle for the seamen and that the same might work for them. The Courier stated, 'The dockers relied on the active support of the seamen, stewards, and others ... and in this they were not disappointed, although the men to whom they looked for support had already secured settlements of their own grievances. It is feared that the carters will redeem their pledge and join the strikers.'

At 9 a.m. the crew of the *Empress of Britain* came out in support of the dockers. The Courier carried the story. "Yes, I admit we have got what we wanted," said a steward; "we have no grievance with the company, but there is a question of honour at stake. The dock labourers struck purely in sympathy with us, and now we are going to do the same for them". With that the *Empress of Britain* men began a triumphal march from dock to dock, calling out the men from every Atlantic ship in the north-end docks.

The remarkable fact was that almost overnight the working force was organised and unions which had struggled with mere hundreds of members could suddenly count them in thousands. Unorganised workers became union men and the employers had to gave way to the demands. Tom Mann believed that it would bring about the end of capitalism and that there would be a workers' republic. That dream suddenly seemed possible.

The Courier wrote on 29th June, 1911:

'As a result of the contagion of yesterday's developments, there was a record influx of men to the unions, especially the dockers' and its affiliated coal heavers' branch. The enthusiasm was quite extraordinary, and what the men may do under its influence is not a pleasant speculation. It would be too much to say that their officials have them absolutely in hand. There is a spirit of revolt, combined with a feeling of federal brotherhood. Whether the latter will prevail throughout remains to be seen'.

However all was not as it appeared to be at first sight. The dockers had not achieved all that they wanted. The seamen found that the shipowners, whilst they had accepted the idea of a union, had not really accepted their union's demand for a change of wages and conditions. The Strike Committee tried to hold things together and asked for a return to work ... this was put into a manifesto. However, the newly enrolled dockers were not prepared to accept that and tore up the manifesto, refusing to accept orders from the union. This naturally was playing into the hands of the employers.

On the 30 June there was a meeting with the Cunard chairman, Alfred Booth, who categorically refused to accept any terms going further than what was already agreed. The presentation of these thoughts to the workers was met with rejection as the Strikers' Committee played for time. For three days the decision was in the balance. Then on the Monday, the north-end dockers reluctantly returned to work and the Strike Committee kept its authority.

The move to become part of a union had spread to other trades and occupations. The tug boat crews were already out; the lightship men joined them. Next the coopers and labourers at Stanley Dock tobacco warehouse rebelled ... cotton porters, scalers, brewery workers, oil-mill workers, the girls at Walton rubber works, tramway men and, perhaps the most important of all, the railway men.

The railway men had an agreement with their Conciliation Board that they would not strike, but their employers had decided not to recognise their unions. It was a strange way to settle any dispute as, of course, the Conciliation Board had always favoured the employer. It could not continue and by Tuesday, 8 August, 4,000 railway men were on strike. As three quarters of the dock goods were handled by train, the effect on the port was immediate. By the end of the week it had escalated into a national rail strike.

The Liverpool City Magistrates called upon the Home Secretary for support. The decision to bring in extra police and troops was taken on the 9th August, even though up to this point there had been no disturbances. The Head Constable of Liverpool had told the Home Secretary on the 8th August: 'No disturbances of the peace took place'.

The Strike Committee allowed some goods to enter the city and although there was some 'hooting and jeering' the police had been in little difficulty. However, the sudden arrival of one hundred policemen from Leeds and then another hundred from Birmingham changed the tempers of the crowds. More police came from Lancashire and Bradford. Contingents of the Royal Warwickshires, Scots Greys, Hussars, and Yorkshire Regiment were stationed in Seaforth Barracks, Sefton Park and other parks. Then the Lord Mayor rather surprisingly asked for an extra battalion and another squadron of cavalry. Mr. Churchill sent two battalions and a whole regiment of cavalry, as well as the squadron requested. The Daily Post estimated that there were 5,000 troops and 2,400 police at the disposal of the Liverpool Head Constable. *H.M.S. Antrim* sat in the river.

Although the shipping companies had reached an agreement as far back as 3rd August, they choose this time to revoke the arrangements and demand that all 'blacked' goods be moved. This was an unfortunate decision. It was obvious that a serious clash was imminent. A demonstration was planned by the Strike Committee for Sunday, 13th

August. It was announced that the troops had been issued with live ammunition.

There is no better description of what actually happened on that Sunday than the words of Captain Edward Tupper, found in his autobiography 'Seamen's Torch'. Tupper was a friend of Havelock Wilson and was to be a staunch supporter of the National Union of Seamen. He was actually in Liverpool on 'Bloody Sunday'

'I arrived in St. George's Plateau at about 1.30 p.m. on that fatal Sunday, to find a massed crowd of tens of thousands of Seamen and Dockers. On the big slope of steps in front of St. George's Hall - Liverpool's Assize Court - women and children were ranked, tier upon tier of them; the meeting was perfectly orderly, although the military and police were mustered in force. Placed among the crowd were five lorries to be used as platforms.

'At about two o'clock, I was speaking from No. 3 Lorry. There was a sudden commotion by the London and North Western Hotel, where Lime Streeet led into the Plateau, and I was horrified to see men being pursued by charging police. The men rushed into the packed mass, and the police followed, batons rising and falling madly. Madly! Those police were mad, raving mad; it's the only explanation of their behaviour that day. What was the beginning of it all I never discovered; I only know they were imported police - the same old trouble! - who had been on duty at the Stadium all night. Their batons forced a way clean through the dumb and astonished crowd; they reached the other side, the foot of the steps to St. George's Hall: they didn't stop - it has seemed to me often enough that there must have been some devil in them that wouldn't let them stop! - they went up those steps, over, and through the women and children!

'I saw all this from the top of my lorry. I have never seen anything like it before or since.

'The crowd seethed, bubbled - exploded. The men were all unarmed, but trees, set around the plateau in big, eight-foot square tubs, seemed to melt in a moment; those trees became clubs, thousands of clubs. The place became a battle-field - what had been one huge unit of motionless quiet was suddenly a tumult of thousands of sailors and police lusting to smash one another. Soon the Riot Act was read from the steps of St. George's Hall - and that gave the military the right to fire!

'There were baton charges and riots all over the city for hours.

Mounted troops pursued some men through Christian Street - and the women threw from windows all they could lay hands on; crazed with battle, they lighted fires in the street. It was mad - mad!

'Liverpool was a shambles that day - but I was able to send a telegram to Winston Churchill, the Home Secretary, declaring with absolute sincerity and certainty that the imported police alone were responsible.

'In any case, there wasn't only my word for it. The Press took a cinematograph picture, and we saw it, privately. The Government never allowed that film to be shown to the public. The inference is obvious.'

It is agreed that the authorities had over-re-acted. On the Monday after 'Red Sunday', the Mayor produced a notice that was distributed in the streets.

City of Liverpool

Public Warning

I, the Lord Mayor and Chief Magistrate of the said City, hereby warn and urge all persons not having any business to transact in the centre of the City, to keep away from those parts of the City, especially in the neighbourhoods of St. George's Hall, Lime Street, Christian Street, Scotland Road, and any other parts where trouble has taken place. Especially, do I request all women and children to remain at home as much as possible during the disturbed condition of the City.

Large numbers of persons have assembled in the disturbed streets for the purposes of seeing what is going on, and I warn all such persons that if the Authorities are called upon to act, innocent citizens are as likely to be injured as those against whom any drastic measures on the part of the Police or the Military are directed.

S.M.Hutchinson.
Lord Mayor.
14th August, 1911

'Red' or 'Bloody' Sunday' was probably inevitable. A large crowd of the working class had gathered. It was like open class warfare. The fighting lasted for three days. Workers, troops and police all clashed. Another battle was also being waged! Around Great Homer Street the Protestants and the Catholics were settling old scores. It had nothing to do with the strike, but naturally hit the media headlines!

Red Sunday, 13th August 1911

Guns were fired on the Tuesday morning in Vauxhall and two men were killed. A crowd of strikers had held up five prison vans which were being escorted by troops. The shooting was headline news. Tom Mann had declared a general strike on that Tuesday and the whole port was closed. The Liberal Government reacted by sending in more troops and a gunboat with its weapons aimed at the city centre. The Mayor strongly requested that the Liberal Government would allow the use of the troops to work as 'blacklegs'. Fortunately, Churchill forbade what he called 'this objectionable step'. It was significant that the Liverpool Territorials were ordered to hand in their rifle bolts! Both sides feared the escalation of the troubles. There had to be a solution!

On Thursday, 17th August, the Government decided to mediate. Both sides were asked to resume normal work, with no dismissals and to await the outcome of a commission which would report on the dispute. The unions accepted, urging that the report be produced with speed. The employers held out for a further two days, objecting to government interference, but gave in on the Saturday. The railways resumed work on the 22nd August. The Strike Committee was wound up on the 24th.

The seventy-two days were over. Lessons had been learned, especially by the workers. Unions had realised that they had strength, if they could organise their workers and also that real power was possible if they could support each other. It had been a show of strength and did bring about the recognition of the unions. It was an uneasy peace. The advent of the first World War was to divert, but not postpone, this power struggle. When it came again, the government of the day would be better prepared.

The General Strike in 1926 arose from disputes between the coal miners and the owners. The pound was over-valued against the dollar with the result that Winston Churchill in his budget of April 1925 returned the country to the gold standard. The effect was to de-value the pound in order to help the export industry and this, in turn, meant that wage reductions were inevitable. Churchill saw the strike as a quasi-revolutionary movement and resisted any attempt at negotiation. This view he made abundantly clear as editor of the 'British Gazette'.

The Government, having learned much from the 1911 Riots, had foreseen the difficulty and in 1920 had not only passed the Emergency Powers Act, which prevented any interference with strike breakers, but had been stockpiling food and coal and petrol. Whilst the miners stayed out for six months and actually failed to win anything, those who had 'come out' in support were mostly back at work within a week. The T.U.C. had been completely outmanoeuvred.

In Liverpool, the violence of the 1911 dockers' strike was not to be repeated. Much had been learned from that confrontation. In 1926, building workers, ship builders and railway men all joined the strike. It lasted nine days and really caused little inconvenience. Only seven people were arrested under the Emergency Powers Act.

The ferries continued to run and, as many seamen still did not belong to any union, there was sufficient labour available for the ships to be manned. Not all the dockers were on strike, so the ships were being loaded. Two battleships had been sent to Merseyside in anticipation of trouble, but the men were not used. *H.M.S. Ramilies* and *H.M.S. Barham* were berthed at the Princes Landing Stage.

One effect of the 1926 strike was that it enabled the owners to refuse re-employment in many instances and allowed them to 'weed out trouble makers'. This story is repeated many times in the history of strikes.

In 1955 there was a seamen's strike, in London and Liverpool, which lasted from May to June. The numbers involved were comparatively small, 1,700.

.Again there was another more serious strike in 1960 which lasted from July to September. Liverpool seamen were fully involved. It started in a small way. Some two hundred members of the catering staff in the *Carinthia* stopped work because four of them had been logged for minor insolence. The next day the crews of the *Reina del Mar*, the *Apapa* and the *Empress of England* joined. An unofficial strike committee was formed and they sent delegates to Southampton, Hull, Cardiff, Manchester, London and Glasgow. At the end of the week, 2,000 men were out in Liverpool.

Eric Heffer in his autobiography, 'Never a Yes Man', makes this observation on the 1960 strike.

'As a result of the dispute an unofficial national committee of thirty-two delegates from all major ports was set up. This was the first time such a committee had met and it was a harbinger for the future. The stoppage was short-lived, but the rank and file had shown their strength. They were fed up with the way they were treated.'

In the first phase some five thousand seafarers were out for nine weeks and then a further four thousand were involved. It was estimated that 123,000 working days were lost.

This strike had been motivated by the unofficial Seamen's Reform Movement and the problems were not to go away. A major strike was almost inevitable.

I was already in Liverpool when the most disastrous strike of all was called in the summer 1966. All the ports in the country were virtually brought to a standstill. The grievances which caused these actions were not just to do with the seafarers' discontent over wages and hours of work; they were as much concerned with union representation on board ship and with the terms of the Merchant Shipping Acts which controlled such matters as discipline at sea.

The problems had been fermenting for a number of years and it became obvious that 1966 was to be the year of confrontation. Outside London, we had in Liverpool the largest foreign-going trade in the country and a strike of seamen was to have a disastrous effect. It proved to be a long and bitter battle.

On the 5th May the Liverpool Members of Parliament tabled a motion asking for immediate action by all concerned to avoid the strike:

'The first call on any industry is the dignity, wages, hours and conditions of those employed in the industry and it urges a reappraisal and full examination of such factors in so far as they apply to the Merchant Navy in 1966.'

Harold Wilson and Ray Gunter were not pleased by this motion. Gunter urged that the employers' offer be accepted, even though it was lower than the government's norm. Seafarers's wages and conditions had lagged behind other workers, so an offer of 3 per cent (the government's norm was three and a half per cent) was inevitably rejected. Gunter promised a full-scale enquiry. This was also rejected. To the amazement of the National Union of Seamen, Harold Wilson went on television and said: 'This is a strike against the state, against the community.' This was truly an extraordinary statement for the Prime Minister to make!

On the eve of the strike call, 12 British manned vessels sailed, leaving 95 in the port. Mr. Roger Woods, the Chairman of the Liverpool Committee of the N.U.S. stated that:

'We are not against the Labour Government or its policies in any shape or form. We want a fair deal out of the community. In other words, in this New Britain that Harold Wilson is talking about, we want a fair share.'

The strike started at mid-night 16th May, 1966, and the dock gates were picketed in London, Liverpool, Manchester and Hull. This was the big one.

In time the basic reason for the strike became clear. The seamen's demand was for £14 for a 40-hour week. The 40-hour week had already been agreed in 120 other trades in the industries in Britain. In fact, the hours, pay and conditions were considered to be worse for British seamen than those of any other major European nation. As it was, the men were actually working a 56-hour week at sea and 40 in port. An able seamen was paid £12.11s.5d, rising to £13.17s.1d after five years. This rate included compensation for having been at sea on Saturdays, and for 16 hours work at weekends when the ship was at sea. The basic rate was thus under 5 shillings an hour; overtime rates at night and weekends were only 6 shillings. Seven out of ten seafarers earned less than that. The men felt that they had a genuine grievance.

On the first day of the strike, the C.P.R. *Empress of England* remained in Gladstone Dock and should have sailed with 940 passengers. C.P.R. booked air-flights for about 600 from Prestwick, Manchester and London. The Mersey Docks and Harbour Company stated that 41 ships had no crews; 27 had crews and there were in addition 39 foreign ocean-going ships and 9 coasters.

These were busy times for the Chaplains as we tried to visit every vessel in order to talk to the men. Tension was high as a seaman feels isolated aboard his ship with little contact with his fellow seafarers. Our job was to listen.

The media debate produced figures from the employers challenging the seamen's claim about the hours and the pay. William Hogarth, the seamen's leader, came to Liverpool on the 19th to address the Liverpool men as both sides began to harden. Mr. Hogarth told the meeting that his members faced a long, drawn-out battle with the Government.

> "The shipowners have dug their toes in. They are hiding behind the Government's prices and incomes policy. In other words they have passed the buck to the Government. ... I would make this appeal to the Prime Minister. Think again. Do not make a hasty decision in this issue because it might well mean the downfall of the Labour Government in the ultimate."

It was no surprise that the local Labour M.P.s did not like this kind of language.

So the strike began to gather momentum and there was no hope of any settlement. After one week the strike pay of £3 per man was paid by the Union. There were 144 ships in port, of which 81 were British. The loading and discharging of cargoes was continuing as normal and special arrangement was made to supply the Isle of Man. With all these vessels in port and their crews idle, it was no surprise that our establishments were well patronised. British seamen were mixing with foreign seamen in a strike situation which was already becoming confused.

"Seamen could not live on £3 a week strike pay for very long." This was

Mr. Eric Heffer, the Labour M.P. for Walton.

"We have got to ensure the strike is brought to a conclusion as soon as possible. This has got to be on the basis of the seamen getting what they deserve. The seamen in this country have never had a fair deal. They have always had to fight every inch of the way."

There was no doubt about the stance of Eric Heffer.

The government declared a state of emergency on 22nd May. Ray Gunter announced a court of inquiry with Lord Pearson as chairman.

The seamen claimed that their productivity had jumped by more than half in the last fifteen years, although the numbers employed on British ships had dropped from 96,000 to 68,000. The offer from the shipowners, as a result of the Pearson Report, was to be a 40-hour week at sea to be achieved in three annual stages. Direct overtime for the weekend and public holidays had been proposed in the Report - again in three stages. Also on offer was 12s. 6d. a month increase. The Sunday-at-sea leave agreement would be withdrawn, which meant an average loss of 37 days paid compensatory leave a year. These were hard terms. No further wage claims would be considered for the next three years. Unsurprisingly, the proposal was rejected and no more communication was being made with either side of the dispute.

By the 2nd June, there were 170 vessels of all sorts in the port, of which 101 were registered in Britain. The strike was into its third week. The Dock Board emphasised that the port was still working with twenty-two vessels with cargo being handled, but that the number of British ships immobilised was slowly increasing.

The Daily Post asked the Liverpool M.P.s: 'Do you feel that the seamen should accept the Pearson Report and go back to work?'

Simon Mahon (Bootle. Lab.) 'The Report is a basis for agreement ... reduce the three stages to be concluded in twelve months.'

James Dunn (Kirkdale. Lab.) 'I would ask the seamen to consider the proposals.'

Richard Crawshaw (Toxteth. Lab.) 'I think it is a favourable report.'

Tim Fortescue (Garston. Con.) 'My view on the recommendation of the Pearson Report is that it is inflammatory and should not have been made.'

Eric Heffer (Walton. Lab.) 'Certain points are acceptable as a basis for negotiation.'

Eric Ogden (West Derby. Lab.) '... it is a better offer than the Union negotiators put to their executive before the strike.'

John Tilney (Wavertree. Con.) 'I feel strongly that they should accept it.'

On the 20th June, the Liverpool seamen in their sixth week of the strike voted to stay out. A total of 171 vessels of all types - 126 of British registry - were in port and 85 were working cargo. The demand for an immediate forty hour week was firm.

An emergency debate was held in the House of Commons on the 20th June after Wilson had met with Trade Union leaders. The Prime Minister made a statement

> "...a few individuals have brought select pressure to bear on a select few on the executive council of the NUS who in turn have been able to dominate the majority of that otherwise sturdy union. It is difficult for us to appreciate the pressures which are being put on men I know to be realistic and responsible, not only in their executive capacity but in the highly organised strike committee in the ports, by this tightly knit group of politically motivated men."

It was at this juncture that I attended an open-air meeting at Pier Head. The speeches were strong and to the point. Time was passing and the seamen were obviously beginning to realise that they had little backing. The Prime Minister had not seemed in sympathy and talk of 'reds under the bed' had not helped It was as though Wilson thought that the men were against the government Anger was just below the surface. When the time came for a vote, my hand went up to continue the strike! Actually elbows were coming in from all directions!! I voted to carry on with the strike!!!

Port emergency committees were set up on the 22nd June in Liverpool and in another eleven major ports. They operated from noon under the Emergency Regulations introduced a month before. This was to prevent the congestion in the ports halting the movement of trade.

George Woodcock, the General Secretary of the T.U.C. gave an indication that the Pearson recommendation on the forty hour week might be acceptable, if the Sunday working clauses were removed. This seemed to add to the confusion.

The Prime Minister, Harold Wilson, had not helped He firmly appeared to be convinced that the strike was Communist inspired. On the 22nd June he met the Leader of the Opposition in order to discuss the allegations. In Liverpool, the seamen were angry at this Communist tag which they felt had been attached to them by Mr. Wilson's statements in Parliament. The men stressed the fact that the strike had been orderly and not politically motivated. This certainly was my impression and the allegations seemed to be totally unfounded.

Finally on the 29th June the executive council of the National Union of Seamen decided by 29 votes to 16 to 'adjourn the strike for a period of twelve months'. It was expected that the government would set up a court of inquiry to 'fully investigate other grievances and allow further negotiations to take place.' There appeared to be no other solution possible. It was not popular.

In Liverpool a special meeting was called. The reaction was 'the strike is still on'. There really appeared to be absolute confusion. On the 30th a meeting was held at Pier Head and the men were advised, amidst the clamour, by their Union representatives to return to their ships. There seemed to be little to be gained by further action. Unsurprisingly, on the following day, in the Philharmonic Hall, all but two of the 1,800 present voted in favour of a return to work. There was no other choice. The men felt that they had been let down by all sides of the dispute and that they had acted in a responsible manner throughout.

The 47 days of strike were over and the return to work was not with enthusiasm. The mood was for continuing the battle to increase wages and improve conditions. The Prime Minister was accused of 'interference' and condemned for his 'statements in the House of Commons on June 28'. In the port over 50 ships were signed on within 24 hours. The strike was really over.

One seaman said to me that they had been 'sold out by the Government, their Union, the ship-owners and the nation'. Perhaps it had been a battle that could not have been won as it had come a century too late.

Eric Heffer summed up the situation.

'The government had done itself a great deal of harm and laid the basis for defeat in 1970. It was the beginning of conflict with the trade unions and an example of how Labour governments can turn friends into enemies.' We have to wait until ministers publish their memoirs to find out the truth. Dick Crossman revealed, for example, that both George Brown and Jim Callaghan wanted to fight the seamen to the death and that only Dick Marsh disagreed, saying the strike was no issue to fight on and the men had a good case. Crossman lamented: '... it is we the Labour Government who have prevented the shipowners from surrendering to the seamen, simply because a surrender would have made nonsense of the three and a half per cent norm and given the men a big increase. We are paying a high price for George Brown and his policies'.

We should have realised that the great era of British shipping and of the British seafarer was quickly coming to an end. The British seafarer was about to face redundancy on a catastrophic scale and he was to endure a constant anxiety about the future, as the demand for his labour disappeared. Foreign flags, foreign ships, cheaper crews, lower standards, all of this was around the corner. The seafarer was to be proved helpless in the face of such change and those who were to survive were mainly forced to 'go foreign'. The result is that in many ways the British seafarer under a foreign flag was to be as much at risk today as he was a century and a half ago. For this country it was too late. No longer were we to be a leading maritime nation.

At the start of the twentieth century, all the agencies involved in the care of the seafarers were expanding. At the start of the twenty-first century, we face a different world, although there is one factor that has remained constant for two centuries ... the seafarer comes last!

12.
The Scandinavian Churches

'Have you got an emigrant ship that's bound for Amer-i-kay?'
'Oh, yes! I have an emigrant ship,
I have got one or two;
I've got the Georgie Walker and I've got the Kangaroo.'

In the middle of the last century, a National Evangelical Society was formed in Stockholm as an expression of the religious revival in Sweden. At the request of the Swedish congregation in London, the Society decided that a Mission was to be established in Liverpool. The year was 1870.

Pastor P.G. Tegner was chosen to be the pioneer on Merseyside. It was an inspired choice. He was warm hearted, zealous and talented ... and proved to be the right man for the post.

On the 22nd August the Pastor came to Liverpool and on Sunday the 28th August he preached his first sermon to about 90 people in the 'South Bethel'. This is another example of the co-operation that was afforded by one Society to another. His text was taken from Revelations 3.20. 'Behold, I stand at the door, and knock'. That door was opened and the work in Liverpool by the Swedish Church was under way. It had often proved to be as simple as that!

Pastor Tegner started working amongst the seamen aboard the ships. However, he was to grapple with a far greater problem. Much concern had been expressed about the emigrants on Merseyside who were waiting for passage to the New World. Tegner needed help. He was to look for and find support from the local Swedish residents. Three or four times each week he held services and prayer meetings, which were attended by local worshippers as well as by the seafarers. Pastor Tegner cared for his people and was endlessly busy.

However, his major challenge proved to be the great numbers of Scandinavian emigrants passing through Liverpool on the way to America. Between 1830 and 1930 nine million people from Europe emigrated via Liverpool, mainly to the United States, Canada, Australia, New Zealand, South Africa and South America. No thoughts about the Swedish and Norwegian Churches can be complete without a consideration of these families voyaging mainly to the New World. For a number of decades it was to be the major concern of the chaplains.

Before 1840, most emigrants went to British North America, now known as Canada, and half of those were to cross into the United States. The earliest Liverpool emigrant vessels were mainly American and were sailing ships. The average journey was fifty-five days. The Australian emigrants had to face ten weeks to four months. With the advent of steam-ships in the early 1870's a new pattern emerged. The Irish emigrants were able to cross to Liverpool and then sail to America. Naturally, this movement to Liverpool resulted in vast over-crowding in the city. Living in lodging houses and cellars, there was a real health hazard.

However, the Swedes were not poor, unlike the Irish and the English, but 'were principally agriculturists, with a sprinkling of tradesmen and mechanics, who, naturally, anxious to get on in life, are prepared to go wherever their chances seem most encouraging.' (Liverpool Review May 5th, 1888). An important reason for their emigration from Scandinavia was the religious problems in their countries. Their State Church vigorously combated non-conformity. This attitude almost encouraged people to leave. Naturally, in the later years, the exodus was mainly to be families joining families.

The normal route for the Scandinavian emigrant in order to reach Liverpool was by rail in Europe and by ship to Hull. The Liverpool Review painted the picture. (May 1888).

'The flocks of wearied Teutons and Scandinavians we see crowding our thoroughfares reach Liverpool after a 3 or 4 day journey, during which have jolted hundreds of miles in 3rd class railway carriages, a little more comfortable than our English ones; however, crowded for a couple of days and nights in the steerage of a small steamboat and then packed in the train at Hull, they have been forwarded to Liverpool. The emigrant train, like other specials, must take its chance and is shunted about to suit the convenience of the regular traffic. Arriving at Liverpool, the emigrants are met by officials of the various steamship companies and interpreters from boarding houses to which they are allotted until they are shipped to the States.'

In the 1860's the number of Scandinavian emigrants passing through Liverpool ranged from 16,000 to 60,000 a year. It was a lucrative trade. The ships returned from America with timber, cotton and tobacco. This enabled these vessels to carry passengers on the outward journey.

As with the seafarers, these earlier emigrants found themselves in dire difficulties in Liverpool, especially from the runners. A report by Sir George Stephen in 1851 included this comment.

'At first the runners play havoc. Actually I do not know how to describe it, except tearing to pieces, only they do not separate their limbs; but they pull them by the collar, take them by their arms, and generally speaking, the runners who are successful enough to lay hold on bags are pretty sure of carrying the passenger with them.'

Once this had happened, the emigrant was invariably cheated. Happily in the '50s these runners had to be licensed and this marginally improved matters in favour of the victims.

The lodging houses in Liverpool in the middle of the century were probably no worse than found elsewhere in the country, but the numbers of people involved created desperation. Charges were from 2d to 4d a night, but the conditions were terrible with 20 to 30 sleeping on straw in a cellar. One house was found to hold 92 lodgers, even though it was only licensed to sleep 12.

The Liverpool Mercury in May 1848 stated:

'It was no uncommon thing for some of the dirty low lodging house keepers, for a fee, to send boxes on board with live people in them, under pretence that the box contained luggage'.

It really was the same activity as the crimps employed with the seamen. Many would-be emigrants lost all their monies and possessions before finding a ship and were to remain in Liverpool. Inevitably, many of the young girls had no choice but to survive as prostitutes.

Probably the first emigrant ship was the *Black Ball* in 1818, an American vessel. In the second half of the century, most were British ... Cunard, Inman Line, Guion, White Star Line, National Line and Allan Line. The rail companies began to work with the shipping owners and offered special package deals. At first the trip could have taken seven or eight weeks, but with the advent of steam the duration and the misery were halved.

The journey was not without danger. Three vessels foundered in 1839. In 1847 the *Ocean Monarch* caught fire off the Welsh Coast and 176 emigrants were lost. The *Tayleur* on the way to Australia was wrecked off Ireland with the loss of 370 lives.

In the early days, the fare on the sailing ships was about five pounds per person and the passengers were crowded together in the holds. They were small ships and the crossing must have been grim. There would be no ventilation, no toilets and very little space. No cooking would be allowed because of the danger of fire. Food was poor and by the end of the voyage in very short supply.

The Passenger Act of 1855 was to limit the numbers carried in each ship and a doctor travelled, if there were more than three hundred passengers. Over five and a half million emigrants left Liverpool between 1860 and 1890.

Brunel's *Great Britain* had sails, as well as steam. Steam was only used to supplement wind power. The vessel was to carry over twenty thousand emigrants to Australia in thirty-four passages. ·

When Pastor Tegner started his Liverpool ministry in 1870, he would have been welcomed by the emigrants as they waited for their ships. He died on the 12th April 1881, but not before he had laid the foundations for the work to continue to the present day. As early as 1873, he had advocated the urgent need for a Swedish centre in Liverpool.

Pastor Sundqvist, after serving for four years in Marseilles, came to Liverpool and on the 1st December 1883 the foundations of the Swedish Gustaf Adolf Church were laid. The Consul for Sweden and Norway, Mr. Harald Ehrenborg, chaired the building committee and negotiated the purchase of a site for the church on the corner of Park Lane and Cornhill. The architect was W.D. Caroe, a young man aged twenty-five.

The Church still proudly stands as an example of Swedish architecture in the middle of Liverpool. Basically, it is a church with a reading room on the floor below and a small residence for the Pastor and his family and a Chapel. Today a sauna is to be found in the basement!

The father of the architect was Mr.A.K. Caroe, the Consul for Denmark. As might be expected, the Danes and the Finns joined in with the project. The Church was opened in 1883 and consecrated by J. Neander, who was chairman of the Mission at that time.

The new building enabled Pastor Sundqvist to offer much more assistance to those in need, but although he continued to work, his health was failing. In 1885 he returned home to Sweden.

Pastor O. Heden became the third minister in Liverpool and he remained for fourteen years. During his time he was able to consolidate what had been started. It was estimated that during 1885, the number of worshippers who had used the Gustaf Adolf Church reached 25,000. Pastor Heden installed the pipe organ and the altar-piece. This altar was dedicated on the day that the Pastor delivered his farewell sermon.

Pastor E.G. Wolfbrandt was already working in Liverpool for a year before he took over the leadership over on the 1st July, 1898. He was full of energy. In his first full year, he visited 2,595 emigrants and called aboard 987 ships. It was also noted that 273 services were held. Two years later Pastor Wolfbrandt reported that 33,000 worshippers had attended the Gustaf Adolf Church.

Swedish Gustav Adolf Church

In 1909 the Pastor left Liverpool and was appointed to be the Secretary of the Swedish Mission Board and, apart from a short time in Hamburg, he was to remain in this post for the rest of his life.

The same year that Pastor Wolfbrandt left Liverpool to return to Sweden, the assistant minister, Andersen-Hetland, retired on pension after 36 years of faithful service. This was a time of great change for the Church.

In the autumn of 1909, Pastor Carl Petri came to Liverpool and remained for fifteen years. I was surprised to discover that during the First World War years he was not allowed to invite the seamen to the church, so he spent his time aboard the ships in the docks.

As with the other agencies in Liverpool the inter-war years were not very easy as the depression affected shipping from all countries, but with the help of the local residents the Church prospered and was naturally very busy during the Second World War.

The work continues up to the present day. The author recalls that during his thirty years of friendship with the pastors and the worshippers at the Gustav Adolf the door was always open. Regular Bible discussions were held there with the ministers from all the other Missions and denominations. The sessions were ever ended with coffee and memorable Swedish pastries.

Pastor Fridtjof H. Asche on the 17th January, 1967 wrote an article about the origin of the Norwegian Church in Liverpool.

'As long ago as before the first World War, traffic of Norwegian ships at Liverpool was so great that there was need for a Christian movement among our seamen. The reason why the Norwegian Seamen's Mission, however, did not take up its own regular work before the autumn of 1918 is because of two things. The first being that the Swedish Seamen's Church had for many years had its Norwegian assistant. Secondly, the Norwegian Seamen's pastors from the other stations in Great Britain, namely Glasgow, Shields, London and Cardiff, took it in turns to hold church services in Liverpool.

'After a trial period of one year with Pastor Sigurd Gundersen as leader, the General Assembly decided in 1919 that Liverpool should become a permanent station. The seamen's Pastor worked during this period in direct co-operation with the Swedish Seamen's Church.

'On the 5th December, 1920, the new Norwegian premises in their own building in Great George Square was consecrated by General Secretary Sven Schartum. The funds came from the merchant Kjerland in Bergen and the firm Vogt and Maguire in Liverpool.

The consecration ceremony took place with great formality in the presence of the Bishop of Liverpool, the Norwegian minister in London, representatives of the highest authorities in Liverpool, together with Norwegian seafarers and local Norwegian residents.

'The years that followed showed that this new station had a great need to meet. Seafarers and local Norwegian residents and faithful English friends rallied round the Church. There were many testimonies that the work was to the enjoyment and benefit of all those who called there.

'Once the Norwegian Seamen's Mission had got a footing in Liverpool, the question arose as to what could be done in Manchester. A room was rented there in the Missions to Seamen. The idea was that the Norwegian and Swedish Pastors in Liverpool should hold meetings there every Wednesday evening. There was, however, little satisfaction in having a reading room without constant supervision. In 1926 the problem was solved by an anonymous gift. Two houses in the vicinity of Dock No.9 were presented to the Norwegian Seamen's Mission. There was plenty of space for a reading room on the ground floor and living quarters for the new assistant on the first floor.

'Both in Liverpool and in Manchester, the Church's premises were badly damaged at the start of the second World War. In Manchester, the work was not renewed after the war. In Liverpool, new and larger premises were rented in 1941 in Upper Parliament Street. The lease was terminated in 1947. In 1948 the purchase of an old mansion in 22, Southwood Road, right beside St. Michael's Station, was entered into. Here the work prospered. The house was altered to suit the Norwegian Seamen's Mission' purpose. It is surrounded by a large and beautiful garden, well suited to garden parties and athletic arrangements in the summer.

'The Church is open every day till late in the evening with free service of coffee and waffles. Here our seafarers can enjoy themselves with newspapers from all corners of their homeland, television, letter writing, billiards, table-tennis, darts, etc. There are three regular social evenings during the week, namely Evening Service and social gathering every Sunday, entertainment evenings with film shows every Tuesday and social evenings every Thursday. The programme varies with music and song, games and competitions, showing of slides with discourse. In order to observe our object, devotions are always said. Every first Sunday in the month we gather for a united Scandinavian Church Service,

The Norwegian Seamen's Church

alternatively in the Swedish and in the Norwegian Seamen's Church. In addition to all this we arrange sightseeing and outings as often as the opportunity arises.

'As colleagues the seamen's Pastor has an assistant and a house-mother or hostess. Every day the Pastor and his assistant go round the docks on ships' visits. In addition to Liverpool and the Birkenhead side, we cover the whole of the Manchester Ship Canal to the extent that it is practicable. We greet everyone personally and welcome them to the Church. We bring with us newspapers and post, give diverse information and try to be of spiritual help. We also carry out an extensive personal service, see to the developing and printing of rolls of films, various repairs and shopping, also the sending forward of parcels, letters and money. The Seamen's Church works in close co-operation with the Norwegian offices in Liverpool, such as the Royal Norwegian Consulate-General, the Norwegian Government Welfare Office for the Merchant Navy, the Norwegian Seamen's Union, Shipping

Office and Medical Office, and with the Swedish Seamen's Church. 'It is first and foremost the contact with the Norwegian ships and the Norwegian permanent residents that keeps up the Church's colony. In addition we have some support from English firms that are in touch with Norwegian shipping. Nevertheless, we are dependent upon a regular grant from the head office in Bergen.

'There has been a marked increase in the Norwegian ship's traffic during the last year. During the year that has gone we made 928 visits on board 601 ships, whereof 65 ships in the Manchester Ship Canal. We held 58 Evening Services and 123 social occasions. We undertook 76 sick-visits, arranged 924 long-distance telephone calls and 3562 letters for seafarers.

'The Seamen's Church wants to be a home both for our sailing and residential countrymen. The work has moved from house to house during the time it has been in existence. Ship's traffic and trends have gone up and down during the years. But what has stood firm and unchanged is that seafarers constantly have use for us. We are happy every time we can be of help and guidance to them and remind them of that which the heart deep down inside longs for.'

During my time at the Mersey Mission to Seamen we co-operated very closely with both the Norwegian and Swedish Churches. Every month we shared a morning of Bible study over coffee and pastries. We became good friends and where possible we helped each other with any transport problems. Often all three organisations carried seafarers to the airport. The Norwegian Veterans, who had fought during the War from this country, had formed an accordion band and they held monthly 'get togethers' at the Mersey Mission in James Street. It was a good sound!

Occasionally we also shared our worship on Sundays. Perhaps our greatest joint venture was when for one week every year we co-operated, under the leadership of the Norwegian Government's Welfare Service, in an International Seafarers' Sports Week. It required much preparation and could only have been possible because we really were a team.

Early in the '90's the Norwegian Mission was closed and they joined forces with the Swedish Church in Park Road. As this was the way in which they had started, it was a natural marriage.

13.
The Akbar
The Protestant Reformatory Ship

At the turn of the century, the only means of crossing the Mersey was to board a ferry. You had the choice venues, Rock Ferry, New Ferry or Eastham. Eastham boasted an hotel with tea-gardens and a dance hall, but the main attraction must have been the group of old warships, moored just south of Rock Ferry Pier. The last remaining warship was to be the *Conway*, which was removed to the Menai Straits in 1941.

The four warships were independent of each other, but had the same aim ... the training of young lads. *Conway* was the officers' training ship and lay a little south of Rock Ferry Pier. The *Akbar*, a Protestant reformatory vessel lay midway between Eastham and Rock Ferry. The next in line was the *Indefatigable,* an old sailing frigate, housing orphaned sons of seamen and other boys in poor circumstances. The southernmost berth was occupied by the Roman Catholic reformatory ship *Clarence.*

Liverpool Life ran an article in 1857 on the *Akbar.* 'On hailing the vessel, a boat was put off immediately, pulled by six boys, in charge of the boatswain. They were clean looking làds; the day being warm, they were lightly clad, and rowed with the utmost regularity. The boatswain was a stout, ruddy-faced tar, evidently from the south of England, and his sharp-spoken, "Give way, give way, youngsters," met with a hearty response from his boat's crew, and in a few moments we ascended the steps leading to the deck of the *Akbar.* The place was in excellent order, the deck remarkably clean, and an air of comfort, cheerfulness and contentment was manifested by everyone we saw.

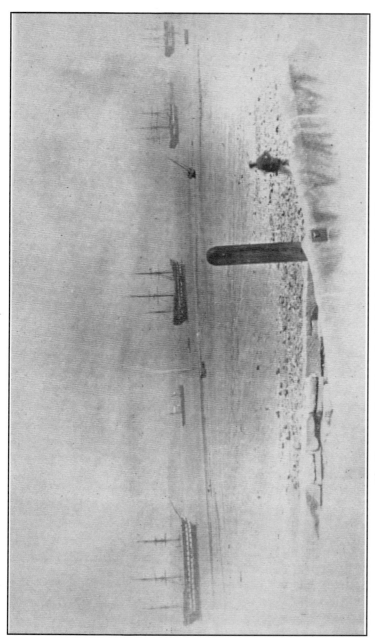

The Conway, the Akbar, the Indefatigable and the Clarence

'The vessel is calculated to contain 150 boys, and the number will be gradually increased until it reaches that point. The wisdom of such a step is apparent. When fifty boys are got into 'good trim', have learned their duty, learned to respect their officers, to submit to discipline, which is very strict, and have - which is more important than all, for it involves everything else - learned to control themselves, and stifle or keep under those outbursts of temper which so strongly mark the class from which they spring, then, but not till then, twenty-five more boys may be introduced with some hopes of successful treatment. The staff of officers consists of the superintendent, a schoolmaster, a boatswain, a boatswain's mate, a purser, steward, carpenter, cook, and two seamen, who all reside on board.

'Whilst between decks, we first visit that portion devoted to educational purposes. The boys have three hours instruction from the schoolmaster daily. Some of them in a short time have made great proficiency. The lesson books used are those of the Irish School Society. The master, a mild-spoken, elderly man, takes great delight in his work, and pointed out, with honest pride, the progress that several of the pupils had made under him.

'We pass on now to midships, where the tables are just being let down, and on which the captains of various messes are arranging tin plates for dinner. We descend to the lower deck. Here is the dormitory; the hammocks are all rolled neatly up, and laid in the centre of the floor. By these are bags, marked with large numbers. On inquiry we find that these bags contain the change of clothing for each boy.'

John Smart read a paper at a meeting of the Liverpool Nautical Research Society on the 10th December, 1959. It was entitled *The Story of the Akbar.* Much research was involved and it deserves repetition within the context of the Reformatory Ships and the history of the Mersey Mariners and the care of the seafarer. Many a 'Liverpool Jack' was to start his seagoing days in the old wooden lock-up, the *Akbar.*

'Typical products of an age of charity were the reformatory ships, which were founded with the dual purpose of suppressing juvenile crime and of providing discipline and training for those boys who had transgressed against the law as it then stood. The first organisation to undertake this duty on behalf of such boys was the Liverpool Juvenile Reformatory Association.

'During the period 1855 to 1907, when the establishment moved on shore and became known as Heswall Nautical Training School, there were two vessels which bore the name *Akbar.* The first was originally an East Indiaman built of teak in Bombay in 1800. She was bought into the Royal Navy in the following year as His Majesty's Frigate *Cornwallis.* Renamed the *Akbar* in 1810, she came to Liverpool in 1829 and served as a quarantine hulk in the Sloyne until acquired in 1855 by the newly formed Liverpool Juvenile Reformatory Association. Between that year and 1862, when she was broken up, she did duty as a reformatory ship, the first vessel to be so used. During subsequent years a number of similar ventures were undertaken elsewhere and by the 1870's there were in the country no less than fourteen vessels classified as industrial ships, reformatory ships or charity schools.'

This first *Akbar* had served in the Dutch East Indies before coming home to Milford Haven to act as a quarantine ship. When she came to the Mersey to fulfil the same role, she was one of many. There were to be at least ten quarantine vessels in the river ... at one time there were six together. The fear was bubonic plague, cholera, typhus and small pox. When Captain Clint and four members of the committee first inspected *Akbar,* they were appalled. The upper deck was rotten and much work was required: The estimated cost was £1,000 - the eventual amount was £2,000. Her condition was never satisfactory and she was described as a hazard!

The name Clint is associated with much of the caring activity in Liverpool. He was a remarkable character. He came to Liverpool from South Shields, where he was born in 1786. He spent twenty-four years at sea, beginning as an apprentice and coming ashore as a master. He bought a vessel named *Cherub* and settled down as a successful shipowner. One of his friends was John Cropper, another well-known Victorian philanthropist. Cropper was an enemy of slavery and a promoter of work amongst unfortunate boys ... and very much behind the *Akbar* project. Clint became the deputy chairman of the new Shipowners' Association in the port, a member of the pilots' committee, a benefactor of the Northern Hospital and the Sailors' Home, and a pioneer of steam tugs in the river. He also was to join in the *Conway* project and was the prime mover in launching the *Indefatigable.* Clint died in 1868.

'The second *Akbar* had a rather uninteresting history. A product of the Royal shipyard at Deptford she was laid down as *H.M.S. Hero* of seventy-four guns. During building her name was changed to the *Wellington* and she was launched in 1816. Like so many other vessels built at that time, she never served at sea and for the first thirty-two years after her completion she lay undisturbed in the dockyard. In 1848 she was commissioned as a Depot Ship,

Sheerness, for a time; then she had a short period as Coast Guard District Ship and finally became Flagship and Guardship at Devonport in 1861. During her forty-five years in the Royal Navy she served four years in commission and forty-one in reserve. In 1862 Captain Saulez of the old *Akbar* took fifty boys to Plymouth to assist in bringing her around the coast to Liverpool. She arrived in the Mersey on the 5th May in tow of the Liverpool Steam Tug Company's iron paddler *Blazer.*

'Detention in the *Akbar* was not intended as a punishment. Those boys who were committed had served short prison sentences for a variety of crimes. The period served on board was intended to inculcate discipline and to provide training in a variety of ways, which would be of advantage in later years. The ages of the boys upon entry varied between twelve and sixteen years. They arrived in many cases ragged, barefooted, underfed little scare-crows and usually spent three years on board. The possibility of committal to the *Akbar* rather than to a shore school rested not necessarily upon the gravity of the new entry's crime. It depended upon his physical condition and ability to undergo the rigours of life at sea. Despite the protests of successive captain-superintendents, from time to time a number of boys were entered whose poor health was a constant source of anxiety. All too often the neglect and semi-starvation which they had suffered since birth, left them with insufficient strength to resist the ravages of pneumonia and consumption.'

In many cases the parents were expected to make a contribution towards the up-keep. It could have been as much as five shillings a week, which was a large amount at that time. The local authority began to finance these reformatories in 1857 and the short-fall was met by the public and the Liverpool Juvenile Reformatory Association. The response was never enthusiastic, but help came in various ways. The captain in one annual report made a pertinent comment:

  · 'Many thanks to friends for various presents including fruit and vegetables. I would like to remind friends who have gardens, that, much which they throw away, if sent to *Akbar* would be gratefully received by me and equally gratefully consumed by the boys.'

The article in Liverpool Life of 1857 describes a scene from *Akbar.*

'The boys are frequently sent on shore - sometimes in charge of an officer, sometimes alone; but no attempt had up to this time been made at an escape. A few days before this, a boy had been sent across to Liverpool, and had to wait at the pier-head a very considerable time, and was thus afforded every opportunity for desertion; but he wisely set a proper value on the industrial training which he was receiving aboard the *Akbar,* and stood to his colours. What is most to be regretted when the boys are thus sent on shore is not their conduct, but the conduct of those whom they meet, and who in many cases, by coarse jokes and heartless jeers, remind the lads of their position. This never fails to irritate and create feelings of resentment. Yet, notwithstanding this, their behaviour, all things considered, is most exemplary. On Sunday, the boys frequently are sent to the Floating Church, Birkenhead, and their conduct is spoken of by the superintendent in terms of commendation.'

Other remarks in an Annual Report tell the story of life aboard. 'January 11th, 1858 - Try beef at five and a ha'penny a pound: April 1862 - Cook to undertake the barber's work which will save 15 shillings per month: 1863 - Committee understands that new boots can be bought cheap for cash at 5/6d and appear as good as those for which we have paid seven shillings, eight shillings and nine shillings. Try them. Understand that potatoes can be bought for one shilling and ten pence a bushel equal to those for which Hall and Son are paid four shillings and three pence - change supplier.'

Keeping the boys occupied could not have been easy. The deck was endlessly scrubbed with stone in summer and in winter. The lads made and repaired their own clothing. As far as possible they found their own entertainment, and by the light of oil lamps they read what books were available. Sing-songs were ever popular and in 1858 Captain Fenwick bought musical instruments with a gift of ten pounds! This developed into a Brass Band and proved to be a popular attraction in Birkenhead.

The Minute books record some grim accidents.

'Thomas whilst employed in blacking a portion of the rigging was accidentally jerked off and thrown down from a height of 16 feet on to the deck, dying three hours later ... Alfred fell from the main top deck and received concussion and partial jaw fracture, was recovering ... Henry lost his finger by carelessly placing his hand between a boat and the ship ... Benjamin fell from the main top, died same day ... William, while manning the working boat, slipped and was crushed between the boat and the ship side. His body was washed up on the shore ... Ebenezer fell from the main top - a height of 60 feet and was taken to hospital where he has progressed favourably.'

The boys were always hungry and cold.

'Food was locked away and it was a puzzle in April 1864 as to how Matthew, one of the 203 boys on board, managed to obtain and hungrily wolf down a great deal of porridge. So unaccustomed was his stomach to food in such quantity that the lad collapsed and died! The body was handed over to his mother for burial.

'Meat was an expensive item and there was consternation among the Committee in 1871 when the supplier reported that he was compelled to raise his meat prices from seven and a ha'penny to seven and three farthings!'

By present day standards existence in this grim, old ship was extremely hard. There was little or no comfort on board. The work was hard and the discipline strict, but life was nevertheless far superior to the vagrant existence which many boys had previously experienced. Food was far from plentiful for growing boys living an active open air life. In accordance with the prevailing system as operated in ships of the day, messing was on a 'pound and pint' basis. For breakfast at 7.30 a.m. the boys received a pint of porridge and four ounces of biscuit. Dinner consisted of four ounces of beef, one pint of soup, three ounces of biscuit and twelve ounces of potatoes or four ounces of rice. For supper, dished out at 5.45 p.m. there was a pint of porridge or, on Thursdays and Sundays, a pint of coffee. Tuesday's menu offered pea soup and pork and on Thursdays and Saturdays pudding was substituted for potatoes.

This uninspiring diet was criticised by H.M. Inspector in 1875 when he reported that, 'The boys are not very robust and there have been three deaths in the year. Salt beef, soup and biscuits comprise too large a part of the dietary. I recommended two or three solid fresh cooked meat diets in the week, and more bread instead of biscuits and a regular supply of potatoes and vegetables.' Five years later the boys were being given soft bread twice a week. In 1895, they received a two ounce smear of margarine four times instead of twice a week, and a meat dinner to replace one dinner of bread and cheese. The possibility that they should have milk in their tea and coffee was deferred for further consideration.

The Inspector reported in 1904;

'The boys in the mass look far from well. There are too many puffy pasty faces and skin eruptions. The boys are being dosed with lime juice, but what is wanted is not the means to deal with the trouble when it does arise, but measures to forestall the trouble.' Under his watchful eye, the situation gradually improved with the addition of fresh fish twice a week, doses of cod liver oil, vegetables, and in 1914 the feast of bread and scouse dinners! By 1924, the results of the more satisfactory diet were reflected in the quarterly reports showing weight increase of three pounds a lad and a growth in height of half an inch, with the observation that 'the boys are now looking healthy and stout.'

Extremes of temperature were felt more severely on board the *Akbar* than in any of the shore schools. The suffering from the elements in winter was acute, with chilblains, diseases of respiratory organs, consumption, pneumonia and asthma. Colds, influenza and hacking coughs spread like wildfire among both the lads and staff in the cramped confined area, so that infections at times debilitated 50% of those on board. Ventilation on the sleeping deck as late as 1904 was appalling, especially in winter when ports could not be opened as freely as in fine weather. In summer, the boys were berthed midships in a sort of sweat box but even this discomfort was preferable to the horrendous cold of 1894, the year Queen Victoria opened the Manchester Ship Canal. The weather in that winter was so severe that the Canal remained frozen for about 13 weeks, and some of the river as well.

John Smith's article continues.

'Seamanship instruction occupied a considerable portion of their daily life and in summer-time "Turn out, lash up and stow" was at 5.00 a.m. In winter-time it was two hours later, and all hands turned in at 7.45 p.m. in winter and 8.30 p.m. in summer. When one watch was at school, the other was undergoing instruction in knots, splices, bending and unbending topsails and so on; and the procedure was reversed during the afternoon period. With the exception of uniform caps, all items of clothing were made on board and clothing was washed on Tuesdays and Fridays, in the afternoon in winter and before breakfast in summer. Every Thursday evening all hands were mustered for a bath in tepid water. At 8 o'clock in the forenoon during summer-time one deck was washed daily, except on Sundays, but in the winter each deck was scrubbed only once a week. One wonders if the ship was ever really dry and whether these damp conditions were, at least in part, the cause of so much sickness and the relatively high numbers of deaths which occurred in all similar vessels in the early days.

'To go to sea was a more difficult task then one might perhaps imagine. In the sixties, for instance, it was difficult to obtain berths in British ships. This was in part due to a slump, but also due to a lack of interest on the part of British ship-owners, possibly on account of the history of the candidates. The boys preferred to ship in Scandinavian or German ships, as rates of pay were better, but the Association preferred to find them berths in British ships if at all possible. Service in the Royal Navy was barred to boys from reformatory ships, although in later years a few were accepted as stoker ratings.

'When first opened in 1855 the original *Akbar* was moored in the Great Float, Birkenhead. But dock works there led to her removal to a berth off Rock Ferry. The other training ships were later arrivals. The *Conway* arrived in 1859, the *Clarence* in August 1864 and the *Indefatigable* in 1865. The situation of these ships, although well up river, was exposed, but it enabled the boys to obtain their full share of practical boat handling in all states of the weather. There are a number of instances upon record of prompt and efficient boat handling being responsible for some very dramatic rescues from the cold waters of the Mersey. For individual acts of rescue the Liverpool Shipwreck and Humane Society medal was awarded on various occasions to *Akbar* boys.

'Life both within and without the ship was not altogether devoid of excitement from time to time. There was the ever present prospect of one or the other training ships breaking adrift from her moorings. The *Akbar* herself was in trouble a time or two from this cause, and during a wild January night in 1877 she dragged and ran ashore between Rock Ferry and New Ferry. The duty run to New Ferry could be very hazardous at times and on one occasion a boat on the Rock Ferry run met with disaster. Having left the ship at 4.00 p.m. one afternoon, the boat was blown off course and carried up river until she eventually grounded on Frodsham marsh eighteen miles away. Her occupants spent a miserable night without any shelter and the episode ended in the death of a boy who had been visiting his brother on board. On more than one occasion various ships on the moorings were run down by careless merchantmen.

'If not young and hardened criminals the boys were, at the very least, 'hard cases' and on one occasion caused considerable trouble. A handful of vicious and depraved youths gained the upper hand for a time and mutiny was in the air. The stores were broken into and finally seventeen of the ringleaders lowered a boat and absconded. They were eventually recaptured and ten were tried before Mr. Justice Day at the Liverpool Winter Assizes in 1887. He declined to punish them further on the grounds that the discipline in the ship was defective. Considering the type of boy with which the officers had to deal, it is remarkable that there were not more outbreaks of a similar character.

'As far as possible the boys were taught trades, and the carpenter and his crew built boats, made spare spars and so on and were responsible for the maintenance of the ship. The ferry undertakings which in the early days were private ventures had always been interested in the *Akbar.* Messrs. Hetherington and Thwaites of the Rock Ferry Steam Packet Company gave use of their vessels without charge on many occasions. Reciprocally, when in 1866 the seamen of the Rock Ferry paddlers went out on strike, the *Akbar* boys manned the steamers.

'Friends were invited to visit the ship on any day except Saturday, and the ship's boat met the New Ferry steamer if the master sounded his whistle when passing. In the early days of 1855 the boys had landed from the first *Akbar* in the Great Float to attend Sunday service in the Mariners' Church, Birkenhead. In later years a resident chaplain was appointed and part of his duties strikes a very modern note, that of attending to the voluminous and increasing correspondence. For the convenience of visitors who wished to attend Divine Service on board, boats left Rock Ferry slip at 10.45 a.m. and 6.15 p.m. on Sundays.

'To discipline and train 200 boys was no easy task and the provision of spare time amusement was quite a big problem. Originally there had been nothing to do after hours. This state of affairs invariably led to a fairly large defaulters' list and by the 1880's efforts were made to organise sporting events. A rather humorous note creeps into a report about this time, when it was decided to raise the pumps from the orlop to the lower deck, so that the pumping parties would be under the eyes of an officer. Evidently sky-larking had been the order of the day. Cricket and football were played in season and a certain amount of amusement was provided on board during the winter months. When first introduced the results were not too promising. With typical good humour Captain Hicks commented that the majority of his lads were quite ignorant of games and preferred to do nothing, for which they evinced much talent.'

It is no surprise that there were occasional problems aboard. There were several attempts to set the *Akbar* on fire. The captain reported in 1877: "A little after 6 a.m. I was awoke by an alarm of fire and immediately slipped on a dressing gown and ran down to the seat of the fire which was in the after hold and in three distinct places. The fire was made up on a lot of odds and ends of rope which we call shakings and which were saturated with tar. Mr Webb and Mr Allen were most energetic at the seat of the fire, the latter almost exhausted and smothered with smoke. Fortunately having fire quarters and stations every night we had the evening before filled wash deck tubs with water, so that being very prompt we had got the fire well under before we got the hoses from the pumps and I think it must have been discovered almost immediately it was lighted. This, of course, was after the boys were up in the morning, they behaved well and there was no sort of panic, but had it happened in the night things might have had a very different result." The lad responsible was sentenced at Chester Assizes to eighteen months imprisonment with hard labour. There was another fire in 1903, but it was firmly dealt with and there was no great damage. Five years earlier, *Akbar* broke from her moorings in a heavy gale and collided with *Conway*.

Insubordination was inevitable and was severely handled. In 1898 thirteen lads absconded, but were caught and spent a week in prison on remand. Three of them received three months hard labour and the rest were dealt with aboard *Akbar*.

Health was always a problem In one year six boys were to die and the cause was invariably consumption, pneumonia or pleurisy. Accidents could not be prevented. An inspector in 1893 made this comment. 'The one weak point in the ship is her record of sickness. The fact that health on board during the past ten years, as judged by the vital statistics, does not appear to be up to the level of other ships, demands the careful consideration of the Committee.' This was the report that resulted in the boys spending a fortnight in the Cholera Hospital in New Ferry, which happily was empty at the time.

The old ship was fumigated and cleaned, new timber was installed to replace the old decaying wood. The captain reported:

> 'The result of the experiment was most successful, not only has the condition of the ship been improved but the boys have benefited greatly from the change and the run in the grass field during the magnificent weather. Relaxation of discipline was unavoidable in such a place but the lads could not have behaved better and in no instance did they take advantage of the almost absolute freedom. They returned in the best of health and spirits.'

The ravages of time and the effects of long service were becoming increasingly apparent and for years repairs and maintenance had been a constant drain on the resources of the Association.

But the *Akbar* was very old! In 1906 it was estimated that she was taking in a ton of water every twenty-four hours. Age and weather were taking their toll. It was unsafe tò rig the main sail. This was the end.

By 1907, it was considered totally unsafe to risk another winter in her and on the 30th October the majority of officers and boys left her. She was then over ninety years of age, had figured in the Navy List for forty-five years and had served a further forty-five years in the Mersey. She was towed into the West Float in December, 1907, sold to Messrs. Thos. W. Ward Ltd., and towed away to Morecambe, where she was beached and taken to pieces.

The boys moved to new premises in Heswall where they remained until the school was closed by order of the Home Office in February 1956. Perhaps the only relics of the *Akbar* which remained were her mizzen topmast, stepped in the school grounds, and the decayed jaws of her mizzen boom. During the hundred year existence of the Association almost 8,000 boys had passed through the two ships and the shore school.

With the demolition of the *Akbar* there passed yet another of that fleet of wooden warships which for so long remained as interesting survivals of the craft of the shipwright and of the outmoded system of juvenile education and training.

Another picture of the *Akbar* is given by a Benjamin Blower, who in 1878 produced a book entitled 'The Mersey' and in a chapter called 'The Estuary' he added a footnote about the reformatory ship, *Akbar.*

'Instead of being confined to the cells of a prison, here are 160 lads, of the age of twelve and upwards, undergoing the most close and vigilant supervision. Their habits are watched, their morals guarded, their minds cultivated, and their hands taught the useful trades of tailoring and shoemaking, their bodies well fed and exercised by their being put through all the lessons of a seafaring apprenticeship, climbing masts, hoisting and lowering sails, taking in reefs, etc.; and above all, their souls are cared for, being brought in daily contact with the lessons of God's Holy Word, and taught to sing the praises of Him whose name they had formerly been accustomed to dishonour and blaspheme. "This is the finest sight I have yet seen," was my involuntary exclamation as I was present at morning prayers, and saw the occupants of this prison home listening to the Bible read, then kneeling on the deck as prayer was offered, and last of all joining in singing their Maker's praise; the sweet tones of the harmonium accompanying their voices. The day thus begun, the deck was transformed into a school. On one side were three different Bible classes, one of which I was asked to conduct, which I did for a few minutes with the greatest satisfaction, being vastly pleased with the intelligent answers of the pupils. On the other side was one knot of boys making their own clothes, while the cobblers and shoemakers were busy beside them. Standing for a few minutes beside the teacher who was drilling his class, the business was interrupted by a young man who came up, and shaking the master warmly by the hand, said "Good-bye, Sir, I'm just going off." A few words of Christian counsel were spoken to him, and then he went round the whole class, shaking hands with each and saying farewell. His time was out, and he had got a berth as ordinary seaman in a ship going to India. In his chest he had a clean comfortable outfit and a Bible.'

The Mersey Mission to Seamen was well involved with the Training ships and in 1897 a sub-committee was elected by the Mission to interview candidates for the various chaplaincies. The idea of training boys to serve at sea goes back at least to 1756, when Sir John Fielding, the famous author and London magistrate, had collected a number of urchins who had been brought before him and had sent them to serve on board *H.M.S. Barfleur.* He also requested the Marine Society, which had just been established, to take any boys he sent to them and to this day that Society assists lads in nautical schools.

The Marine Society was founded in 1756 by Jonas Hanway, a London based philanthropist and a member of the Russia Company. The aim was to encourage poor men and boys of good character to join the Royal Navy at the start of the Seven Years War ... Britain and Prussia against France and Austria. By the end of the war in 1763 the Society had recruited 5,451 men and 5,174 boys. It was incorporated by Act of Parliament in 1772 to apprentice poor boys into the Royal Navy and the merchant service; it equiped them with clothing and set out to provide a pre-sea education. The Society commissioned the first pre-sea training ship in the world, the *Beatty.* On 13 September 1786 the 350 ton sloop took onboard 30 boys. This was the start of the era of pre-sea harbour training ships.

The Mersey Mission's interest in *Akbar* was underlined in 1889 when the Reverend F.E. Hicks, chaplain in *Akbar*, was appointed as an honorary chaplain in the Mersey Mission to Seamen Another chaplain was the Reverend Digby Bliss Kittermaster whose title was 'Superintendent of Shrewsbury School Mission to Boys in Liverpool and Chaplain to Reform Ship *Akbar*'. His stipend was £100 per annum from the Mersey Mission and £160 from *Akbar.* He was a powerful character, not afraid to speak when moral conditions were unsatisfactory. On the 3rd January, 1907, he reported to the Mersey Mission's Committee on the conditions aboard *Akbar.* This led to the retirement of the Captain, the dismissal of the Chief Officer and the temporary withdrawal of himself from the ship. He was congratulated on the stand he had made for the purity, discipline and proper care of the boys. Kittermaster was a remarkable man. He was to become the Archdeacon and Rector of the Pro-Cathedral in Buenos Aires, a Chaplain in the Great War (winning the Military Cross) and then for twenty-four years a Master at Harrow. He ended his days as Chaplain to a Borstal Institution in Rochester.

Another picture of Liverpool emerges from an article in The Porcupine, dated February 12th, 1876. The problem of the homeless orphan boy is discussed.

'The Newsboy's Home appears to us to be one of these institutions that might admit boys of this kind. We are not quite certain whether the managers confine the lads to selling newspapers only, but we rather think they are allowed to shine boots until the time arrives for them to purchase the evening papers. Boot-shining will be the most profitable, a lad being obliged to work hard to sell four or five dozen papers before he can realise sufficient to clear his day's board and lodging (about 4s.6d. per week). The committee appears to be fully aware of the necessity of giving these lads, at a small charge, a substantial dinner of roast meat and vegetables, with a slice of bread, and a cup of tea to drink with it; and by this means they are helping to lay the foundation for the boy's future health.

'The Shoeblack Society is one of the oldest institutions we have. Probably it is the only one that deals with the lowest class of street-arabs, and trains them to become useful members of society. The cost of living for each boy is about 3s.6d. per week.

'The Children's Friend Society is a home for destitute boys engaged in shops and offices; and as the inmates appear to us to be anything but children, we think the name is a mistake. The working of the home, if we are rightly informed, is quite different to any other, and will be new to many of our readers. As far as we understand it, every youth is obliged to contribute the whole of his weekly earnings, from 5s. to 12s. Out of this the committee keeps 8s.6d. for board and lodging; the remainder, if any, is kept in the bank for clothing and pocket-money. The object, we believe, of the youths working in the home is to fit them for stewards on steamers, etc. The institution does not appear to have any resident superintendent and matron ... averaging forty boys weekly, we think such supervision is absolutely necessary.'

The conditions of life in Liverpool were never easy for the strays. The dangers were many. Whilst *Akbar* was outmoded at the end of her days, the old warship had rescued those in need. Thousands of young boys found a decent way of life and were ever grateful for a second chance. *Akbar* had succeeded for the majority.

Akbar had certainly been tough and when today we reflect upon the harshness of life in the training ships - and that cannot be questioned - perhaps, at least, the boys were given aboard security and protection from the evils of life on land. The existence at that time of so many reform vessels in the country certainly indicated their value.

14.
The Clarence
The Catholic Reformatory Ship

Just below St. George's Hall in St. John's Gardens there is a fine statue of Monsignor James Nugent (1822 - 1905). His hand protects an urchin lad. The inscription talks of an Apostle of Temperance, Protector of the Orphan Child, Consoler of the Prisoner, Reformer of the Criminal, Saviour of Fallen Womenhood, Friend of All in Poverty and Affliction. On one side are the words ... An Eye to the Blind, A Foot to the Lame, the Father of the People; on the other side you find these words ... Speak a Kind Word, Take Them Gently by the Hand, Work is the best Reforming and Elevating Power, Loyalty and Country and God. This beautiful monument was erected by public subscription and was unveiled on the 8th December, 1906 ... it had been an immediate response to his life.

The story of this remarkable man has been well written by Canon Bennett and was published in 1949 by the Liverpool Catholic Children's Protection Society. Today we talk of the Nugent Care Society working with and for all people of goodwill. Father Nugent played an important part in the story of Liverpool's waterfront. His rallying cry was - Save the Boy!

It is difficult for us to comprehend the plight of ordinary people 150 years ago in Liverpool. Shimmin in a book entitled 'Liverpool Sketches' knew all about the degradation and despair of so many as they fought for mere survival.

' ... there is a beer-house, and in this were carousing a set of ruffians, the like of which could not be excelled. Women, without shoes, and a very few garments on, were their companions; whilst brawny

195

loafers skulked about, and vicious cripples stammered out blasphemy at the door. The street was sloppy and strewed with decaying vegetables, and yet amidst it all, young children tried to gambol about; and old people sat at court-entrances, at windows, or on door-steps, with their elbows resting on their knees, in every state of dirt and disorder. But the blear eyes - the wolfish glance - the tawny skins and stunted forms of youth seen around, indicated the life struggle in which they were engaged, and the result could be clearly seen.'

This was the world of Father Nugent.

He was born in 1822 and was ordained into the Catholic ministry in 1846. St. George's Hall had just been built, together with the Royal Infirmary and the William Brown Library and Museum. The real Liverpool was less grand. The first Medical Officer of Health, Dr. W.H. Duncan, the first in the country, had just been appointed. Three hundred thousand refugees, all hoping to emigrate, landed in Liverpool and almost a third stayed in the city. A seventh of the population died in one year in Vauxhall ... 5,845 from the fever and 2,589 from dysentery. Of the twenty-four Catholic priests in the city, ten were to die in the year. All this happened in the first year of Father Nugent's ministry ... 1846.

He joined the staff of St. Nicholas, behind the original Adelphi Hotel. In 1849, 5,245 people died of cholera. Father Nugent accepted the challenge and within four years he had founded a Catholic Institute in Hope Street and there he was to remain for a further ten years before his appointment to Walton Prison as Chaplain. That Hope Street Institute was to become a great centre of learning and excellence in Liverpool.

The city was a place of desperation. Children roamed the streets in abject poverty. It was estimated that twenty-three thousand were wandering in dockland. Nugent promptly opened a Ragged School in Spital-fields, between Dale Street and Whitechapel ... a tumble-down house was adapted. Four years later there were thirty-three such establishments! However, regrettably, the children had nowhere to sleep apart from the streets!

A French visitor to Liverpool in 1873 wrote his 'Notes on England' and he included a vivid picture of the children in the streets.

'It is now six o'clock, and we return through the poorer quarter. What a sight! In the vicinity of Leeds Street there are fifteen or twenty streets across which cords are stretched and covered with rags and linen, hung up to dry. Bands of children swarm on every flight of steps, five or six children are clustered on each step, the eldest holding the smallest ... in tatters, they have neither shoes, nor stockings, and they are all shockingly dirty; their faces and hands appearing to be encrusted with dust and soot. Perhaps two hundred children romp and wallow in a single street. On nearer approach one sees one of the mothers and a grown-up sister, with little more covering than their chemises, crouching in the dusky passage. What interiors! ... the smell resembles that of an old rag shop. The ground-floor of nearly every dwelling is a flagged and damp basement ...some of the younger children are still fresh and rosy, but their large blue eyes are painful to behold ... many of their faces are scrofulous, being marked with small sores covered with plaster. As we proceed the crowd is more dense. Tall youths seated or half-crouching at the side of the pavement play with black cards. Old, bearded hags come out of the gin-shops; their legs totter; their dull looks and besotted smile are indescribable; it appears as if their features had been slowly eaten away by vitriol. The rags which they wear are falling to pieces, displaying their filthy skins ... Rembrandt's beggars were far better off in their picturesque holes. And I have not yet seen the Irish quarters! The Irish abound here; it is supposed the number 100,000; their quarter is the lowest circle of Hell.'

This truly was the world of Father Nugent, who was to be Chaplain in Walton Prison for twenty-two years. He said: "There is no more practical school to study mankind than within the walls of a prison." Father Nugent not only understood, he was a man of action. Action was needed!

To the surprise of many Catholics in Liverpool, Cardinal Wiseman suggested a fact-finding visit to *Akbar*. The Cardinal had opened the first Catholic Reformatory for boys at Hammersmith in 1855. He had come to Liverpool to give a lecture on his work at the Philharmonic Hall, but must have had previous knowledge of the *Akbar*. A group of interested people, accompanied by the Bishop of Shrewsbury and Father Nugent, were well received aboard. The year was 1858. That visit was to bear fruit.

The first Annual General Meeting of the Liverpool Catholic Reformatory Association was in 1864 and it was no surprise when Father Nugent was asked to be the first president. The decision had already been taken in 1863 to establish a Ship Reformatory in the Sloyne, off New Ferry. The time had come to implement that decision. Father Nugent was asked to make contact with the Lords of the Admiralty.

The Admiralty was persuaded to loan a suitable man-of-war for the purpose. The warship, *Clarence*, had been launched in 1827, a 84 gun vessel of 2,279 tons. She had been laid down at Pembroke Dockyard as the gunship *Goliath* and as she was launched by H.R.H The Duke of Clarence the vessel was renamed *Clarence*. She was never commissioned and lay in Devonport until the decision to loan her to Liverpool.

Clarence began her new role in the Mersey on the 15th August, 1864. She had been towed from Devonport to Liverpool and work was started to fit her in Sandon Dock to accommodate some two hundred and fifty boys.

Money was an immediate problem. Meetings were held in Preston, Wigan and St. Helens in order to meet the cost of equipping the ship. Fortunately, the Corporation of Liverpool came to the rescue with a grant of £1,500.

Much was to be achieved along the lines of the *Akbar*. The main purpose was to educate the young lads ... compulsory school attendance was not instituted until the 1870 Education Act. The majority of boys, after completing three years in the *Clarence,* were to be employed in the Merchant Navy.

The first Commander was Captain Edward Algar, R.N., who supervised the alteration to the vessel in Sandon Dock before she took up her mooring in the river. The boys were instructed in seamanship, carpentry, shoemaking, tailoring, etc., and were taught reading, writing, arithmetic, and geography, whilst their religious instruction and practice was in the hands of a chaplain appointed by the Bishop of Shrewsbury.

Canon Bennet in his book on Father Nugent includes a chapter on the reformatory ship, *Clarence* and expands on the problems faced by the Committee.

'Father Nugent had placed illiteracy as a major cause of crime, and statistics bore this out on the *Clarence*. Of sixty-six boys admitted in 1867 thirty could not read at all, forty-one could not write, and fifty-one could not cipher, i.e., do sums. True this was before the 1870 Education Act, but in 1885 of forty-nine boys admitted eight could not read, write, or cipher, and twenty-seven only imperfectly.

'Disposal of the boys after three years or so presented little difficulty, as they were nearly all taken into the Merchant Navy (not the Royal Navy) and except in times of depression very many made good. One problem which gave concern to the managers was the ease with which they were robbed of clothes and money when they were paid off. A shore hostel was suggested for their protection, but a welfare officer was appointed as a compromise.

'The Association was always preoccupied about finance, dreading heavy outlay on disasters beyond their control. On one occasion a large steamer just launched collided with the *Clarence,* but the cost of repairs was met by the owners of the steamer. In February

1880, the ship broke away from her moorings, and to restore her to her anchorage cost the managers £250. In November of that year a boy set her on fire, but prompt action by both officers and boys averted catastrophe.

'They were not so fortunate in 1884 when a few boys set fire to her on the night of 17th and 18th January. In spite of the efforts of officials of the Dock Board, the Liverpool Corporation, and the owner of the New Ferry, Mr Thompson, she was completely burnt out with all equipment and stores. Happily all those on board were able to get to shore safely, and no lives were lost. Six boys responsible for the fire were sent to the Assizes and sentenced to five years penal servitude.'

After a short stay in the Port Sanitary Hospital in Bebington, everyone had to be evacuated again because of a cholera threat. The school moved to a land-based reformatory.

'Meantime the committee of the *Clarence* in their quandary turned to Father Nugent to use his good offices once more with the Admiralty for the loan of another ship. The Admiralty insisted that first the insurance money be paid over to them, but the committee had only insured for a sum sufficient to outfit another ship in case of fire. They further made known that the loan of another ship would be dependent upon the committee's ability to insure the hulk against fire, and it was some time before a company could be found to take this risk. By November all difficulties seemed to have been met when the *Royal William* was made over to the committee to be renamed the *Clarence*. She was a 120-gun ship launched in 1828.

'At the request of the Admiralty, the Dock Board had removed the wreckage at a cost of £2,734, which was reduced by the sale of the salvage to £1,509. The Admiralty claimed the salvage money, and held up all work on the new *Clarence* until they got it, so that she did not come into commission until November, 1885'

The new regime, under Lieutenant E.P. Statham, was very strict and in February, 1886, there was a serious mutiny. Thirteen boys were sent to the Assizes.

Canon Bennett gives a vivid picture of the events.

'The previous evening a conspiracy by ten boys to abscond was discovered, so they were locked up for the night. Next morning they refused to obey orders, and were joined by three others. The leader, named Scully, armed himself with a long sharp knife, while the rest picked up belaying pins, broken oars, and pieces of wood. They attacked two senior boys who tried to make them see sense, and various officers. When the officers who lived ashore tried to come aboard efforts were made to upset their boat by crashing down other boats on top of them. The ringleaders were prepared to kill the captain, who was still below decks, so their wrath fell most heavily on Frederick John Potter, head schoolmaster, who received three head wounds from belaying pins and was stabbed by Scully within an inch of his life. At this point the captain, known by the boys as 'Hot Soup', came on the scene, and cowed the mutineers by threatening them with an old pistol, for which in fact he had no ammunition. The disturbance was then quickly put down, and the boys concerned given in charge.'

The whole affair caused serious questions to be asked about the reform system in general. The thirteen boys involved were firmly punished. Scully received five years penal servitude, and the rest twelve months hard labour.

Father Nugent had not been a committee member since 1877 and had been obviously distressed by the whole affair. The Bishop responded by appointing a committee of entirely new members.

For the next thirteen years all continued as normal on board the *Clarence*. However, the end of the vessel was to be dramatic. Canon Bennett continued the story.

'Captain G.H. Yonge, R.N., followed Captain Statham in 1895. The end came with disastrous finality when she was set ablaze by some of the boys, after weeks of preparation, in the very early hours of 26th July, 1889. All the two hundred and thirty-five boys and staff were got away safely, as well as the Bishop of Shrewsbury, Dr. Allen, who was spending the night on board preparatory to holding a Confirmation service the next morning. By 6 a.m. the ship broke her back and sank. The survivors had nothing but the clothes they stood in.

'They were housed in St. Anne's School, Rock Ferry, until they could be transferred to St. Vincent's Working Boys' Home, Liverpool, 105 Shaw Street (known as Father Berry's Homes), whence they went to a disused jail at Mold, and later from there to temporary premises at Kirkedge, near Sheffield.'

This was the end of the experiment with floating reformatories for the Catholic Reformatory Association. They set about establishing a nautical training school on dry land to be known as St. Aidan's, in Farnworth, Widnes. The title 'nautical' was quickly to disappear.

Canon Bennett adds a charming post-script to his chapter on the *Clarence*. 'Monsignor Pinnington told me how he hid one of the boys responsible for the fire until he could get him away safely to Canada. No doubt he compounded a felony, but there were many others besides himself who breathed more freely once the *Clarence* was at the bottom of the river.

'Father Nugent owed something to the *Clarence*, for it provided him his finest peroration in his campaign to save the boy. "If you saw a child fall into the river would you not make some effort to save him? This is the common instinct of a noble heart. In 1864 I established in Liverpool a Reformatory School Ship where boys under sixteen years of age are instructed to be sailors instead of being sent to prison. Last summer one of the boys fell overboard from the ship into the river. Instantly a cry was raised, "A boy overboard! A boy overboard! Save the boy!" rang across the waters, from ship to shore, and was re-echoed from the deck of every vessel that lay at anchor. As quick as lightening, one of his companions leaped from a port-hole into the dark and angry flood. With dauntless courage he breasts the surging waves, gaining ground at every stroke. Now his companion exhausted sinks, again he rises to the surface. Already he is borne by the flood half a mile down stream. See! See! His strength has gone, his hands are motionless. He sinks again for the third time. His little companions having swarmed upon every part of the ship look on with breathless anxiety, and now their voices are lifted in solemn prayer: "O God, Save the Boy!" When the noble heroic boy, James Ward, seizes his sinking companion, one joyous shout rends the air: "He's saved! He's saved!" In the Sacred Name then of the One Redeemer and Father of all, help me save the boy who is perishing on your streets, borne along to destruction by the torrent of neglect, ignorance and crime."

'It seems ungracious to mention that the Commander of the *Clarence* noticed that this falling overboard and rescuing always occurred in the summer and never in the winter. He threatened to flog the next boy who fell overboard and the boy who rescued him!'

15.
The Indefatigable

The name is a proud one ... there have been five ships bearing it in the Royal Navy. Two of them became schools for the training of boys for the Royal Navy and the Merchant Navy. Some twenty thousand young men were to learn their trade in *Indefatigable*.

In 1864, a Liverpool seaman and shipowner, Captain John Clint, conceived the idea of providing means of training destitute and orphan boys in the ways of the sea. He was concerned about the poor boys in the city. Clint was an enthusiast. With his friends and the help of the Mayor a meeting was called and a subscription list opened to produce the required monies.

The first committee decided that boys of all denominations and faiths should be accepted for training, although there should be 'daily readings of the Bible and morning and evening services in the form of the Church of England'.

In 1863 Clint applied to Sir James Graham, First Lord of the Admiralty, assisted by Captain Alfred Ryder, R.N., then a member of a Commission of Enquiry into the state of Navigation Schools, asking for a smart, neat, masted ship-of-war for the Mersey.

The Admiralty agreed to loan *Indefatigable*, a fifty-gun frigate, built at Devonport and launched in 1848. The shipowner, James J. Bibby, contributed £5,000 to transform her from warship to training ship. This was a vast sum of money and a remarkable gift.

Indefatigable had served off Portugal and in the West Indies. Her last commission was in South African waters. Back home in 1857 she joined the Reserve Fleet in Devonport. It was the time when sailing ships were being converted to engine power and most were to end their days as floating barracks or store hulks. In 1864 *Indefatigable* came to the Sloyne, off Rock Ferry, and the work started.

Her main deck became a classroom, a tailor's shop and quarters for the captain and his wife. The first master was Captain Groom; it was part of the scheme for training boys that there should be a maternal influence and so Mrs. Groom joined her husband on board. Their cabin, its ports decked with plants and flowers, became a familiar and homely sight to passing ships and a haven to which boys could come with the kind of problems on which only a mother could advise.

The portholes in the lower deck were enlarged to provide better living conditions for the 200 boys the ship was intended to accommodate. The lower deck also provided classrooms, the lower hold became the practice room for the band and the upper deck was used as a drill space and for a galley and a hospital.

It was a brave sight of wooden-walled ships ... *Indefatigable, Conway, Clarence* and *Akbar.* Another famous old ship, the giant *Great Eastern*, was also moored off Rock Ferry as a show ship. The *Great Eastern's* compass was removed and housed aboard *Indefatigable* and used for instruction.

At the end of the first year in 1865, just forty-eight boys had been accommodated, but slowly the numbers grew as money was obtained. The aim was still for 200 lads, although the ship could actually house 300.

In 1873 *Indefatigable* broke her moorings and was badly damaged. The dock repairs took eight months. No new boys could be accepted. However, back on station, the work continued with the launch of a floating bath for the use of the boys who were able to combine·sport with cleanliness. There were 149 boys aboard with the captain, a chief officer, a carpenter, a cook, two school masters and four seamen instructors. There was no State aid, but the venture was viable with voluntary support sufficient to meet expenditure.

The Annual General Meeting in 1875 concerned itself about the needs of the boys aboard. Mr. Shallcross, a ship-owner, proposed that the lads should leave *Indefatigable* and take apprenticeships aboard vessels. Mr. Bushell, whilst agreeing in principle, thought that it would not be possible until better wages could be paid. The fact was that boys were placed in vessels when they left *Indefatigable*, but remained for one voyage only because they could receive better wages elsewhere as ordinary seamen.

'While an apprentice boy received perhaps £40 in four years, boys who went out as ordinary seamen found that they could obtain £1 a month, and in about twelve months were able to ship for £2 10s. or £3 a month. Apprentices receiving only £6 or £8 in their second year therefore became dissatisfied, though the committee pointed out to them that probably at the end of five years they would find themselves in a better position than boys who went out at first as ordinary seamen.'

A letter was then read to the Meeting.

'My conviction is that some decided action must before long be taken to maintain the standard of our British seamen, otherwise they will most certainly cease to exist. The rapid deterioration in the quality of our sailors I attribute to the following causes:

1. The best of them settled in California and Australia between the years 1849 and 1860.
2. The abandonment of compulsory apprenticeships.
3. The loss of the best of all schools for training seamen ... the coal trade on our east and west coasts ... it being now chiefly carried on by steam in lieu sailing vessels.
4. The increased demand for boys in the iron ship building and boiler yards of the country, which hold out greater inducements to them pecuniarily, than going to sea.

Hence, unless better pay is given to apprentices ... as suggested by Mr. William Inman - and the system made once more compulsory, I can see but a gloomy future for the efficient manning of our ships.'

A report written in 1881 continues this theme. It concerns Messrs. Balfour, Williamson and Co.'s Apprentices' Home which was situated in Duke Street.

'It gives me great satisfaction to be able to state that the number of Apprentices received into the House during the twelve months is far in excess of any year since the opening of the Institution. The total is 621. Compared with the preceding year, 1879, there is an increase of 72. Compared with 1878 the increase is 184. I think the increase in our numbers is attributable mainly to the fact that the Institution is now much more widely known than it was some years ago.

'I make no apology for directing your attention to a notice of our work which has appeared in the New York Sailor Magazine. In the March number ... there is an article on the subject of the Seamen's Chaplaincy at Honolulu, from the pen of the Reverend S.C. Damon, D.D., the Chaplain. Dr. Damon remarks that in his labours he is constantly coming into contact with British sailors and officers, and, after referring to the Sailor's Rest in Devonport, he says: 'But another Institution for the benefit of British seamen has its head-quarters at 151, Duke Street, Liverpool. With this Home for Apprentices on board merchant British ships, I am well acquainted. When I was in Liverpool, in February 1870, the Institution had just opened. The Founders of this Home laid out their plans in the most generous manner for the improvement of seamen.'

This report on the Balfour Home in Duke Street then makes sad reading.

'I regret to state that the list of the apprentices, known at the Home, who have been lost at sea during the twelve months is a very long one. At least 40 lads, who have from time to time visited us, have perished. In one wreck alone, that of the *Galatea,* three of our boys were lost. The second and third officers of the ship, who also were drowned, had, during their apprenticeship, been inmates of the Home, and the master, Captain John, was a friend of the institution. The loss of this ship so near home, and with so many persons on board intimately associated with us, cast a deep gloom over the house.'

There had been some comment that, whilst the Balfour Home had been funded by the generosity of the founder, the Institution had confined itself exclusively to foster the apprentices for the company's ships only. However, the Report of 1878 made it quite clear that it was open to apprentices in the Merchant Service generally and that many other ship-owners had inspected the Home and directed that their boys should be sent to it. In that year 456 boys had been received. The Secretary also thanked the Sailors' Home for the help and co-operation they had been afforded.

Twenty years after the beginning of the school in *Indefatigable,* the main theme at the 1885 Annual General Meeting was 'care of the boys'. The Honorary Secretary, Mr. Charles J. Bushell, reported that, in spite of the intensity of the commercial depression, *Indefatigable* was prospering. Describing the boys, he stated that 79 of the lads aboard had lost both parents, 93 had no fathers, 19 had been deserted and only 31 had fathers living. Sadly the numbers shipped as apprentices had slumped to eleven.

H.M.S. Conway, Akbar and Indefatigable (with practice canvas set) about 1900

Again the problem of training was discussed and pin-pointed by the Mayor in his address. 51 lads became ordinary seamen and 15 of them joined the R.N.R., 8 were sent to sea as stewards, 1 entered the Royal Navy, 13 were sent to occupation on shore. The grand total of boys on board on the 31st December, 1885, was 222. Captain Miller, R.N., thought the vessel was beautifully clean, and the boys seemed healthy and happy, and were neat, tidy and respectable wherever one happened to meet them. This statement was greeted with applause!

It was reported in 1890 that 200 boys off *Indefatigable* were taken in the armed cruiser *Teutonic* to witness the Spithead naval review. The Mayor again noted that there was an urgent need in the country for the training of boys in practical seamanship and that the advent of steam had dramatically reduced the apparent need for every ship to carry apprentices. This was a recurrent theme. It was also noted that Captain and Mrs. Groom had retired and that they had been 'presented with an illuminated address and a handsome gong from the Officers, and a silver-plated crumb scoop from the boys.' Captain A. Bremner and his wife assumed command.

The 27th Annual General Meeting was held on the 22nd March, 1892 in Liverpool Town Hall and the Mayor, Mr. James de Bels Adam presided. It was reported that the number of boys aboard at the end of 1890 was 231 and an extra 94 arrived in 1891, making the total compliment of 325. 31 had been sent to sea as apprentices, 30 as ordinary seamen, 14 as cabin boys, 4 into the Royal Navy, 9 to occupation ashore, and 2 had died, leaving on board at the end of 1891, 235. Of this number 111 were fatherless, 11 motherless, and 62 without either father or mother; only 28 had both parents living.

In 1912 an Inspecting Officer of Training Ships confirmed what was already obvious. 'The ship is worn out and unsuitable for further service.'

The Admiralty was not in a generous mood. The hull of *H.M.S. Phaeton*, thirty year old, was available for £15,000. The *Phaeton* was a second-class steel cruiser, not on loan this time, but for sale. Again the Bibby family came to the rescue, not only buying the vessel but providing the money for the refit.

Phaeton, built on the Clyde, had been commissioned in 1886 and had served in the Mediterranean and in the Pacific. Although she was a steamship she was also one of the last ships in the Royal Navy to carry sail and occasionally even to use it. She had been paid off in 1903 and had since been used as a parent hulk for destroyers and as a training vessel for stokers.

Towed to the Mersey, she was fitted out at Birkenhead and moored off Rock Ferry Pier on 15th January, 1914. She had been rigged as a barquentine, but the yards and booms had long gone, together with the engines and boilers. There were two funnels left as reminders of her past The vessel was renamed *Indefatigable*, the third of her line and the first steel training ship in commission. The old *Indefatigable* was broken up in West Float.

At this time another training ship, the smaller barquentine, *James J. Bibby*, which had been used by the boys for sea training, was requisitioned by the Admiralty and was used as a Q ship, fighting submarines in the North Sea.

In the much loved magazine, Sea Breezes, Arthur Plumridge wrote two articles about his days in *Indefatigable* just after the First World War. The Spartan conditions, uninteresting food, control of pocket money and censorship of letters, which he records, have to be judged against the background of the times.

'I arrived at New Ferry, Birkenhead, where a stage hand made the recognised eight bell signal to the ship and a cutter came across and I was on my way. My mother came with me to New Ferry but she was, of course, left at the landing stage. The parting was rather poignant.

'Once on board, I thought, 'Well, here I am for better or worse' ... The main deck I thought looked very austere and bare looking but the planked deck was nice and clean; I later found out how this was made so.

'Of inevitable interest to a growing lad is food and therefore away to the galley. It was quite spacious and equipped with a coal-burning range. There were also two enormous cauldrons (possibly originally used for boiling intrusive missionaries in the more backward countries!) but now used in the less drastic operation of making stews and beverages. These cauldrons were heated by steam from the boiler room via a steam jacket.

'This little kingdom was ruled by the cook, one Murphy, (inevitably 'Spud') who furnished the best example of an expressionless face I have ever seen. I never saw his expression change no matter what circumstances. He had two boys to assist in his labours; I often wondered whether they grew up to be as equally dour as their mentor.

'Our meals were taken at bare wooden tables, 10 or 12 of us to a table, all seated on long forms and the practically unvarying menu was as follows.

'Breakfast consisted of a slice of bread some four inches or so square by a fraction over one inch thick which was adorned by a knob of margarine (known to all us boys as 'spottom') stuck in the middle: in cold weather this was impossible to spread. This delicate piece of tempting food was placed on a bare table opposite one's allotted space, by a 'cook of the mess' which exalted chore was undertaken by most of us on a rota basis.

'To assist in the assimilation of the food, we were issued with one of 'Spud's' beverages which we dubbed 'cocoa flush' and which had been prepared in the galley by the dropping of solid slabs of cocoa, unsweetened I may add, into one of the cauldrons I have mentioned, this having been previously filled with boiling water. A couple of tins of milk (we never saw fresh milk) were tipped into the cocoa and water, together with a very meagre quantity of sugar, the mixture then drawn off into 'kettles', utensils similar in shape and size to a large domestic wash bucket (the mop bucket type) prior to being dropped by the hoist to the mess deck, there to be rationed out using basins as balers. These basins were used as drinking vessels too, cups being completely non-existent.

'Dinner for each day except Fridays and Sundays consisted of 'buzz'. 'Spud' Murphy concocted several kinds of 'buzz'. There was 'pea buzz', 'Irish buzz', 'mystery buzz' and another variety which I have forgotten, although at the time, I never thought it would be possible. These 'buzzes' were neither soups nor stews but partook of the characteristics of both and were served in those same basins as was our 'cocoa flush'.

'A small pile of broken ship's biscuits was put beside each basin at table and sometimes these were quite palatable, especially to hungry boys, when a new sack had been opened, but if allowed to go stale, they turned soggy and tastelessly horrible, under which circumstances the ever present sea birds benefited. The biscuits were circular, three inches in diameter and about half an inch thick and bore the name 'Ixion'.

'Dinner on Fridays was usually boiled cod, served on a plate, with the usual biscuits, but on Sundays 'Spud' really triumphed. On this high day we had two slices of roast beef and a couple of boiled potatoes, also on a plate, with 'duff' for 'afters'. This latter 'Murphy Special' was of a dark brown hue, but had the texture of cheddar cheese and contained the occasional lonely currant and raisin. This had to be eaten all the way, but we were all blessed with a good set of grinders. Each portion was about four inches by three and just under an inch thick and was 'served' by being dropped on to the bare table, as we had used the plates for the beef and potatoes. To drink, we had water obtained from a tank on the main deck.

'For tea, we had the usual square of bread - we called it tack but in place of the breakfast margarine, we had a small dollop of jam spooned on to the middle of the piece of 'tack'.

'Sometimes in winter, we had slight addition to the foregoing menu; breakfast, for instance, would be varied by the serving up of a thick porridge known as 'burgoo'. A small quantity of sugar was added in the making but we had no milk. On the whole not a popular dish. Occasionally we would be issued with boiled rice for dinner. This, scantily spotted with raisins, was also not popular.

'Our cutlery, knife, fork and spoon was lodged in a locker with our kit-bag and carried to the mess deck when the bugle summoned us to a meal. Except for the Sunday beef, knife and fork were superfluous and the spoon was the only tool necessary.

'All the time I was in *Indefatigable*, I never saw eggs, fresh milk, fruit, vegetables (other than potatoes), bacon or anything other than what I have mentioned; there were dried peas and such for the 'mystery buzz', but it remains a great mystery to me how we boys maintained our health and strength on this Spartan diet!

'We did have occasional 'treats' though, for instance if one missed dinner through being adrift in a boat on some exercise or other, we should then find 'Spud', on our return, was ready with a round of 'tack' which he would dip in beef dripping, of which he seemed to have an inexhaustible supply. This delicious piece of fat-soaked bread would be carted off like a dog with a bone, to some secluded corner to be devoured away from covetous eyes.

'One unwelcome chore for us boys was coaling ship. The coal was taken from a lighter moored alongside and this operation came around once a year. All hands would be employed. The coal was raised with the aid of baskets and a block and tackle. This was an unpleasant task as we and everything else got filthy. After the lighter shoved off, all hands would have to clean the ship and themselves. As usual there wasn't an abundance of either soap or hot water and a rather miserable time was had by all.

'The daily supply of coal for the boiler had to be raised from the bunkers twice a day and this chore was allotted to wrong-doers as a form of punishment, but more of this later.

'The ship's complement of boys was divided into two watches and four divisions, first and third in the starboard and second and fourth

"We all managed to pull an oar"

in the port watch. Each day, Mondays to Fridays, one watch would be on deck learning seamanship and attending to routine duties, while the other would be in school doing normal lessons as in shore schools but in addition navigation in the top classes, so that one week a boy would spend two days in school and three days the following week.

'Punishment would vary from being placed on a coaling party for one, two or three weeks for minor offences, loss of leave, strokes of the cane and what was considered to be the most disgraceful of all - 'canvas'. The unlucky recipient of this had to wear a white canvas jumper for the period of his sentence, so that his shame and disgrace would be apparent to all, much in the manner in which a 'dunce's cap' was once used in schools.

'One particular punishment which to me seemed more fitting for the 19th century was meted out (and probably concocted by) a certain officer whom we all disliked intensely. This ill-disposed man would patrol the lower deck at 9.15 p.m. and would examine hammocks for any faults such as crossed nettles or an untidy rope in which case he would bellow 'Carry your hammock on deck' and at the same time roughly shaking the foot lanyard, whereupon the unfortunate boy, nicely tucked up, would have to leave his warm but short-lived comfort to stand on the main deck carrying his hammock and associated gear on his back, in which cold and draughty position he would remain for an hour.

'Washing clothes was a problem. We used to spread flannel shirts on the washroom floor and with a ration of soap about half the size of a packet of 10 cigarettes and with a bit of luck, hot water, we rubbed away. Afterwards each garment was inspected by an officer and one's name ticked off on a slate.

'Shore excursions for the boys were rare. I think I once went to play football and twice for swimming lessons at the local baths. One of the ship's rules was that a boy was not allowed to go on leave or even ashore, until he had completed three months aboard.

'On completing my training and finally leaving the ship, I was fitted out with quite a huge kitbag full of clothes complete with a suit of oilskins ... and a pair of seaboots tied outside. I was given a Bible by the chaplain (the one with the handlebar moustache had gone and a more likeable Mr. Danderson had taken his place) and I still have this in my possession.

"I did get some pleasure from being a member of the band when we were able on rather rare occasions, to make visits to some local functions but really apart from this I must say that I cannot recall any happy times I had aboard the Training Ship *Indefatigable.*'

That was a sad picture, remembered in much detail.

It was a happy chance in 1996 that I met an old seafarer who told me of his time as a boy in *Indefatigable* ... his name is Billy Maclean. Billy was born in 1911 and when I met him he was 85, living alone in a spotless flat and he was obviously delighted to find someone interested in his past.

"I first came across *Indefatigable* when with two mates I called in the office in Victoria Street - on the glass door it said Training Ship *Indefatigable.* The man talked to us. "Are you hungry?" There was only one answer to that. "Do you want a wash?" I explained that we went into the park and always had a wash every day in the lake. "Where do you sleep?" At that time we had found an old church and that was fine for us. I must have been about ten at that time and there was nothing at home. We lived in a hovel, my Mam and four children. It wasn't much and we ate what we could find. My Dad was long gone! The best place was Great Homer Street Market. If you helped with hand-carts, you got an apple. Everyone I knew was poor!"

Details were taken in the office and Billy thought that nothing more would happen because he was too young. His life of fighting for survival on the streets of Liverpool continued in the same old way ... but he had not been forgotten.

That chaplain who had spoken to Billy made contact with his mother and on the 5th November, 1925, the indentures were signed by the Commander of *Indefatigable*, by Billy and by Elizabeth Maclean, his mother. Billy was thirteen and a half years old. He continued with his tale as we sipped our coffee.

"There seemed to be about three hundred lads aboard. Along with the other new boys, I stripped naked and washed myself in half a barrel of cold water and carbolic soap. I had my own tooth-brush and was given powder on a piece of paper ... it was great to clean my teeth! We sat at tables, six lads on either side with a top boy with a cane at the end. I'd never come across Grace at meals before, but I remember it now.

We present at the table, Lord,
Let manna to our souls be given,
From bread sent down from heaven.

We all gave a loud Amen and sat down. The food was horrible; I shut my eyes to eat it, but I was hungry.

"The bugle went at six. We slept in hammocks which were great; tucked in the hammock was the only private place aboard the ship. I felt safe in mine. The light was very poor in the ship and because we were for ever scrubbing, it was always damp. But we lads were healthy, so it must have been all right. It was a sad-faced place, but we were fed, safe and warm. Remember we were just street urchins.

"They tried to make us seamen, but I don't think it worked. I did learn how to splice. After three months I was allowed to go home to see my mother for two hours and then had to report back to Rock Ferry. We rang the large bell and the cutter came to get us. We all learned how to pull an oar; that was the only fun that I can remember.

"The Chaplain was a good man. He talked to us and opened all our parcels and divided any food amongst us all. Punishment was three or six cuts over the vaulting horse with a half inch cane ... most of it was for nothing much! Into our hammocks at seven and emergency lights only.

"Never saw the Captain or his wife or his dog. We never troubled each other! We were just a bunch of strays. Another punishment was to stand under the clock with your hammock on your shoulders for two hours. That was hard. I was sent there and told "You're leaving!" I jumped into the tub, then received my kit and was told to join Bibby's *Leicestershire* as a bridge boy. There was no time to go home to tell my mother or wish her good-bye.

"I spent two years in the *Indefatigable* and thirty years at sea. It did me no harm and did teach me to respect God."

Billy was a quiet, courteous gentleman. Like so many old seafarers, he knew that most people were not in the least interested in his years at sea and, even if they were, did not know how to ask the right questions. Taking him back in memory to his *Indefatigable* days made his eyes dance and shine. It had been a wonderful conversation and I shall ever remember him.

The new *Indefatigable* was in full use as a training ship until 1941, when it was decided to evacuate her because the Germans were bombing Merseyside. The old ship was taken over by the Admiralty (not to fight!) and renamed *Carrick II*. After the war she was towed to Preston to be broken up after 67 years at sea.z

Temporary premises were quickly found at Clwyd Newydd, near Ruthin. A very old friend of mine, Ron Wilkinson, spent some time in the new camp and I have recorded his memories. Ron's father had been lost in November 1941 when his ship, *Nova Scotia,* had been torpedoed off East Africa ... only 14 of the crew were saved out of a total of 114.

"We were interviewed in the old Sailors' Home where 'Bandy' Williams gave about a dozen of us a written exam. They sent us by train to Chester and then on to Ruthin. There was no-one to meet us so we all started walking, but the Captain's wife then appeared with a car and picked a few up at a time. Next day we were kitted-out in our sailors' rig. Life was tough in those huts, rough and ready and very cold. I believe the place had been the Merseyside Children's Holiday Camp. I arrived there in March 1944 and it was no holiday.

"We were divided into four divisions with about 50 in each division. We slept in two tier bunks and we were so cold. There was no heat in those huts and it was like the Arctic. I kept all my clothes on in bed and aquired as many blankets as I could. When the weather was desperate we all moved into the school room, the mess deck and the swimming area. That was a little better.

"I never forget the food. Breakfast was porridge, chunk of bread and marg and a mug of tea. Lunch was meat of some sort with potatoes and gravy, followed invariably by a sort of 'spotted dick'. Tea was pilchard pie cut into slices, two half inch chunks of bread and a mug of tea. Supper was a real rock cake and half a mug of milk. We were always starving. One day we refused to eat the stuff and in due course the chef was sacked.

"In one half of the day we did Maths and English and for the other half we worked. The mess deck had to be cleaned, the huts to be sorted, the boiler house supplied with logs ... we called the place the 'bug house'. One lad was in charge of the paint shop and the water boy looked after the pump to get the water up to the huts.

"It was in December 1944 that we moved to Plas Llanfair. Two lorries ferried some of the lads and all the property like the figurehead, the bunk beds and the ropes and that sort of stuff. The job took a week and most of us went by train.

"Llanfair was like a luxury hotel to us! Gone were the oil lamps because we actually had electric light and proper hot water. The food was much better, but I was only there two months because my time was up."

Ron was to train as an engineer and served at·sea from 1950 to 1981. His elder sister, Joyce, was sadly to lose her husband, Ray, in the *Piper Alpha* disaster when the oil platform was destroyed by fire and explosion on the night of 6th July, 1988. Their mother, Lillie, went to sea in 1946 and spent seven years with Cunard as a stewardess. She recalled her time in the *Scythia* carrying displaced persons from Cuxhaven to Canada. My contact with this remarkable family was when Lillie volunteered in the early sixties to look after our Ancient Mariners' Club for retired seafarers in Kingston House. We are all much older, but still surviving and friendship and memories bind us together.

The mansion, Plas Llanfair, which had been used by the Americans to train officers, was well adapted to become the new *Indefatigable*. It was a wonderful site for training and along with many friends I much enjoyed the open days when the boys were put through their paces. On occasions, I was invited to take a Padre's Hour. I talked about the Missions overseas, showed them photographs and explained the advantage of having their own club wherever they went. I also met the lads at the start of their time in *Indefatigable* when they arrived at the Sailors' Home in Liverpool to be 'kitted-out' under the watchful eye of Bill Hobbs. There were normally some 150 boys, aged between 13 and 16. Many of them were to enter the Services or the Merchant Navy.

Education was always the primary objective and subjects were taken up to G.C.S..E. level, together with Seamanship and General Maritime Knowledge. Uniform was worn at all times and discipline well maintained. The shore base was a vast improvement on the hardships of the old floating vessels. Times had happily changed. There were three cooked meals a day and I suspect that not one lad had ever heard of 'buzzes' and Ixion biscuits and burgo and spottom!

Indefatigable is no longer in existence except in the memories of many old seafarers. The school closed in 1996 as the demand for sea-going had almost ceased and the original purpose lost in the changes of time. An Old Boys' Association has been formed and periodically a news letter is sent to members. Friendships will remain to the end.

16.
H.M.S. Conway

'QUIT YE LIKE MEN , BE STRONG'

In 1857, the Mercantile Marine Service Association was founded and still exists today. The original purpose was 'to take every legitimate step to elevate to their proper position the officers of the Merchant Navy, and to promote the interests of that service generally'. The prime mover was again Captain John Clint, and the Committee with James Beazley as chairman, and Ralph Brocklebank, S.R. Graves, Robert Rankin and Samuel Rathbone as members, obtained the Frigate *Conway*, and were able to bring the vessel into use in 1859. This was achieved with remarkable speed and expertise.

The Royal Navy, having a regular staff of instructors and much leisure for its midshipmen, naturally did not feel the need so much for training ships;

but it was otherwise in the Merchant Service, which had grown to such enormous proportions since the introduction of steam. It was not a day too soon. The first chairman, Mr. James Beazley, applied to the Admiralty for a disused man-of-war to be turned into a school for young officers; and that summer the *Conway* was made over to the Association. Two years later the success of the experiment was so conspicuous that a frigate of 28 guns was proving to be far too small for the number of cadets who sought entrance, and the Admiralty, at the instigation of the Duke of Somerset, then First Lord, gave the 51 gun *Winchester* to take the place of *Conway*. This ship was, of course, renamed *H.M.S. Conway* and served till 1876, when the Admiralty replaced it with the *Nile*, a screw line-of-battle ship of 4,875 tons and 92 guns. The new ship was much larger and more suitable. She was fitted out and then towed round from Devonport to the berth in the Mersey and was the largest sailing ship at that time to enter the Mersey.

The *Nile* had served on the North American and West Indian stations and had carried the flag of Sir A. Milne. In Devonport the machinery was removed and she was ballasted with 220 tons of copper dross and 175 tons of iron. The topmast and topgallant masts, yards, rigging etc. were all in perfect order for the instruction of pupils in manning yards, and making and shortening sail. There was ample space for school rooms, a hospital, a wardroom and all other needs. The main deck was regarded as light and airy with a height of seven feet from deck to deck; it was all painted white with skylights extending over fifty feet in length and averaging ten feet in breadth. The large cooking range was forward with the cooks' and stewards' accommodation; the range had been removed from the nearby *Great Eastern*.

Much has been written and could be written about the school ship *Conway*. A correspondent some twenty five years after the arrival of *Conway* in the Mersey gives a lively picture. The year is 1883. The writer is not identified.

> 'One bright morning last Autumn I found myself on the Rock Ferry slip. Four line-of-battle-ships, 'hearts of oak', strangely thick and heavy looking in comparison with an iron-clad Cunard liner lying near them, were anchored out in the broad river, and I was waiting for a boat from one of them.
>
> 'Presently a cutter, manned by thirteen smart boys ... the inevitable bull must be excused, for the boys are learning to do men's work ... came to shore, but not for me. A Police Officer landed from it, and, seeing him drop something heavy, bright, and gruesome into his pocket, I understood that he must have come from the *Clarence* or the *Akbar*. On inquiry it appeared that he had been to both

ships, leaving four juvenile offenders on the one floating reformatory and two on the other, to be trained for honest seamen in the three coming years. Let us wish them and their two or three hundred companions all success. Looking at the crew of this boat (it was from the *Akbar*, the Protestant reformatory ship, but one from the *Clarence* would have presented much the same appearance) one could see that the law was giving these boys a noble chance of reaching honourable manhood.

'A few minutes later, another cutter came in, crowded with about thirty boys of quite different style, the sons of happier mothers. Half of them leaped ashore, in good order but eagerly; well-dressed, gentle, manly looking lads, and hastened off to enjoy their Saturday holiday. Some who carried tidy little valises were not to return until Monday morning .... but the crew of their companions who brought them in were not to take me out, for that was the mail boat, and must perform its proper function punctually.

'The leave-boys were scarcely out of sight when a handsome barge of sixteen oars drew up at the pier in splendid style. "Fenders out! Port oars in!" shouted the coxswain, and the boat lay ready for me, with eight oars perpendicular and the stern sheets gay with crimson cushions. The bit of water was crossed swiftly, and we were brought to the side of the *Conway* with that dextrous precision which tells of discipline, active hands and clear eyes.

'Arrived on the upper deck, you find the *Akbar* to be your nearest neighbour, the *Clarence* the remotest of the four. Between these lies the *Indefatigable,* of which a word must be said. It is not a reformatory, but receives the orphans of seamen, sons of struggling widows, adventurous boys who will go to sea, and whose friends seek by two or three years' training here to give them a much better chance of success.

'The distinctive position of the *Conway* will by this time be understood. It is a school for the sons of gentlemen, taking that much-abused word as representing a certain social status, and is intended to give them such education as shall make them gentlemen in education and personal character. To this extent it is the same as many another boarding-school.

'I shall refrain from any attempt to describe the good ship, standing in wholesome dread of the ridicule which might be incurred by very probable mistakes in the use of nautical terms.

'The Commander, every inch a gentleman and a sailor, experience in both the Merchant and the Royal Navy, and conducts the business of the ship with enthusiasm. His post can be no sinecure, involving as it does the care by day and night of some 170 spirited lads; but his efforts, heartily seconded by an excellent staff of teachers and officers, seemed decidedly successful. The discipline is strict, but that is no fault; and it is enforced and accepted with good will.

'I ventured to ask the Commander, as we were standing on the poop, to give orders for 'Fire quarters', an amusement to me of rather a fascinating character. Calling a lad, he directed him to ring the fire-bell, and whispered that the scene of fire was to be the lower deck aft. Instantly on the second stroke following the alarm the lads ran helter-skelter from the places where they had been reading, playing, writing home letters, working, to their appointed stations, a particularly tight and bright young gentleman taking his place at the Commander's elbow as his messenger. Going to the main deck and the lower deck with the dignity of a 'special' (not to say of a Commander) we found ports and scuttles closed, crews standing by each boat with the tackle for lowering it in their hands, fire-engines, pumps and hose rigged and manned; and as we neared the spot where the fierce enemy was supposed to have begun his attack, rows of lads, each with a full bucket at his feet, and a smothering party, each of whom had a hammock on his shoulders ready for prompt application. Everything was done, without a word spoken and quite within four minutes, precisely as if a fire had been a real one, except that I was relieved to find that the port-watch of the forecastlemen (the smouldering party) had not proceeded to the serious extremity of wetting their hammocks for my entertainment. An operation like this, performed swiftly and thoroughly and withal very suddenly, by 150 boys, is satisfactory proof of the training and discipline which renders it possible.

'The life on board seems to be pleasant. Six hours of direct study, with drill in the practical operations of seamanship connected with masts, sails, and ropes, leave plenty of time for amusements between rising at six and going to bed at nine. I was so unfortunate as to miss a Christy Minstrels' entertainment which has taken place on the evening preceeding my visit, and the laughter from which had not quite died away the next forenoon. The solemn presentation of razors, among other things, to the two chief prizemen of the School, about to leave, seems to have furnished no little mirth. Lectures, concerts, and the like are frequent after the days have grown too short for cricket and football on shore.'

This account of a visit to *Conway*, some twenty-five years into its life, ends with a salutary tale.

'Many years ago a boy went in a wooden ship from Nith to Calcutta. He kept up during the outward voyage the regular habit of kneeling for prayer before turning into his hammock, ignorant of the fact that he was doing anything unusual, and that an able seaman, one Bob Shearer, who knew his parents, was watching to protect him from the rude comments of the forecastle. At Calcutta some fresh hands were shipped, among others a blackguard from Whitechapel, called English Bob to distinguish him from the Scottish Bob already on board. The home-ward voyage was scarcely begun when English Bob, seeing young Jamie at his prayers, swore and shouted, 'I declare, here's a younker praying!' and flung a shoe with excellent aim at his head. Thereupon, Scotch Bob took the coward and bully up on the deck and thrashed him wholesomely. Next night, the boy, who had not thought his prayers of much importance, went into his hammock without kneeling; but presently Scotch Bob got him by the heels and pulled him out, saying, 'Say your prayers like a man. Do you think I'm going to fight for a coward? I'll need to thrash you next'. Sir James Anderson, late Commander of the *Great Eastern*, which laid the first Atlantic cable, received in this rough fashion a lesson which he never forgot.'

Amongst the Nautical Jottings of the archives of the Mercantile Marine Service Association in 1887 was the following account of life in *Conway*.

'Two important events have taken place on board the good old ship within a month. The first was the highly interesting and instructive Lecture on the 'Great Ice Age,' by Sir Robert Ball, the eminent Astronomer-Royal for Ireland. By the aid of the powerful oxy-hydro light, the lecturer was able to convey to the minds of the cadets the wonders of the pre-historic age, when the great ice king reigned supreme over much of the surface of the earth. So much was told to the boys on the subject as to engage their thoughts for the rest of the term, if strict attention was paid to what fell from the lecturer's lips. The other event was perhaps the most acceptable to the boys, being always welcomed with outbursts of joy ... the 'Break-up Supper'. This time-honoured custom on the *Conway* is an occasion of much festivity, and is almost as eagerly looked forward to by the invited guests as by the boys. The attendance is always good, when weather permits, and the programme generally includes an Entertainment by the boys, dancing on the main deck led by the *Indefatigable* band, with the Supper at the conclusion. The evening of the 19th saw a goodly company assembled on the old frigate, both guests and boys 'footing it right merrily' to the inspiring strains of the band. Then followed the Supper, marked as usual by those spirited speeches which are looked upon as one of the most notable events of the evening. The ever popular Commander leads off with his address to the boys, his speech being delivered in his own free and hearty style. Mr. Clarke Aspinall (who honoured the company with his presence at some little inconvenience to himself, having come specially from Manchester for the occasion) gave one of those rattling speeches which always seem to 'hit' the mark wherever he goes. Altogether the 1887 Supper was a great success - excelling, perhaps, even those of years gone by - and it was with regret that the guests were reminded by the lateness of the hour that it was time to return ashore.'

One of the most famous cadets in *Conway* was without contradiction, John Masefield. His book, *'The Conway'*, was written in 1933 and is more than the story of the vessel. His time aboard was 1891 to 1894.

'We watched ships being built and launched and floated. We saw them going forth in splendour and coming back shattered by the sea, listed, shored up, dismasted, red with sea-rust, white with sea salt, holed, dinted, ruined, all pumps still spouting, just limping into dock with three tugs, or just crawling to the mud and lying down.'

And still young lads chose the sea!

Life continued aboard *H.M.S.Conway* for the many thousands of cadets who were trained for command. It was the well tried mixture of seamanship, discipline and hard work. At dawn the diesel generators would rumble into action, followed half an hour later by the bugle for reveille. Then came the command for all hands to bathrooms and a speedy lashing and storage of hammocks. "All hands clean ship!" Off went the first boats to collect the catering staff from shore and the tables were rigged for breakfast. All too soon was heard the pipe, "Rig school!" and another day in *Conway* had started.

In 1937, *Conway* was taken into dry dock in Birkenhead, because she was in need of urgent repair, new equipment and classrooms were added. Copper had to be replaced on her bottom and many timbers were to be renewed. A figure head of Nelson was fitted. The dedication ceremony was at Pier Head in the presence of Lord Derby, the Lord Mayor and shipping dignitaries and *Conway* returned to her mooring at the Sloyne in Birkenhead.

However, the war clouds were gathering and as in the First World War life was to change dramatically.

It soon became obvious that Liverpool was really not a safe anchorage, as the German Luftwaffe found the Mersey a very visible target. May 1941 was an important month in the story of *Conway.*

A convoy had arrived and as there were too many vessels for the dock system to hold, a number of ships had to lay in the river. The *Tacoma City* was nearest to *Conway.* The senior hands were on watch during the night's blitz and a parachute mine was observed dropping between the two vessels. Captain-Superintendent Goddard called 'reveille' at about midnight This roused the ship's company and the next command was 'motor-boat crew man boats'. The aim was to remove the 150 cadets to safety ashore and they spent the rest of that night in the Royal Rock Hotel. The bombs and the shrapnel continued to fall and a Dornier was shot down over Rock Ferry Pier. It was a hard night.

The lads returned to *Conway* after lunch and then were transported by buses to Mostyn House School in Parkgate. That afternoon the mine exploded and *Tacoma City* was sunk!

It was decided that *Conway* should be removed to a safe anchorage for the duration of the war and an obvious mooring was off Bangor where the *Clio* had been anchored. This was effected ten days later.

The Training Ship *Clio* has started life in the Mersey anchored between *Indefatigable* and *Akbar*, but was the first to leave the line of training ships and was moved to Bangor. There she remained for a number of years. The *Clio* was a twenty-two gun corvette, built of African oak and launched from Sheerness as a screw vessel. After two commissions in the Pacific, she had been permanently loaned to the North Wales, City of Chester and Border Counties Training Ship Society and was dismantled in 1938.

This was to be the new home for *Conway.* Many will still recall the sight of the vessel as she departed the Mersey. The date was 21st May, 1941. It was a rare opportunity for the cadets to handle a fully rigged ship of the line. The new berth was different. The busy river with all its war-time bustle of Merchant and Royal Navy vessels was replaced by flying boats and motor torpedo and gun boats. The backdrop was Snowdon and green hills.

Obviously, there was great demand for trained young officers for the Royal and Merchant Navies. The solution was for the young cadets to spend the first year of training at Gordonstoun School. This doubled the numbers of cadets attached to *Conway.*

After the war, life returned to normal. No longer was the link with Gordonstoun School maintained as the demand for young officers

Docking at Liverpool for overhaul, July 1937

H.M.S. Conway at the landing stage

decreased, but the training continued. A new and exciting venture was a month for the cadets at the Outward-bound School at Aberdovey. This must have been very popular.

The Outward Bound School was the contribution of Blue Funnel Line and three distinguished men were responsible for its foundation. They were Lawrence Holt, chairman of the Blue Funnel Line, Dr. Kurt Hahn, headmaster of Gordonstoun School, and Brian Heathcote, training manager of the shipping company.

The Menai Straits afforded every opportunity for the young men to learn skills at boat handling in quieter waters than the fast running Mersey. However, there was no way in which the old ship could have returned to her berth on the Mersey as much of the land which had been used for sporting activities had meanwhile been requisitioned for other usage. There were also problems off Anglesey as the Bangor Town Football Club reclaimed the First Fifteen rugby ground. Other playing fields were near Beaumaris and were a long way from the Gazelle Slip where the cutters landed.

The decision was taken to move the ship across to a new mooring near to Plas Newydd. Here the Marquis of Anglesey was able to offer better accommodation. On the 13th April, 1949, *Conway* left Bangor for Plas Newydd. She was a very large vessel for the Straits and the move took one and a half hours.

Quickly two new buildings were erected for the new entrants. The accommodation housed one hundred cadets and staff. The stables became the instruction block. Happily, the dock was dredged and put to excellent use. All seemed to be well.

A new Staff-Captain was appointed when Captain T.M. Goddard retired at the end of the summer term in 1949. He was Captain Eric Hewitt, R.D., R.N.R., who had been a cadet in *Conway* from 1919 to 1921.

On the 14th April, 1953 at 0830 hours the *Conway* sailed on what sadly was to be her last voyage. She was towed by two tugs and was to be taken to Liverpool for a major refit. Much careful planning did not avoid disaster. She was due to pass under the tubular bridge at 0920 as it was vital to beat the tides and make use of the slack water. There would be little space as the channel was only 90 feet and *Conway's* beam was 56 feet.

They were five minutes late at Britannia Bridge and the ebb tide began to run strongly. It could not have been known that the build-up of water was to be greater than normal. The after-tug joined in the tow as *Conway* made no headway. The hawser between the tugs parted, *Conway* swung away to starboard and the end was inevitable. This was a fearful moment

The Clio off Bangor

for Captain Hewitt and the crew of seventeen. *Conway* was aground on the Caernarvon side. The tide receded and *Conway's* back was broken. The loss was to be total.

Captain Hewitt felt this disaster very keenly, but could not be held responsible. The towage had been the entire responsibility of the towing master as *Conway* had no motive power of her own and was classed as a hulk. Hewitt knew the strait and its currents and had asked for three tugs, but had been over-ruled. The memory never left him.

The committee of management in Liverpool, chaired by Lawrence Holt faced the problem. Two hundred and fifty cadets were in training and the immediate reaction to the tragedy was to create a tented village. This was followed by a hutted camp. Life continued.

In September 1956 it was decided to dismantle the remains of the ship. The figure-head was rescued, together with a mast. The demand for mementoes was world-wide as the work continued. Disaster struck again on the 16th October when a workman's torch set the vessel alight. This was the end of a legend.

A new college was proposed and on August 1st, 1961 Mrs Hewitt laid the foundation stone. On the 6th May, 1964, the splendid buildings were opened by H.R.H Prince Philip. The rescued mast was erected at the southern end of the parade ground and the figurehead of Nelson at the northern end. Whilst the college was an era away from the previous environment, much effort was made to ensure that the routine resembled life aboard ship. Some things could not change. Queen Victoria had instituted the Queen's Gold Medal in 1866 for the 'finest sailor'. A short list of five was produced by the staff and all the cadets then voted for the recipient. This award was eventually to be taken over and presented to the best cadet in the Canadian Coast Guard Service and was known as the Queen's Conway Gold Medal. Sailing continued as a major enterprise and the gig races were well battled. There were also the annual rugby fixtures against *Worcester* and *Pangbourne* Nautical Colleges. Swimming in the outdoor pool in almost sub-zero temperatures was remarkably popular!

One visit that I made to *Conway* is well remembered by my family. It certainly was not the sermon that I delivered at the morning service! It was the large jug of fresh cream as we sat at table with Captain and Mrs Hewitt to enjoy an excellent lunch and listen to nautical tales. Children remember food.

Sadly, time was catching up as the shipping industry was changing rapidly. The demand for young officer cadets was falling and the majority of companies no longer supported *Conway*. Captain Hewitt retired in July 1968 and the end was inevitable.

Grounded on Platters Ledge

The MMSA relinquished control of the school to the British Shipping Federation and the Cheshire County Council. By 1972 the number of cadets in training had fallen to the uneconomic level of 170 and the Cheshire Council gave notice that it wished to cease running *Conway* as a grant-aided school as from August 1974.

One hundred and fifteen years of nautical training were over. The final inspection was in June 1974 and the salute taken by the President of the Conway Club, Commodore David Smith, R.N. The ship finally paid off on the 11th July, 1974.

Captain Hewitt reached the grand age of 91 and was in remarkable health. Sadly he died as the result of a fire in his home which he thought he had extinguished, only for it to ignite again after he had taken to his bed for the night. The Captain is still held in high regard by old 'Conways' around the world. It truly is the end of an era.

The 3 ton teak figurehead of Lord Nelson was moved to the R.N. Base in Portsmouth at the same time as it was changing its name from *H.M.S Victory* to *H.M.S. Nelson*. The *Conway* colours on 11 July, 1974 were laid up in the Anglican Cathedral in Liverpool. The anchor was laid to rest in the Liverpool Maritime Museum. This school had provided thousands of officers for the Royal and Merchant Navies during its proud one hundred and fifteen years and produced four holders of the Victoria Cross and one George Cross and care has been taken to ensure that its memory is not to be obliterated by the passing years.

The Archbishop of Wales used these words when the colours were placed into the care of the Anglican Cathedral.

"The sum of the story is that the *Conway* has indeed taught the technical skills that we now take for granted in ships' officers. It has done more than that. The *Conway* has been concerned above all with the formation of character."

In the early 80's the *Conway* mast had been dismantled and had been put to one side. The Conway Club decided in 1989 that it should be refurbished and brought home to Birkenhead. It was in a bad condition. The Canadian Conways ... in particular Mr. A. Sissons (Conway 56 - 57) ... came to the rescue and three 50 foot long Douglas firs were shipped from Vancouver to Liverpool.

With skills that are almost lost, the repairs were effected under the guidance of Shipwright Jimmy Gregory in the Cammell-Laird's Apprentice School, and the mast was assembled at the side of the old Egerton Dock in Birkenhead. A *Conway* stone was erected and a time capsule with the complete story was buried beneath it.

1859 H.M.S.CONWAY 1974
To the many thousands of Cadets Trained to Command
not forgetting those who lost their lives at sea.
'I must go down to the sea again
to the lonely Sea and the Sky'
John Masefield, OM, Conway 1891-94

On the 25th September 1993 there was a Service for the Blessing of the Mast as a symbol of the brotherhood of the sea and in memory of those who gave their lives. Never were the words of Psalm 107 more poignant.

'They that go down to the sea in ships, that do business in great waters;
These see the works of the Lord, and his wonders in the deep.'

The last act of the story was the placing of the memorial and honour boards to rest in the St. Mary's Chapter House Scriptorium at Birkenhead Priory. Now becoming known as the Conway Chapel. There could be no better home as the first *Conway* had been berthed nearby.

Conway will not be forgotten.

17.
H.M.S. Eaglet

On the 1st of November, 1958, the Royal Naval Reserve and the Royal
Naval Volunteer Reserve were amalgamated into one organisation to be
known as the Royal Naval Reserve. This is part of the waterfront story in
Merseyside and my contact as a Padre involved over thirty years of work
in *H.M.S. Eaglet* and friendships with the men and women of the R.N.R.
It is one of the finest 'clubs' in the world ... and I was proud to become
Eaglet's Chaplain in 1966.

Eagle was launched in 1804 and was destroyed by fire in 1927. During
her service afloat, the *Eagle* wore an admiral's flag three times. She was
flagship off the Texel in 1804, again on the South East Coast of America
Station in 1844 and yet again seventy years later when she became flagship
in Liverpool between 1914 and 1919. She was never involved in action,
but gave sterling service to the Royal Navy.

During her service, *Eagle's* complement had been about 600 men. Her officers were the captain and five lieutenants, a master and his mate and a lieutenant of marines. The Marine detachment consisted of about ninety scarlet-coated rank and file. The non-service officers were the surgeon and his assistant, the chaplain and the purser ... these gentlemen carried no rank.

Originally, her seamen ratings numbered some 556 men and thirty boys exclusive of officers' servants and 'widows' men'. These latter were non-existent and in theory amounted to 1% of the actual crew. The books of *Eagle* carried about six as her share of these mythical sailors, whose pay and allowances, by very old naval custom, provided a fund to pay pensions to the widows of officers. These fictitious 'men' continued to be borne on the books of H.M. Ships until about 1830 and their rate of pay was that of an able seamen. Nelson's 'blind eye' was put to good use and must have saved much paper work and bureaucracy.

The Fleet Reserve was instituted in 1852 and continuous service in the Navy in the following year. Obviously it was finally realised that there would be a dearth of trained seamen in the Navy for some years, and particularly in time of war. Permanent service was a new idea.

Recruitment of merchant seamen into the Royal Naval Reserve commenced in 1861 and officers in the merchant service were first offered commissions in the following year. Times change and today there are no merchant ratings in the R.N.R., although the officers remain. To train the newcomers in the ways of the Navy, three drill-ships were established - in London, North Shields and in Liverpool. So commenced the long association of Her Majesty's Ship *Eagle*, the Naval Volunteers and the port of Liverpool. The first Liverpool drill-ship was the old warship *Hastings* which had been District Ship of the Liverpool Coast Guard District, but she did not remain long here and departed for Queenstown upon the arrival of her successor, *Eagle*.

The story of *H.M.S. Eagle* has been written by John Smart and Edward Jones and was presented as a paper on the 13th November, 1958, to the Liverpool Nautical Research Society. I was privileged to be the President of that illustrious Society for a number of years and have received permission to recall some details from that paper.

'The drill-ship *Eagle* arrived from Spithead in tow of H.M. paddle sloop *Geyser* at 4.40 a.m. on Sunday, June 29th, 1862. In the excitement of reporting the fraternal conflict between Confederates and Federals, Monday's paper overlooked any mention of her arrival, but a few days later she took up her berth in the north-east corner of the old Queen's Dock. In those days the layout of the docks in that area differed considerably from that which now prevails. Entrance was by means of the Queen's Basin leading into Queen's Dock. King's Dock, much smaller than the present dock, was entered by a short passage on the north side of the Basin. Despite her having been in Liverpool for over sixty years, very little information is available with regard to the ship or her berths. One supposes that being such a familiar feature of the dockland of her day she was taken very much for granted.

'The R.N.R. continued to drill aboard her until 1911, although her captain was a commander, R.N. Between 1862 and 1908 this appointment was held in succession by nineteen officers, and she had the honour of claiming that, of all the R.N.R. centres in operation in 1898, those of Liverpool and Stornoway had trained a number of men far in excess of any others in the country.

'The Royal Naval Volunteer Reserve may be said to be descended from the Royal Naval Artillery Volunteers. Hitherto, such volunteers as had been available were professional seamen, but the R.N.A.V. opened enlistment to young civilians who were interested in matters naval. The Liverpool Corps of the R.N.A.V. was formed in 1873 with headquarters in *H.M.S Eagle.* Each Corps was composed of two or three batteries, each consisting of a sub-lieutenant, a chief petty officer, 1st and 2nd class petty officers and from fifty to seventy gunners. The combined Liverpool and Southport Corps united to form the Liverpool Brigade in 1876. A brigade comprised from four to six batteries with an establishment of about 450 men.

'The volunteer gunners were intensely enthusiastic and at its zenith the Brigade had units in Liverpool, Southport, Bangor, Caernarfon and Birkenhead. By this time the *Eagle* had changed berth from Queen's to King's Dock and in the 1880's lay at what is now the berth of the Booth Steam Ship Company at North 2 King's Dock. Unfortunately, as had happened with the Sea Fencibles (men recruited for the defence of U.K. only and dating back to Nelson's time) and again with the Royal Naval Coast Volunteers (started in 1853), official encouragement was lacking. The guns were vintage pieces, the gear scanty and there was little or no provision for sea training. In effect the gunners were soldiers dressed as seamen. An interesting feature of the uniform was that the blue jean collars had waved tapes, the officers' silver stripes were waved and both these features were revived in later years upon the formation of the

R.N.V.R. The waved lace, in gold instead of silver, continued to distinguish R.N.V.R officers until recently replaced by the regular pattern, but can still be seen upon the sleeves of officers of the Sea Cadet Corps.

'In 1892 the Admiralty who, in truth to tell, had never cared for anything less than the genuine article, saw fit to disband these eager young men and today an In Memoriam notice preserved aboard *H.M.S. Eagle* proclaims that the R.N.A.V, 'Died of Neglect'.

'In view of the volunteer spirit so evident in the latter half of the last century, it is indeed strange that the Board of Admiralty were not as ready as the War Office to direct it into useful channels. Even the formation of the R.N.V.R. in June 1903 was accepted somewhat sceptically by authority and not with the enthusiasm which its sponsors had expected. Tradition has it that the first enrolment into the Mersey Division of the R.N.V.R. took place on board *H.M.S. Eagle* in King's Dock on New Year's Day 1904. The target of 300 men was very soon reached and the first drills were held on board the old ship on the 8th March. It was then a few days over 100 years since she had been launched, and her appearance was such that her three admirals would have not recognised this Noah's Ark-like structure as a once proud seventy-four gun sailing ship of the line.

'The Royal Naval Reserve had continued to use the *Eagle* as a drill-ship for forty-one years, but forsook her in 1903. In that year was introduced a more realistic scheme of training in sea-going cruisers, but this only lasted for two years and in 1905 the R.N.R. returned to the *Eagle*. In the meantime, owing to the proposed rebuilding of King's and Queen's Docks, she had been moved to the north side of Salthouse Dock in 1904. When the R.N.R. re-occupied the ship in 1905 the Volunteers moved across to the Custom House in Canning Place and although that grim pile lacked the naval atmosphere, it had at least one advantage. The drill hall was in the north-east corner of the building and was large enough to accommodate the whole of the Division when mustered for drill and inspection.

'On the 31st March, 1911, the R.N.R. vacated the *Eagle* and she was turned over to the Volunteers for their sole use. The Division comprised seven companies of 100 officers and men, four at Liverpool, two outlying companies at Birkenhead and one in Southport. They were not however to enjoy possession for very long.

'International events were moving to a gigantic climax which, among its lesser results was to embroil even the centenarian *Eagle*. Shortly after the outbreak of war she was once again on active service, although in a stationary capacity. Captain H.H. Stileman was appointed to her.as Senior Officer, Liverpool, and upon the 2nd of November, 1914, he received his flag. Thus once again, and for the third time in her long and somewhat chequered career, she became a flagship. This duty she performed for the duration of the war.'

Edward Jones continued his thoughts as he recalled his own observations on *H.M.S. Eagle* during his time aboard during the first World War.

'On the lower deck, in the orlop, were the cells, very dark and small and not at all inviting. In the early hours of a cold February morning the alarm was raised. A prisoner had escaped from his cell. The guards were called out and stationed at all exits, but upon examination it was found that he had gone out by removing the bars from the port in the cell and dropped into the dock with the aid of his blanket and dare not let go. The water was perishing cold and it was freezing hard. He was told to come on board but with chattering teeth he answered, "I c-c-can't, there's no foothold. I can't hold on much longer." He was unable to obtain a foothold owing to the turn of the bilge and a rope was lowered to him, but he was so cold that he dare not let go of the blanket to tie the rope around his waist. He shouted, "I can't come up" then a vast voice from out of the darkness shouted, "Come up, or I shoot". Eventually a dinghy was lowered and he was picked up more dead than alive, a very sorry man.

'In one of the breast-hooks or stringers on the port side was cut: Built by Sir Wm. Rule at Northfleet in 1804, 74 guns, 1723 tons.

'This particular beam was fifteen inches square and it was amazing how the frames and diagonals were fitted together in the forepeak. Above the quarter-deck was the figurehead but unfortunately it was in a dark place and could easily be missed. I believe that the ship's wheel was aboard somewhere but I never saw this. The handrails of the companion-way leading down to the wardroom were covered with coachwhipping complete with turk's head and stopper knots, a beautiful piece of work.

'The old boatswain was always pleased to get someone interested and give them a few lessons in passing the ball to and fro. Very interesting, but very tedious. He was quite a character, that old

The old Eagle

H.M.S. Eaglet in Salthouse Dock, 1922

bosun. When he piped, "Everyone aft!", he would stand at the top of the midship companion and say: "Come on, my dears, come along, my dears. Come along, gentlemen, come on you scallywags. Come on, you lazy louts", and many other terms of endearment followed if we were slow enough to hear them.

'In the wardroom on the sideboard stood a beautiful model of a seventy-four in bronze, complete with guns, anchors, cables, masts, yards and all the details. It stood on a four-wheeled carriage and I admired it many times. I wonder what became of it?'

Eagle continued as the base ship in Liverpool throughout the war, as accommodation for ratings in transit. During this time there was little if any contact with the R.N.V.R.

At the start of the First World War, a battleship called the *Almirante Cochran* was being built by Armstrong, Whitworth and Co., Ltd., for the Chilean Navy. Work had stopped until 1917 when she was purchased by the British Government. She was redesigned as an aircraft carrier and destined to be called *Eagle*. When the carrier was launched on the 8th June, 1918, our old friend, the *Eagle*, was renamed *Eaglet*.

By the end of the First World War with her new name, *Eaglet,* she was in serious disrepair. Gone was the familiar white streak broken by her gun-ports and her black hull had been repainted in standard navy grey. What remained of her masts had at some time been cut down to the level of the roof ridge over the upper deck, and she looked more like Noah's Ark than ever.

In 1921 the Mersey Division of the R.N.V.R. was reformed with a strength of 400 men under the command of Commander William Maples, R.N.V.R. The composition of the Division was by companies, each 100 strong, of which numbers one, two, three and seven paraded in the ship at Salthouse Dock. Number four company was located at Southport, number five mustered at Caernarfon and number six in Birkenhead. In 1922 the Southport company was disbanded but in September 1923 a new Sub-Division came into being in Manchester. For its accommodation the war-time sloop *H.M.S. Sir Bevis,* now re-named *Irwell,* was berthed in Fairbrother Street Wharf, Salford. The local wits referred to her as H.M.S. Neverbudge.

John Smart and Edward Jones continued their memoirs.

'By 1926 the old *Eaglet,* which had now been afloat for almost a century and a quarter, was deemed to be unfit for further service and was ordered to be paid off for disposal. It was originally intended to replace her by *H.M.S. Goole,* a war-time minesweeper, but the *Goole* was too small for this duty and was transferred to Manchester. In August 1926 time, all three drill-ships, the *Irwell* (the war-time sloop) on the west side and the *Eaglet* with the *Goole* alongside, lay in Salthouse Dock together for a short time, a unique occasion. Without going into too much detail regarding the change-over, the *Irwell* from Manchester became the present *Eaglet* and the *Eaglet*-designate, late the *Goole*, became the *Irwell* which we know today (1959).

'A farewell banquet had been held aboard the old veteran on the 2nd of June and upon the evening of Thursday, the 2nd of September, 1926, the Division was mustered aft and at eight bells, as the notes of the Last Post echoed across the quiet dock, her ensign was slowly lowered for the last time and her service as one of the King's ships was ended. She had served under a queen and five kings in the 126 years which had elapsed since Sir William Rule designed her. Her ship's company marched away to the new ship and she was left, silent and deserted as she had been left so frequently before. Again the bugles rang out across the still waters, signalmen aboard the new *Eaglet* hoisted her ensign and the change-over was completed.'

The old *Eaglet* left Liverpool one misty morning in the following February and was towed to Mostyn, where she was beached preparatory to the difficult task of taking apart her aged timbers. On the 19th of April she caught fire as she lay and was burnt out. Her epitaph is contained in a few pages of verse preserved aboard her successor.

'Now not a vestige of her remains,
the old ship has gone for good
To some special Valhalla for seventy-fours
and the ships which were built of wood.'

The old ship's magnificent figurehead, a bearded and helmeted warrior, her wheel and an original door and door-frame still remain intact today in the shore-based *Eaglet*.

During the Second World War officers and men of the Mersey Division mobilised for service with the Royal Navy; 120 lost their lives in the conflict. *H.M.S.Eaglet* was commissioned as Base Ship Liverpool wearing the flag of Commander-in-Chief Western Approaches, Admiral Sir Percy Noble and then Admiral Sir Max Horton.

An excellent book entitled 'The Sea Chaplains' by the Reverend Gordon Taylor, a wartime chaplain himself and the R.N.R. chaplain of the London Division until 1970, includes a section of especial interest to Merseysiders.

'In September 1939 the Royal Navy began its blockade of Germany in Northern waters by using the older cruisers to cover the exits to the Atlantic, the Denmark Strait and the Faeroe Islands Passage. In the October the ships were augmented by the first of the liners which had been converted into armed merchant cruisers (A.M.Cs).

'In February 1940 twenty A.M.Cs. were on the Northern Patrol, four were with the Halifax Escort Force and twelve were in the Mediterranean.

'A chaplain for the A.M.Cs. was appointed in August 1940 in order to minister to the men who had the arduous work of the Northern Patrol, and he was a particularly good choice. He was Eric Evans (R.N.V.R.), then Vicar of Crossens, near Southport, Lancashire, who for five years before the war had been the Senior Chaplain of the Mersey Mission to Seamen, and who therefore knew well many of the merchant service officers and men who were serving under the T.124 (or T124x) Agreement. Such to a large degree were the ships' companies of the A.M.Cs., though their captains and commanders were generally Royal Navy officers who had been brought back from fairly recent retirement and a considerable proportion of the seamen were also from the Royal Navy.

'Evans made his first patrol in the former Bibby liner *Cheshire*, and followed this with others in the former P.& O. *Chitral*, the former Anchor liners *Cilicia* and *Circassia,* and the *Wolfe,* which was the former Canadian Pacific *Montcalm* as renamed. He remembers spending Christmas 1940 in northern waters. From early in 1941 he worked from the base at Halifax (*Seaborn*) on a roving commission with the A.M.Cs. of the Western Patrol, before returning to Britain in the former Cunarder *Alaunia*.

'As Evans' ships in the North Atlantic reduced in number, his suitability for work in such ships was again recognised by his appointment in October 1941 to the base-ship which was anchored permanently at Freetown, Sierra Leone, the very old former Union-Castle liner *Edinburgh Castle,* for sea-going duty with the A.M.Cs. operating in the South Atlantic in the South American Division.

'He joined the former Union-Castle liner *Carnarvon Castle* and stayed in her at the captain's request until March 1942 when he took passage to Cape Town to join, first the former Furness Withy liner *Queen of Bermuda* and the former Royal Mail *Alcantara*. After almost three years in A.M.Cs. he returned home to Britain and in due course joined the cruiser *Bermuda*, which became engaged in Russian convoy work. He ended his service on the staff of the admiral at Bombay. Few clergy who joined the Navy as Temporary Chaplains, R.N.V.R., can have seen more sea-time then Eric Evans. After all his voyaging he returned to parochial life in West Lancashire, and saw many arduous years as Rector of North Meols and Archdeacon of Warrington. He died on 25th of December 1977.'

When I arrived on Merseyside in 1961, Eric was a member of the Mersey Mission to Seamen's committee. He never talked about his wartime adventures, but proved to be a mine of information and a loyal friend.

Sometimes memories are brushed down and given an airing. Happily as the years passed, I joined the 'old and bold' on many festive occasions, when anecdotes were spun out to amuse and little was made of the suffering and hardship of wartime at sea. *Eaglet* was a great meeting place for 'swinging the lamp' and telling the tale.

After World War II the Mersey Division was reformed under Commander, later Captain E.N. Wood, DSC, VRD, RNR. A mine-sweeper was attached to the Division in 1947 as Sea Training Tender and named *H.M.S. Mersey*. She was to be replaced a number of times.

The R.N.V.R. wavy stripes were replaced by straight stripes with 'R' in curl in 1952. In 1958 the R.N.V.R was amalgamated into a new unified Royal Naval Reserve. I joined the Division as Chaplain in 1966, having been an Officiating Royal Navy Chaplain since 1961.

My memories of the 'floating hulk' are fond, but distant. The first duty of the Chaplain on Drill Night in *Eaglet* was to conduct prayers at Divisions. The drill deck was large and decidedly ill-lit. With the full ship's company assembled after much shuffling and restrained shouting, the order came ... "Off caps". Forward I went and for two minutes or so the stage was mine. It was a challenge. Quickly I realised that a piece from the Liverpool Echo was more likely to grab their attention than Cranmer's best prose. I knew that I had communicated when during my tour of the ship, my leg was pulled and the topic dissected. There was one bit of Cranmerian prose that never failed. Too often the lights invariably dimmed from fatigue and old-age. That was the cue for me to make use of the Evensong Collect, "Lighten our darkness we beseech Thee, O Lord ... " and there was always a fervent "Amen".

When in 1972 the old ship was declared redundant and we moved to the new shore Headquarters in Princes Dock, the official opening was conducted by Vice Admiral Sir Gilbert Stephenson. The Service took place in the Cathedral and from that distance I read the Dedication Prayer for the new *Eaglet*. The ship's company marched proudly through the City to our new home.

One of the privileges of being the R.N.R.Chaplain is that, even in retirement, I maintained my contact, not only with *Eaglet,* but with the various retired officers' associations and in particular with the Walker's Old Boys Association and the Submariners' Association and the Sea Urchins.

In my book, 'A Dog Collar in the Docks', I told the story of the death of my brother Petty Officer Frank Evans, in 1940 in the submarine *Thistle* and how in 1965 I came across Arthur Briard, who had missed that last fatal trip because of a severe cold. My story ended with the words ... 'We never saw or heard from him again.' Time has moved on and I would like to continue the tale.

In the spring of 1996 I was invited to a 'bit of a do' in the Hanover Hotel and was warned that I would have a surprise. It was a good evening as we ate 'babies heads' and dug our bread in the gravy. That dish was common food aboard the boats - a mixture of everything wrapped into a ball of suet! At the appropriate time I read to the company the story of my brother and Arthur Briard, and ended with the words, "We never saw or heard from him again ... until tonight!" There was Arthur, 76 years old with Parkinsons' Disease. We talked well.

A few months later in the August, the Parish Church of Liverpool was packed as I conducted his funeral and at last was able to tell the full story ... the story of Arthur Briard, submarine gun layer extraordinaire!

"Arthur joined the training ship, *Exmouth,* at the age of twelve and enlisted in the Royal Navy in 1935. He became a submariner in June 1939 and luck was with him when his first boat, *Triumph,* survived after striking a mine in the Skagerrak in December 1939. Next came *Thistle* which was sunk off Norway in April with no survivors. His next boat was *Trident* and for his part in the sinking of a U-boat on the 8th October 1940 he was mentioned in Despatches.

"In May 1942 he was drafted to the newly built P212 (later the *Sahib)* which was nearing completion in Birkenhead. The navigator was Lt. Commander I.E. Fraser, V.C., D.S.C., R.D., R.N.R., (*Conway* '36 - '38). The boat was armed with a 3" gun and he was the Gun Layer. One night an 1,500 ton Italian troopship was attacked, *Sahib's* gun knocked out two of her 4.7" guns and crippled the engine room before the Italian even opened fire! This was later described as one of the finest single gun actions of the war.

"For his part in the sinking of U301 and several supply ships he was awarded the DSM on 6 April 1943. The *Sahib* carried out many other gun actions, including an attack on an Italian armed tug, towing a barge on 22 April, 1943. In his own words, 'Out of 72 rounds fired, we scored 70 hits, 45 of them on the tug, which was so badly damaged that it was forced to beach itself and its tow'.

"On 24 April, 1943, following a successful torpedo attack on a heavily escorted Italian merchant ship, the *Sahib* was repeatedly attacked with a total of 51 depth-charges, but managed to surface before she sank. With the rest of the crew he was placed in captivity by the Italians. Taken to Germany for interrogation, he was returned to an Italian prisoner-of-war camp, where his immediate aim was to escape (in common with many other *Sahib* P.O.W.'s - 19 managed to escape and 14 successfully got back home).

"Arthur was involved with the digging of an escape tunnel when the camp was taken over by the Germans with the intention to move all the P.O.W.'s to Germany. On the morning of the camp evacuation he hid down the partly-dug tunnel, and covered up the entrance. After being concealed for a long hot day, he emerged and simply walked free out of the abandoned camp's open gate!

"The next couple of months he spent fighting alongside a band of partisans until in November 1944 he walked through the German lines to the advancing Allied 5th Army and freedom. His escape received a 'Mention in Despatches' on 12 June, 1945.

"After the war he remained a leading seaman until 1949 and then joined the Merchant Navy. Finally he 'swallowed the anchor' in 1973 ... a remarkable record of service. His last five voyages in the M.N. were in the *Atlantic Conveyor* which was lost in the Falklands affair.

"Arthur Briard was a typical seaman, completely unassuming, a quiet professional. It was a privilege to have known him."

When I retired as the R.N.R. chaplain, my successor was the Reverend John Strettle Williams. He is much loved on Merseyside. Most families have nautical connections and the Padre is always accepted by them.

As I write, plans are in being and the foundations in place for a move from Princes Dock to make way for a commercial development and the new home is alongside Harry Ramsden's Fish and Chips emporium in the South Docks. As one wag put it ... "At least they can save a dollar or two on the galley!" The new building ... *H.M.S .Eaglet* ...will house not only the Royal Naval Reserve, but the Royal Marines from Birkenhead and the Sea Cadets.

Times ever change; the work continues.

18.
Summerlands and the Ocean Club

'A time of war, and a time of peace.'
Ecclesiastes

No story of Mersey Mariners can be complete without some information about the Liverpool Seamen's Welfare Centre and Summerlands and the Ocean Club. However, when I came to Liverpool, the Ocean Club had been long closed.

It was at the height of the Second World War, when the Battle of the Atlantic was taking its deadly toll of British merchant ships and seamen, that the Liverpool Seamen's Welfare Centre was formed.

John Booth was chairman and with M.R.B. Paul, the Liverpool seamen's welfare officer, he formed a committee of seven, drawn from all sides of the industry.

The Council of Management believed that, in view of the ever increasing number of seafarers passing through Liverpool, which had assumed the status of the premier port of the United Kingdom, some form of welfare centre to cater for their needs while their vessels were in the port was an absolute necessity.

With the backing of King George's Fund for Sailors, shipowners, and other interested bodies, the Ocean Club, Lord Streeet, in the centre of Liverpool was opened in October, 1942 by Her Royal Highness the Duchess of Kent, and was an immediate success, soon becoming known in every port of the free maritime world.

245

Fifty years on, I still meet people who remember with immense pleasure all the fun of that Ocean Club, when men fresh from the Atlantic were able to unwind and share the normality of Liverpool ... in spite of the bombs, the shattered buildings and the black-out. Wilfred Patterson, who was responsible for so much of that activity and who later became the General Secretary of the Liverpool Seamen's Welfare Centre, is still with us in 1997, aged ninety. They were demanding days for the people of Liverpool.

Wilfred Patterson retired in 1970 and he was succeeded by Les Ridyard. The work continued, but the need was diminishing as the shipping industry was dramatically moving to foreign flags and foreign crews. The Centre closed in 1977 and Les Ridyard became the Secretary of the Liverpool Sailors' Home Trust, the local agent for the Shipwrecked Mariners' Society and Secretary for Indefatigable. He was a busy man.

The Liverpool Seamens' Welfare Centre was situated in Corinthian Buildings in South Castle Street, adjacent to the Queen Victoria monument. When I started my ministry in Liverpool in 1961, Wilf Patterson was not only responsible for the Welfare Centre, but also acted as the local secretary for the Merchant Navy Welfare Board. The local committee of that organisation comprised all the heads of the voluntary societies involved with the care of the seafarer on Merseyside, together with representatives from the unions and the ship-owners, the port police and the medical doctors. We all shared information and aimed to work as a team. It was much more than a committee with a set agenda; its real value was to be a useful sounding board for ideas and a gathering of friends, all with a concern for the well-being of the seafarer.

At this distance from those dark days, it is hard to convey the pressures and conditions under which the merchant seamen had to survive. I find the list of contents in the average ship's medical chest in 1939 less than encouraging. ' ... a few rolls of bandages, a bottle of iodine, Black Draught for constipation, Cough Linctus, tins of Stabichlor for purifying doubtful 'fresh water', jars of zinc ointment for scratches and abrasions, a jar of mercurial ointment for crabs, aspirin, toothache tincture and a couple of lances for boils.' No wonder the book, which was provided to give medical advice, actually had a last page with 'A Form of Burial at Sea'!

It was a battle to the end. On the last day of the war U-2336 sank the Norwegian steamer, *Sneland*, (1,791 tons) and the British freighter, *Avondale Park* (2,878 tons) off the Firth of Forth on the east coast of Scotland. U-1023 sighted a Norwegian minesweeper off Lymme Bay on the south coast of England and sank her. No wonder the men of the Merchant Navy never forget ... seamen burning and choking in oil, sailors instantly freezing to death in Arctic waters, flashing explosions as ships were blown to pieces! We are the people who forget.

The Battle of the Atlantic was waged every day of the war years and it quickly became apparent to the Council of the Centre that something more was needed than simply a club in the city where seafarers could relax in their off-duty hours. Considerable numbers of men were being laid off for varying periods through illness, accident or injury. All of this was the result of the strain of being attacked by bomb, shell, torpedo and gunfire, of having their ships sunk under them, spending many days in open boats and all the other rigours of the war at sea. The Council took the view that what was really needed was a quiet rest centre, somewhere out in the country, away from ships and ports, where Merchant Navy personnel in need of a recuperative holiday could be sent to forget their war experiences.

Winston Churchill wrote these words after the war.

> 'Battles might be won or lost, enterprises succeed or miscarry, territories might be gained or quitted, but dominating all our power to carry on the war, or even keep ourselves alive, was our mastery of the ocean routes and the free approach and entry to our ports ... the only thing that ever really frightened me during the war was the U-boat peril.'

Over fifty years later it is not easy for the majority of people to understand the nature of the men in the Merchant Navy. At this distance from the events, I still wonder at the courage of men who escaped the horrors and dangers of a tanker being torpedoed in the middle of the Atlantic, then reporting to the Shipping Federation for yet another trip in tankers. Men such as these were the unsung heroes without whom the war would have been lost in a matter of months. As you walked the streets in wartime you might just spot the small, insignificant metal M.N. badge in the lapel. They wore no uniform and were too often ignored. I once asked such a man to speak of his memories.

> "Nothing really", he replied. I pressed him further.

> "Well, two things. First, the voice of people in the streets grumbling about shortages in the shops ... and then the cries of seamen in the water at night and we could not pick them up."

This was typical of a Merchant Navy man!

One such person was Captain Edward John Tucker, who became a good friend of mine, but I never heard his story until I was privileged in January 1997 to conduct his funeral. His wife, Dorothy, has allowed me to recall the events of the war years. Eddie was born in 1920 at Nevis in Alberta, Canada. His childhood was tough and, at the age of seventeen, he came to England to find work and a better way of life. So he went to sea on deck with Blue Funnel. In 1939 he joined Anglo-Saxon Petroleum (Shell). With war around the corner it was not a good time to become a tanker seaman.

When Liverpool was being bombed and set on fire, Eddie was sitting in his tanker at the Dingle Oil jetty with too close a grandstand view of the pyrotechnics. His luck ran out when in March 1941 the *Simnia* was sunk off the Azores, but Eddie was a survivor. The Germans transferred him to a prison ship and he was taken ashore at La Rochelle.

Many months after Eddie's funeral, I read his account of the events of the 15th March, 1941.

'The *Simnia* left Liverpool on March 5th, in ballast for Curacao and on the 13th March orders were received from the Commodore for the convoy to disperse. We therefore shaped a course under the Master's orders and two days later, on the 15th March, we contacted a Norwegian tanker that had also been in the same convoy as ourselves. She passed us and when some distance ahead it was observed that she had altered course 180 degrees and was approaching us on an opposite course, eventually passing astern.

'At this time, which was about 1550 hours, the two masts of a vessel were sighted on the horizon, about two points on the port bow. I was keeping gun watch on the 4" L.A. gun and about twenty minutes after sighting the two masts it was observed that the masts were bearing off the port quarter, indicating that there had been an appreciable alteration of course on the part of the *Simnia*. We loaded the gun in readiness for action but received orders from the bridge not to fire until receiving instructions to do so; apparently the Master was still uncertain as to whether the strange vessel was friendly or otherwise.

'Soon after the *Simnia* had altered course the vessel, which turned out to be the *Gneisnau*, opened fire, firing six rounds in rapid succession; the first and second rounds wide of the target but the four remaining shots struck the vessel in way of the stern, the last shell wrecked the steering engine with the consequence that the *Simnia* became unmanageable, thereupon the Master gave orders to abandon ship.

'One shot had destroyed the port after lifeboat and also when lowering the starboard amidships boat the forward davit collapsed, precipitating the boat into the water, where the falls were cut adrift. Difficulty was also experienced in launching the starboard after boat. As far as I can recollect the sheaves in the blocks became seized up and although oil was poured over the sheaves they failed to function. However, the boat was eventually water borne and was released by cutting the falls. The port boat amidships was successfully launched. The starboard amidships boat being empty a few men were transferred into it from the starboard after boat, which was overloaded.

'By this time the *Gneisnau* had closed the distance to within 100 yards of the *Simnia* when we were ordered to board the *Gneisnau*. This was safely carried out, and soon after boarding, the *Gneisnau* opened fire on the *Simnia* with her 5.9 guns, firing probably 14 salvos into the ship. I saw the *Simnia* practically on the point of sinking when the *Gneisnau* altered course obstructing my view, but I was told that she quickly sank.

'The Chief Engineer was injured by shell splinters when a shot struck the vicinity of the engine room. His injuries were not serious although he lost the top of the index finger of his left hand and also had numerous small shell splinters about the body, which caused him considerable pain.

'The Chief Cook, Second Cook and Messroom boy were killed on board, the Chief Engineer carrying the latter from his room up on to the boat deck where he died. The Chief Steward received injuries to his heel from shell splinters, and was unable to walk, and was assisted to the boat by two of his Chinese shipmates. His injuries must have been severe as some time elapsed before recovery.

'We were on the *Gneisnau* for about four days, when we were transferred to a prison ship where we remained for a further four days until being landed at La Rochelle. On arrival at La Rochelle we were taken to a vacated dance hall in La Pallice where we spent the night, and next morning were transferred by cattle truck to Stalag 221 in the neighbourhood of Bordeaux. We remained at this prison camp for about six days pending arrangements being made for our transfer to Stalag 10 B in Germany. When I left Germany, as far as I know the staff and crew of the *Simnia* were in good health.

'Captain Anderson was not transferred from the *Gneisnau* at the same time as the rest of us, but was eventually landed at Brest and brought to the same prison camp.

'I met two army gunners on board *Gneisnau* and they told me they were ex the *San Casimiro* and that the Captain was also on board. The Army gunners were landed at the same time as myself but I understand that the Captain of the *San Casimiro* was landed at Brest with Captain Anderson.

'The names of the two gunners were Wadcock and Gibbons.

'During the short time I was on board the *Gneisnau*, she sank nine vessels.'

This statement was dated 3rd August, 1943.

So along with many others Eddie was bundled into a cattle truck with no food or water and set out for an unknown destination. After some days, the train arrived at Bremerhaven and a prisoner-of-war camp. However, the men of the Merchant Navy were regarded as non-combatant civilians and were not acceptable in the normal camps. So, Eddie's first task was to help build a Merchant Navy Camp. He was to remain there for two years and used his time studying under the guidance of his fellow seafarers.

Without any warning or any information, one day Eddie was picked with a number of other men and placed in covered trucks for a journey across Germany. At night they were allowed off the lorries and given water. They had no idea of where they were heading or why. It was June 1943. A few days later they emerged, to their immense surprise, in Lisbon. He had been selected for a 'rank for rank, age for age' exchange and was to be sent back to England. So Eddie boarded the *Samaria*, hardly believing his good fortune.

Safely home he was granted four weeks 'survivor leave'! Apparently, his two years in the prisoner of war camp were irrelevant. Then it was back to sea on tankers for the rest of the war. Just another Merchant Navy man! I was privileged to be his friend.

I first met Tim McCoy early in 1962 when he walked into Kingston House. Tim was in trouble and his shipmates had advised, "Go see the padre!" He had just been made redundant by the Dock Board, having served for some years in the dredger, *Hilbre*. We talked for a long time and it resulted in a friendship which has well survived to this very day. Tim once wrote a song about 'Padre Evans and his Mission by the sea'. It was recorded in the famous Cavern, but we sadly never made the charts!

In March 1941, Tim crossed on the ferry for an interview with the Master of the Harrison ship, *S.S. Logician*. He was bemused to find the deck cargo was a mixture of army tanks, aircraft and ammunition boxes. Captain Jones took him on as a coal-trimmer in the boiler-room.

Back home he excitedly told his dad that he was starting next morning in a Harrison boat.

"That's a hungry so-and-so of a company, son; two of fat and one of lean."

POW's in Malug and Milug. Eddie in second middle row.

"I've got to go, dad."

For five days he crossed the river and each morning his mother sent him off with the same words.

"Bless yourself ... and your dinner will be in the oven, son."

At the end of the fifth day he was going over the side when he was stopped by the mate. By seven that night they were out in the river and leaving Liverpool 'scupper-deep with amunition'. Four years were to pass before he was home for that dinner.

The ship called to coal in Freetown, next came Durban and finally via the Suez Canal she arrived off Crete. It was the second week of May and they were discharging ammunition when a German Stuka neatly dropped a bomb alongside the funnel (that's where the well-worn comment 'two of fat and one of lean' comes from). Tim regained consciousness in the General Hospital ashore. A week later the Germans 'dropped' in and Tim was a prisoner of war.

P.O.W Camp at Sanbostell

The prison ship, *Santa Catherina,* deposited them in a gaol at Salonika, before an interminable train journey across Europe ended in Austria at Sanbostell. There Tim found some two thousand Russian prisoners and about fifty Merchant Navy men. After about eight months the Russians were dying of typhus and it was found that they were keeping the bodies in order to claim their rations. The merchant men, including about fifty Liverpool seamen, volunteered to build their own camp. This was in Malag und Milug Nord, between Bremen and Hamburg in Germany. They survived by farming and growing their own food; a chapel was built and eventually Canadian food parcels were delivered.

This was the same camp where Eddie Tucker off the *Simnia* was living. Many Liverpool men were there and amongst them was the Second Mate of the *Simnia,* Tom Ferryman. Tom helped with the instruction classes and was in time to become a lecturer in the Nautical College in Liverpool. The Churchill Foundation was able to supply the camp with the necessary books and this was never forgotten.

Near the end of the war, they painted large letters, M.N., on the roof and an allied plane dropped a message, 'We know you are there'. Tim recalls that the Welsh Regiment came down the road and he well remembers eating a loaf of Hovis all to himself!

The next day they were flown to Belgium and back to England where they kissed the ground and ate for two days. Back home in Liverpool, Tim took a taxi to the Dingle and there in Hill Street were the flags ... 'Welcome Home, Son.'

I am proud to count Tim as a friend.

It was for this calibre of seafarer that the Council of the Liverpool Seamen's Welfare Centre began examining the prospects of acquiring suitable premises, and after a considerable search, Summerlands House and estate were offered and purchased through a gift made by King George's Fund for Sailors.

When I visited Summerlands, we travelled from Liverpool to the mansion, which was about four miles from Kendal in Westmoreland - the Gateway to the English Lakes - where it stood in an estate of some 55 acres. But all this did not come into being quickly.

It was decided to make as little alteration to the house as possible, and after the completion of the preliminary work, Summerlands was officially opened on September 23rd, 1944 by Mr. George Tomlinson, M.P., J.P., then Joint Parliamentary Secretary to the Minister of Labour and National Service. Grants for its subsequent developments were made by British Shipowners, King George's Fund for Sailors, the Merchant Navy Comforts Service and many others.

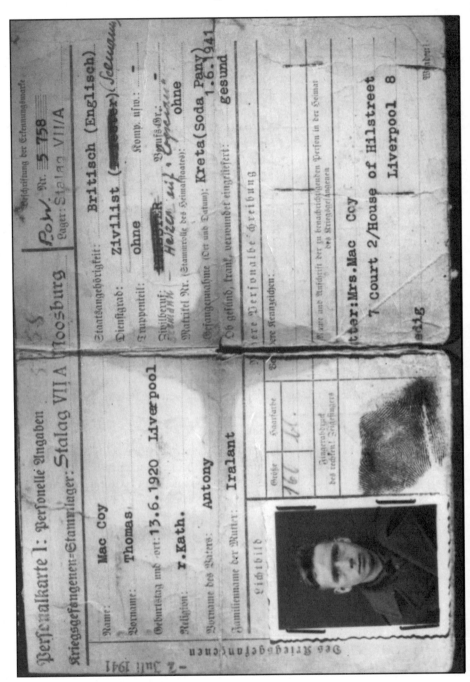

In the initial stages, Summerlands was run purely on the basis of a guest house where seafarers, having completed their medical treatment, could stay for a fortnight or so before rejoining their ships to return to sea. When you entered the house, there was a spacious hall with a large fire-place; carved in the stone were the words ... 'When friends meet, hearts warm'. It was a good start.

As a result of their experience with various individual cases, it became clear to the Council that quite a number of personnel who came to the centre were disabled to such an extent that they would never be in a position to return to sea again. Something had to be done to rehabilitate these men. There was to be an answer.

Workshops were opened in April, 1945, in the old stables of Summerlands, and disabled men, unfit to return to sea, were given work making children's cots. Later, modern wood-working machinery was set up and the workshops expanded to create an extensive factory manufacturing a wide variety of furniture for the home.

Although the strain of war-time life at sea no longer existed, the Council of the Liverpool Seamen's Welfare Centre was fully aware of the fact that there would always be men in need of a recuperative holiday as a result of illness or accident and that there would be many unfit for further seagoing service. It was a right decision.

Summerlands had accommodation for 36 men. There was no regimentation. The house was fully licensed and operated like any first class hotel. It had become a working estate with cattle and pigs and hens and an extensive market garden and horticultural section. This was a new world for a seafarer.

A disabled man worked for a probationary month and then underwent nine months training. There were three main departments ... the machine section, the assembly section and the polishing department. Wages were paid at the normal union rates. At the end of his time contact was made with the Resettlement Officer of his home town, so that assistance was given with the placement into local furniture factories. The system worked.

Some men were invited to remain at Summerlands, if they wished, and houses were built on the estate for the married men. Over thirty houses and bungalows were eventually provided and this venture was called Summerlands Village.

The factory was to produce furniture of the highest quality ... dining suites, dining tables, bookcases, television tables, occasional furniture and a whole range of kitchen furniture. Everything was on sale in stores throughout the country. It was a thriving business.

The Workshops

Sadly, in the late seventies the economic and social atmosphere changed. The Convalescent Home closed in 1977 and the factory was closed in 1980. As the need for the facilities in the Summerlands House was over, it became obvious that the work of the Liverpool Seamen's Welfare Centre was at an end. The House in the Lakes and the Centre in Liverpool were no longer needed.

Arrangements were made to ensure the future of the residents and to safeguard their homes in Summerlands Village. It was a sad end, but inevitable. No longer was there a need for rehabilitation centres as the numbers of men employed in the Merchant Navy plummeted.

I was to make a number of visits to talk to the residents in order to ensure that they would not be uprooted because of the closure. Happily, the properties were bought by the local authority and the little community survives to the present day.

19.
The Chinese Seafarers

'But there is neither East nor West,
Border nor Breed, nor Birth,
When two strong men stand face to face,
though they come from the ends of the earth!'

Kipling

It is no surprise to find that Chinese seafarers in the last century were present in Liverpool in great numbers and that this led almost by chance to the formation of an 'unorganised' Chinese community.

When the East India Company's Charter was revised and the monopoly broken, it opened trade, first with India in 1813, and then with China in 1833. The pioneer ship, *Symmetry*, was sent from Liverpool to Canton and at the end of 1834 she returned with an assorted cargo. This was to trigger an enormous commercial empire.

The Ocean Steamship Company (renamed Ocean Transport & Trading Ltd. in January 1973) was formed by Alfred Holt and his brother Philip. It was registered on 11th January, 1865. The first ship, *Agamemnon*, sailed on her maiden voyage to China on 19th April, 1866, to be followed by *Ajax* and *Achilles* and thus establishing a long tradition of trade with the Far East. It was in 1893 that the Company first employed Chinese seamen.

Alfred Holt had been trained as a railway engineer with special knowledge of steam propulsion. As a result of his work, the steam-ship was to prove, not only profitable, but with the opening of coaling stations, to be a great advance on the sailing ships.

William Laird had opened an iron-works in Birkenhead in 1824; four years later with his son, John, he built the first iron ship, a 60-foot lighter for the Irish Inland Steam Navigation Company. The first screw-driven vessel was the *Robert F. Stockton*, built in 1838. Other ships quickly followed. Lamport and Holt in co-operation with James Moss and Company used small, iron, steam ships to carry cargo from the Eastern Mediterranean. The first iron ship to cross the Atlantic was the *City of Glasgow*, which was owned by the Liverpool, New York and Philadelphia Steam Ship Company, founded by William Inman. Towards the end of the 1850's, the Cunard Company were planning iron, screw-driven ships. In the same way, Harrisons were extending their coastal European services and in 1866 inaugurated a Liverpool-New Orleans service. Pacific Steam Navigation Company traded with the western coast of South America.

There were problems. Coaling restricted the length of voyages. The safety of the engines and also the pressure required in the boilers were yet to be mastered. The screw propeller was imperfect because of the low tensile strength of cast iron. Alfred Holt with his knowledge as a railway engineer was well placed to solve most of these difficulties.

So Holt's opened their Far-Eastern service with three ships ... *Agamemnon, Ajax* and *Achilles*. This was the Ocean Steam Ship Company.

By the end of the 1860's, Liverpool ships with steam and iron were trading with the five continents. The Liverpool docks and warehouses were creating untold wealth.

It was Alfred Holt who introduced steel girders to support the upper deck of a ship. This did away with the rows of pillars in the hold and increased the carrying capacity of vessels. Costs of voyages were drastically cut and the size of vessels soon increased to some 10,000 tons deadweight.

The result of all this endeavour inevitably led to the creation of Liverpool's Chinese community as seamen left their ships to find work ashore. Most were probably 'Blue Funnel' men. They quickly settled in Liverpool; many worked as laundrymen or in boarding houses and some were to open grocer shops selling Chinese goods. Many were eventually to receive Home Office permission, not only to work but to marry English girls.

Captain Edward Tupper in his book, 'Seamen's Torch', explains the way in which so many Chinese seafarers came to this country. Tupper was the National Organiser for the National Sailors' and Firemen's Union (later the National Union of Seamen) and along with Havelock Wilson was in constant touch with the Government during the first World War. He was alarmed at the numbers of Chinese entering the British Mercantile Marine via Hong Kong. As long as they spent twenty-four hours in that British

Colony and passed the language test, they were accepted. In his book he describes that language test.

"Where are you from?"
"Hong Kong." (That made him British!)
"What are you?"
"Fireman."
"Where do you live?"
"Cardiffi."

'That was the language test. On the face of it, it did not prove much; I knew it didn't prove anything. I bullied the Board of Trade shipping master, and I asked the questions after a dozen or so had given the same replies.

"What are you?"
"Hong Kong."
"Where do you live?"
"Fireman."
"Where are you from?"
"Cardiffi."

As a result of this, questions were asked in the House of Commons and the official answer was that they had an 'indisputable and inviolate right to serve in the British Mercantile Marine'.

Incidentally, in 1989 we picked up from the airport fourteen 'seamen' from the Maldive Islands and after feeding them in the Mission, we placed them aboard a foreign ship. I discovered that they had no experience of seafaring! Times do not change.

By the end of the First World War there were over 6,000 Chinese living in Liverpool. Most lived in the Pitt Street, Great George Square, and the Nelson Street areas. This became our 'Chinatown' and at the end of the twentieth century we are busy restoring Chinese road signs and producing an oriental atmosphere for the millenium!

During the 1939 - 1945 war the Chinese Seamen's Reserve Pool was established in Liverpool, and the Liner Section was administered by Alfred Holt & Co. for the Ministry of War Transport. For this purpose the Company was faced with the huge task of recruiting large numbers of Chinese seamen and arranging their passages to the U.K. Many were brought from Bombay and Calcutta in the early 1940's. There were usually about 2,000 men registered in the pool at any time, and men from the pool were supplied to any shipping company needing them for ships sailing from the U.K.. Hostels were opened in Liverpool to accommodate the seamen while they were ashore. These hostels were managed by independent persons, but the seamen's welfare and the general running of the boarding houses were supervised by Alfred Holt & Company, who also arranged travel from Liverpool to the ports where the men were required.

George Musk in his excellent history of Canadian Pacific writes about the Chinese crews.

'At the beginning of the war there was considerable trouble with the Chinese crew. They raised objections to sailing in a war zone and demanded double pay. They also held the conviction that soldiering was the lowest type of employment and they would 'lose face' serving the troops. More important perhaps was the lose of 'cumshaw', as the officers had batmen who would serve their morning tea! This led to an amusing situation. Morning tea was usually served at seven o'clock. The first day out the Chinese bedroom boys anticipated the batmen by five minutes. Next day the batmen started earlier, so the stewards stepped up by another five minutes. Eventually, some people found themselves being wakened at 5.30 with a most unwelcome cup of tea.'

After the war, by arrangement with the British Shipping Federation and the National Union of Seamen, Blue Funnel employed its own pool of Liverpool domiciled seamen for service on board ships in the U.K and Home Trade waters.

The Company also continued to help in maintaining two boarding houses for the Chinese seafarers, and a Chinese Seamen's Social Centre, attached to one of the boarding houses in Nile Street, was opened and proved to be a popular meeting place. The Chinese crew department extended its offices over 'The Nook', a public house, but was in 1970 merged into India Buildings, the head-quarters of the Holt Company and following a marked reduction in the number of seamen needing shore accomodation the Company ceased to be financially interested at the end of 1969 in the boarding houses.

As a result of changing patterns of trade and a decrease in the number of ships using the port of Liverpool the Company's pool of locally domiciled Chinese seafarers was disbanded at the end of July, 1972.

Liverpool's Chinatown suffered badly during the bombing in 1940-41 as did most of the inner city and dock districts. After the war, the pattern of Chinese life changed. The old image of opium dens and gambling haunts faded, all to be replaced with modern Chinese restaurants. Today all this is taken as normal as we buy instant and take-away Chinese food. This is a long way from 1904 when Ping-Long was hanged for shooting Co-Hing in a quarrel, arising from a gambling dispute.

There had been a Chinese Seamen's Welfare Centre in Bedford Street from 1917 to 1943. Whilst other organisations were caring for seafarers of all nations, the Chinese seamen rarely visited our establishments and it was assumed by us that they were absorbed into the local Chinese community. However, my experience was that most foreign residents very quickly acquired a life-style so different from their homeland that they tended to disassociate themselves from visiting seamen. This fact was recognised in 1961.

With the support of the Merchant Navy Welfare Board and of Blue Funnel, a new Centre was opened. One Chinese put it this way.

'We need a Centre ... for Chinese seamen who come into this seaport, strangers in a strange land; how they long for a place ... to have a rest and refreshment while they are ashore.'

I had been in Liverpool just three months when Stewart MacTier of Alfred Holt declared open the Centre in Rathbone Street, Liverpool 1, and the new work began. The Warden was the Reverend James Ma. James became a friend.

James produced a booklet with a little of his story.

'Like all the other Chinese people, we have an historic background of Confucianism, Taoism, and Buddhism; all of my people worship their ancestors. Believe me, when a Chinese is converted to Christ, it is indeed a great miracle.

'The outbreak of the Sino-Japanese war had its effect upon my native town as well as upon many other towns and cities in China. Alone, I fled for my life to Kwelin, Kwangsi province. Thereafter, through love for my country, I joined the Chinese Expeditionary Army and went to Calcutta, India, where I completed the radio system training courses. In the summer of 1945 a few months before the surrender of Japan, I returned to Chungking, the war-time capital of China. The Japanese were making their final attacks by means of continuous bombing raids of that mountainous city. A small bomb descended upon my position and though it was not exploded it cut the man who was next to me in two pieces. People found me amongst the dead bodies; there were just a few wounds on one side of my body, but most damage was inside. I lost my memory with the heavy shock'

Slowly James recovered and in a sanitorium became a Christian ... it changed his life.

'Several years later, in 1948, I was baptized in the Lutheran Church in Hankow, the central city of China. At the time I was twenty-one years old and ended my service as a radio officer in the army. As an ex-serviceman I then attended Wuhan University to finish my Chinese Classic studies.'

James next lived in Hong Kong (1949 - 1957) and spent four years in the Lutheran Theological seminary. He became the joint editor of a magazine called, 'Light and Salt Periodical'. One of the subscribers was Miss Gladys Aylward and he discovered that she had worked in China but had returned home to Liverpool in 1948. She became famous as the 'small woman' in the film 'The Inn of the Sixth Happiness'. Gladys on a visit to Hong Kong in 1956 encouraged James to come to Liverpool to work amongst the Chinese population.

Arriving in Liverpool on 2nd February, 1959 James lodged in the Y.M.C.A. and joined in the worship there.

'Later on by kind permission of the Mersey Mission to Seamen, from March 8th, 1959, our services have been held in the Chapel of Kingston House. On week-days, we also use one or two rooms of Kingson House for meetings.'

Life was not easy as he had no real income and depended upon the kindness of his growing circle of friends and supporters. In this way he survived for two years. His life changed when the Chinese Seamen's Centre opened on April 11th, 1961.

The Centre consisted of a ground floor only and was not very big. However, it functioned well as a social meeting place and was very comfortable. Part of the objective was to help the seamen with English lessons and also an understanding of the laws of this country. Television was still a novelty and helped with the language barrier. Another attraction was the provision of Chinese newspapers and literature.

Of great interest to me was the catering area. Chinese food was still a novelty and I was a willing pupil! It seemed to be a happy place, but I always felt that the Chinese had a great ability to produce an atmosphere of calm and to accept all that you had to say, whilst reserving their thoughts lest they caused offence.

I joined occasionally in their Christian worship. The chapel was always full! Sadly after a comparitively short time the centre closed and James Ma left Liverpool. His departure was so sudden that I failed to make further contact with him

The Chinese Cultural Revoltion created problems for the seafarer. A friend, Ralph Owen, told me that most of the men belonged to the Hong Kong Seamen's Union and they tried to bring the U.K ships to a stop in July, 1967, but the men were very loyal to the Company and not one of Blue Funnel or Glen Line ships failed to sail on time. Some of the crews were militant, yet always remained polite and courteous in the negotiations. Many of the Chinese-owned ships in Liverpool made it quite clear that we were not welcome on board and some even pulled up their gangways at the end of the day 'lest they be contaminated by the capitalist West'! I used to carry a small, yellow book, 'The Sayings of Chairman Jesus', and raised many a smile as I went about my business! My own observations were that the conditions of employment and certainly the wages were much superior on the British ships and I was not surprised that the men remained loyal to their companies.

One of my contacts was with the Liverpool Chinese Gospel Mission which was situated between the Joy Hong restaurant and the Seeyep Chinese old people's centre in Nelson Street. It was a small congregation sitting on old cinema seats in a converted drinking bar of a former political club which had supported Nationalist China. The man in charge was Mr Stephen Wong and he lived there with his wife and family. It was a friendly place. As you opened the door it rang a bell like a village store and there would be Mr Wong in his slippers, all smiles and welcoming.

Mr Wong would talk of his youth, running away from home, drunkeness and meeting with Gladys Aylward and, above all, his Bible. He had gone to a Bible College after dismissal from a Liverpool shipyard because he refused to work on Sundays.

An article in the Guardian told his story in the February 18th, 1969 edition.

'Mr Wong is 47 and has an English wife and four children. His wife started teaching recently. He has no income, but finds that money comes in, sometimes from people he has never met. "Someone in New Zealand heard about us, and sent a cheque." A man who heard that he and others had visited the Chinese on foot gave him a new van. It is now nine years old and still in use. Recently a man gave him a washing machine.'

As a result of my friendship, the Chinese children used to come to our chapel in Kingston House on a Sunday afternoon for Sunday School. They were a lively and colourful bundle. Just occasionally I was asked to speak and the children were all eyes and wonderment, although I suspect that they had no understanding and were too polite to ignore me. It was fun. Many of their fathers were seafarers and I felt that they were there by right.

With hindsight I realise that my contact with the serving Chinese seafarer was minimal and as he made no real use of our clubs and facilities, there was no way in which we could exchange our thoughts. He was, of course, used as cheap labour and in the modern world has been superceded by even cheaper labour.

20.
The M.M.S.A. Story

The conditions in the British Mercantile Marine throughout the first half of the 19th century were such a scandal that eventually the Government felt compelled to intervene. It was not before time as there were revolutionary developments in shipbuilding and in particular the introduction of steam propulsion at sea. In 1812 the 25-ton *Comet*, fitted with a four horse power engine, proved that steamboats could produce a regular service. In 1818 the first iron sailing ship was built, and in 1821 the first iron steamship. In 1839 the *Archimedes* became the first steamer to be fitted with a screw propeller.

All this development led to an increase in the numbers of vessels at sea and produced a heavy toll of accidents. The loss of life shocked the nation. In the three years between 1816 and 1818 the number of British lives lost at sea was 2,288; between 1833 and 1835 it was 2,682.

In 1836, a select committee was set up by the Government to investigate the cause of shipwrecks and its frank report resulted in the strongest of criticism. The major causes were listed ... the defective construction of ships, inadequate equipment, imperfect repairs, improper and excessive loading, bad design resulting from an unsatisfactory system of tonnage measurement, lack of adequate harbours and faultiness of charts. To all this was added the incompetence of masters and drunkenness among officers and crew.

Drastic remedial measures were recommended and the main proposal was that a Board be established to superintend and regulate the affairs of the

Mercantile Marine. Action was sadly very slow and, inevitably, another select committee was set up in 1843 to examine the causes of shipwrecks and produced an almost identical report.

In 1845 the Board of Trade, in co-operation with the Admiralty, Trinity House, and Lloyd's Register of Shipping established a voluntary system of examination for masters and mates. The passing of the Mercantile Marine Act of 1850 was to enable the Government to establish a Department of the Board of Trade charged with the general responsibility for the affairs of the Mercantile Marine. This was an important break-through and the consequences were far reaching. Examinations for masters and mates in foreign-going trade were made compulsory and there were to be formal inquiries into shipwrecks which could result in the cancelling or suspension of certificates. There was to be no appeal!

A meeting was called in Liverpool on the 3rd April, 1857 at the instigation of Ralph Brocklebank, a leading shipowner and Captain C.H.E. Judkins, of the American Royal Mail service. The objective was to discuss the arbitrary and oppresive powers vested in the Board of Trade. The meeting was well attended and feelings were strong.

It was agreed to petition Parliament. The first resolution expressed concern about the injustice of the courts and lack of impartiality, aggravated by denial of an appeal system against the Board of Trade's decisions. The second resolution was against the composition of the tribunals, suggesting that they should be representative of all concerned. Finally, it was unanimously decided that an association should be formed, to be called the Mercantile Marine Service Association (MMSA) with the primary purpose to

> 'take every legitimate step to elevate to their proper position the officers of the Merchant Navy, and to promote the interests of that service generally.'

In 1859, impressed by the need for a school to educate and train boys for sea service, the Council of the Association obtained from the Admiralty the loan of the frigate *Conway,* to be moored in the Mersey, off Rock Ferry. Four years later the granting of a charter of incorporation by Parliament enabled the Association to carry out its plans with purpose. Amongst these was 'the provision of refuges for aged, sick and worn-out officers of the Mercantile Marine.' This was the beginning of the three main streams of the Association's work - professional, educational and charitable - each complementary to but independent of the others.

With the full co-operation of the representatives of the port of Liverpool, the Association played an important part in shaping the Merchant Shipping

Amendment Act of 1862. Also steps were taken to establish a nautical school for those studying for the examinations for certificates of competency. Members of the Association were given free tuition but other candidates were required to pay a fee.

Another endeavour succeeded in 1880 when the right of appeal against the findings of official courts of inquiry was granted.

Shipowners, merchants and others interested in sea service proved to be so generous that the Association's funds could be spread on philanthropic work. In 1882 a large park on the banks of the Mersey was bequeathed to the Association. Almost immediately a number of villas were built to house aged and necessitous master mariners and their wives. A few months later a large donation from a Liverpool shipowner led to the foundation of a home for aged widowers and single men with past service in the Mercantile Marine and in 1906 a home for widows of seamen was erected.

Sadly many of the seagoing members felt that their professional interests were being compromised or not represented strongly enough. This feeling resulted in a breakaway movement and culminated in 1893 in the formation of a new society, the Imperial Merchant Service Guild, membership of which was restricted solely to certificated masters and officers of British nationality.

At this time there were five societies claiming to represent masters and officers in the United Kingdom, but within ten years the newly formed Guild could claim to be the largest by far and the most powerful with over 10,000 members. The MMSA continued its work as the two main bodies worked closely together. There was work to be done and, in particular, the courts of inquiry were steadily giving way to a more lenient and just feeling towards masters and officers.

There were matters of concern. The problems created by the crimps slowly disappeared as the manning of ships was controlled. Another problem was the ballasting of ships and a special committee of the House of Lords was appointed. No light load line was actually recommended, but valuable suggestions led to some improvement. Thought had to be given to the navigation of large vessels by uncertificated men, the carriage of dangerous goods in winter and the securing of better shipboard accommodation. Of primary importance was concern to safeguard the salaries and conditions of service of masters and officers.

The outbreak of the First World War obviously imposed a great strain on all seafarers and led to the formation of the National Maritime Board in 1917. This Board under the Ministry for Shipping regulated the conditions of service for British seafarers and was retained at the end of the war.

Unfortunately the cessation of hostilities was followed by a reversion to the old standards as the sacrifice of the seafarers was easily forgotten. The depression years led to the formation of another two officer's organisations. One quickly disappeared but the other, the Navigators' and General Insurance Company which was founded to bear the costs of an inquiry and to cover any consequent loss of earnings, was to evolve in 1928 into the Officers' (Merchant Navy) Federation. All the other unions were able to operate through this Federation and in 1933 it secured election to the National Maritime Board. Two years later the Navigating and Engineer Officers' Union was formed along conventional union lines and one of the most important developments was the introduction of the Merchant Navy Officers' Pension Fund in 1938.

The Second World War focused the real need for unity amongst the organisations claiming to represent the Merchant Navy officers and this resulted in 1942 in the MMSA accepting responsibility for masters serving in command.

In 1956 the Merchant Navy and Airline Officers' Association came into being and the Radio and Electronic Officers' Union was formed in 1967. In May, 1970 the Rochdale Report suggested that 'it would be in the best interests of all Merchant Navy officers for the MMSA, MNAOA and REOU to merge as soon as possible'. The Mercantile Marine Association had been formed in 1857 and over the years had incorporated the Mercantile Marine Trawlers Association (1920), the Harbour and Dockmasters Association of the U.K. (1920), the Sunderland British Shipmasters and Officers Protection Society and the Imperial Merchant Service Guild (1925). The Merchant Navy and Airline Officers Association had been founded in 1956 by the 'coming together' of the Marine Engineers Union (1887), the Marine Engineers Association (1899), the Navigators Insurance Company (1921), the Navigating and Engineer Officers Union (1935) and the Grimsby Trawler Officers Guild (1952). The Radio and Electronic Officers Union had emerged in 1967 from the Association of Wireless Teleraphists (1912), the Cable Telegraph Operators Association (1921), the Association of Wireless and Cable Telegraphists (1921) and the Cable Staffs Association (1926).

All of this was finally merged in 1985 into the National Union of Marine, Aviation and Shipping Transport Officers ... NUMAST. It had been a long and complicated journey. Today NUMAST cares for over 18,000 serving officers, although it must be noted that the vast majority are sailing under foreign flags. The international scene is monitored by the International Maritime Organisation and has authority to inspect and control the sailing of all vessels.

Liverpool can boast of many 'firsts' and one of the latest additions to the list in the maritime world must be the founding of the Nautical Institute. The idea was mooted by Captain 'Ticky' Malins of the Marine Society in the Spring of 1969 and the first action was determined by Captain Frank Main, Head of the Navigation Department of the Liverpool Polytechnic (formerly the Regional College of Technology, Byrom Street) and the late Captain Rob Smith, Pilot Superintendent, Mersey Docks and Harbour Board.

That action was to call a meeting in Byrom Street on the 28th April, 1969 with 32 Master Mariners and 6 other mariners. Captain Main outlined the need for a professional body and indicated that the Marine Society had 'floated' the idea for some two years. Other meetings followed and Captain Len Holder was appointed as the local secretary and all this led to a meeting at Trinity House, London, on Wednesday 10 December, 1969 concerning 'The Establishment of a Nautical Professional Body'. The aim was 'to promote high standards of nautical competence and knowledge'. Today there are some 6,000 members worldwide and there are 34 branches around the world with more planned. The Nautical Institute has become a powerful advocate for excellency in the nautical world.

In the last century the MMSA had been facing dire problems. To understand the MMSA Story is to comprehend the privation, distress and injuries suffered by the seafarer. The Mariners' Park Estate in Wallasey was the response to that understanding and the present residential complex with its various facilities and the associated funds is the result of successive appeals and the generosity of many benefactors.

The first of the identified needs was fulfilled when Mr. William Cliff, a merchant and benefactor, undertook to provide a large sum of money to defray the cost of a home. The Liverpool Home for Aged Mariners, later known as Cliff House, was in memory of his daughter, Rosa Webster and the foundation stone was laid by Mrs. William Cliff on the 16th October, 1880. The bands of the 1st Cheshire Engineers and of the training ship, *Indefatigable,* were there. The Home was opened on the 16th December, 1882, by His Royal Highness the Duke of Edinburgh. The MMSA's magazine, Reporter (this chapter is totally indebted to it!) actually describes the day in detail and covers forty pages. The building was in the 'grand' style and with a clear height of 14 feet in the rooms defied any attempt at heating and modernisation.

In the early days the residents wore coarse linen aprons to protect their uniforms and happily porridge and endless stew were phased out. At first uniforms were worn and each man received a tally on which his name and admission number were engraved for identification purposes, and 'to assist the local constabulary in their task of those found blowing for tugs, usually

Cliff House

Gibson House

after 10 p.m., back into sheltered waters.' By popular demand uniform caps gave way to grey felt trilby hats but the traditional blue raincoats were retained, worn over uniforms when outside. Eventually the uniform was abandoned and no longer did it afford an entrance fee and a free glass or two in the local hostelries.

During the last war the residents were evacuated to Llanwrst in the Conway valley and many of the Association's records were lost. Following the introduction of the Welfare State the demands changed, along with the need to modernise the building. Eventually it became evident that Cliff House could not continue and on the 31st August, 1977, the building was vacated and the residents were housed in Gibson House.

During the 95 years of Cliff House, 1,113 seafarers were residents. My memories during my visits are of a magnificent building and the friendliness of the staff and the improbable tales of the seafarers. In time I realised that most of the stories were true, although some of the waves had grown in the telling. It was demolished in 1981.

A few months prior to the completion of Cliff House, on 10th January, 1882, Mrs.G.W. Slack opened the first two cottage homes, which had been erected and endowed in memory of her husband. These remained until 1977.

Further land on the northern boundary was purchased in 1900 including Manor House which became the infirmary wing of Cliff House. This land enabled the estate to evolve to its present size. A generous donation by Andrew Gibson meant that MMSA could build in 1906 a home to accommodate widows and naturally it was called Gibson House. It is a fine building and is fully occupied.

Today in Mariners' Park Estate there are 38 bungalows, 44 flats, 7 houses plus 24 flats and accommodation for visitors in Gibson House. Over the years much of the finance has come from King George's Fund for Sailors, I.T.F., the Seamens' Hospital Society, other nautical charities, many shipping companies and private individuals.

My wife and I were very grateful when in the early 1980's we had closed Kingston House, the headquarters of the Mersey Mission to Seamen, and literally having no place to live, MMSA came to our rescue and we spent a very happy eighteen months in one of the bungalows. It was a grand place to live! Surrounded by retired seafarers, a simple five minute walk to post a letter could take well over an hour as I chatted with cheerful nostalgia to so many old friends. No-one is ever lonely in Mariners' Park.

A great step forward was taken in 1936. The John Davies Memorial Infirmary was erected by Mrs. Jeanette Davies in memory of her husband, John Davies, underwriter of Liverpool. The Infirmary was extensively

The Infirmary and Nursing Home

damaged following the bombing in World War Two. It is now a Nursing Home and cares for up to 30 patients, as well as providing single rooms and two suites for married couples. The Home is really a life-line for the very sick and the elderly residents in the Park and open to other seafarers and their dependants. Many times I have enjoyed visiting patients and have found that the care is excellent without depriving any individual his privacy or dignity. This is a very special place

The NUMAST Welfare Branch is responsible for the maintenance of the Mariners' Park Estate, including the Nursing Home and Gibson House and is ably administered by the Estate and Welfare Officer, Captain Mike Condon. It is quite a task - the routine maintenance and repair of all the properties, including interior and exterior decoration, together with the upkeep of the grounds and gardens. Another responsibility is the distribution and oversight of various Welfare Funds which award pensions, regular grants and lump sum hardship grants. There are currently more than 500 retired seafarers in receipt of pensions and grants.

As we approach the millenium, I was intrigued to read a statement made by a local Member of Parliament at the Annual General Meeting in Liverpool Town Hall on the 30th May, 1900.

'I am not going to weary you with statistics, but I have here the figures from the most recent Parliamentary Report on the subject, which gives us the percentage of foreign as compared with British seamen for the last fifty years. In 1856 the percentage was 7; in 1868 it had increased to 11; in 1878 to 13; in 1888 to 14; and in1898 to 20 per cent. You see, therefore, that the proportion of foreign to British sailors is increasing in our Merchant Service to a very alarming extent, and if not put a stop to in some way there is no knowing where it will end some day; in fact it almost seems that in the course of time the British sailor is going to be superseded altogether.'

Mr.Charles McArthur, M.P., obviously would not be surprised that his prophecy has almost come true just one hundred years later as we have less than three hundred British flagged vessels with a minimum of British seamen aboard. 'Telegraph', NUMAST's house magazine, quoted statistics in the July 1997 edition and states that

'British owned and registered tonnage has slumped to its lowest ever low. The decline in the UK-owned trading fleet last year was more than five times the rate of decline during 1995. In contrast, the world merchant fleet increased by 25 million dwt (3.5%) ... the highest growth since 1979.'

NUMAST pin-points the decline further ... the UK-fleet down to 233 ships of 2.28 million dwt compared with 237 ships of 2.57 million dwt at the start of the year and 1,614 ships of 50 million dwt in 1975.

NUMAST's Biennial Meeting in May 1997 was told by the Deputy General Secretary that a survey was being launched to assess the long-term welfare needs of seafarers nearing retirement. "This will shape national decisions on charitable work for seafarers and will form the basis of any future development of NUMAST's welfare services." He further stated that, "Mariners' Park needs to be upgraded, the nursing home should be more flexible and improved."

The General Secretary of NUMAST, Brian Orrell, deserves the last word on behalf of the seafarer.

"The Sea Sense campaign will continue to press the case for a new maritime vision in this island nation and the need to regenerate the seafaring skills which have served our country so well, both in times of war and peace. Let's hope our new government has the wisdom to recognise that shipping is no sunset industry doomed to extinction, but rather a vibrant, expanding and dynamic industry in which Britain could recapture its once dominant role."

Mariners' Park and the Queen Elizabeth II

21.
British Sailors' Society

On 18th March, 1818, a public meeting was held in the City of London
Tavern, Bishopsgate Street. This eventually led to the Reverend Peter
McGrath coming to work in Liverpool in 1979. In the chair at that meeting
in 1818 was Benjamin Shaw, M.P., and under his guidance a Society was
formed to minister to the religious needs of seamen. The motivation was
obvious as the Wapping district of London was as appalling as any other
city and the plight of seafarers was equally desperate. This new
organisation was given the title of 'The Port of London Society'. The
work started.

There is no doubt that this was the first Society in this country to work
formally amongst seafarers. Actually that 1818 meeting must have been

the result of previous activity. Probably the Bethel Flag had been hoisted on the Thames some four years before. The first Bethel ship was a sloop called *Speedy;* this warship was converted into 'an ark' and anchored in the Thames. It was a new concept and it was to be quickly copied in many other ports in the country.

The first missionary ordained to care for sailors was the Reverend W.H. Angus. He visited home ports and also hoisted the Bethel Flag on the Continent in Belgian, German and Baltic ports. Ships even carried the flag to the Pacific and in 1826 reached Sydney and Melbourne.

For the first fifteen years the Society was known as The Port of London Society, but George Fife Angas, the second treasurer of the Society, proposed in 1833 that the title should be changed to embrace the whole world. Angas shortly afterwards became one of the principal founders of South Australia and also helped secure New Zealand to the British Crown. His son, the Hon. J.H. Angas, became President of the Society and established a fine Sailors' Bethel and Rest at Adelaide.

The proposal in 1833 was that 'the interests and objects of the Sailors' and Port of London and Bethel-Union Societies being the same, they now be united.' It was resolved that 'this institution be called The British and Foreign Sailors' Society for promoting their moral and religious improvement.' The work quickly expanded around the world.

My study on the first floor of Kingston House looked down upon the Shipping Federation Office just across the road and upon the majestic edifice of the Mersey Docks and Harbour Company. Morning prayer, Bible study, coffee and the day's planning over, I invariably looked across the road to observe a familiar figure. It was John Yates walking his quiet way to the Gordon Smith Institute or, to give it its original title, the Liverpool Seamen and Migrants Friend Society and Bethel-Union, which was founded in 1820. This was Liverpool's tenuous link with the nonconformist Sailors' and Port of London and Bethel-Union Society. John was on his way to say his prayers and start his day's work. We all commenced the day in the same way.

John's father had bought a large parcel of land at 6d a square yard in Barnston in Wirral and built his house on it. John Yates was to become a tax inspector and after his retirement he worshipped at Chester Street Mission, Birkenhead, by the old Mersey tunnel entrance. That was when he became a full-time volunteer worker in the Gordon Smith Institute. When I knew him, he must have been well into his eightieth year. My respect for him was complete.

Peter McGrath had served his time in the army and then in 1957 worked with Blue Funnel in Birkenhead aboard the ships. The vessels came into

Gladstone Dock in Liverpool, where the deep-sea crew went ashore, and after discharging part of the cargo, the 'shore crew' sailed to Glasgow for final discharging. New cargo aboard, the ship returned to Birkenhead for final loading, prior to the return of the deep-sea crew. Peter worked and learned his trade. Married to Sheila, they also worshipped at the Chester Street Mission ... and there was John Yates with all his tales about the Gordon Smith Institute in Liverpool! There can be no doubt that he was to influence the direction of Peter's life.

Inevitably, Peter was called to study and train for the ministry in Emmanuel Bible College, Birkenhead. His life was not to be the same again. As a part of their training at the College, every Sunday afternoon the students visited the seafarers aboard the ships in Birkenhead docks. It was excellent preparation for what lay ahead. Amongst the students at this time was Malcolm Owen Griffiths. He was to join the British Sailors' Society in London and then went on to work for three years in Jamaica. Meanwhile Peter, having completed his time at College, joined the local Liverpool City Mission.

At a conference which Malcolm chanced to be attending in Liverpool, he urged Peter also to consider joining the British Sailors' Society. It was sufficient motivation for Sheila and Peter to visit London ... a post in London Docks was offered on the spot! It led to two happy years (1977 - 79) as Port Chaplain there.

There never had been a British Sailors Society presence in Liverpool because the Gordon Smith Institute had represented the Non-Conformist activities in the port. However, with the closure of that Society, London decided that a man should be appointed. That man was to be Peter McGrath.

As the Gordon Smith Institute had ended its activity, all continuity had been lost. It was like starting all over again ... a new man, a new challenge. Happily Peter was advised by London to join the Liverpool Port Welfare Commitee and he decided that his first task was to visit all the members in order to introduce himself.

Peter and I met for the first time in Kingston House in James Street and the friendship was immediate. Within months we were sharing the responsibility for an International Sports Week and as Peter did not have a mini-bus he borrowed one from the Apostleship of the Sea in Birkenhead with the blessing of Father George Brown. This was an ecumenical effort as we worked as a team.

Another example of togetherness occurred after the loss of the Penlee lifeboat. A short newspaper article told the story. The date was 20th December, 1981.

'THE PENLEE DISASTER

16 Perish in Cornish Lifeboat Tragedy

The eight-strong crew of the Cornish Penlee lifeboat today drowned as they battled in vain to save eight people from a wrecked coaster in hurricane lashed seas.

The lifeboat had managed to save four passengers from the 1,400-ton *Union Star,* only for them to die as they were dashed on the rocks. A search by Royal Navy helicopters and fishing ships found no sign of any survivors.

At the tiny harbour of Mousehole, the dead lifeboatmen's neighbours and friends stood ready to replace them. It is thought the lifeboat was holed during a collision with the ship in 60-foot waves.'

A memorial service was held in the Stella Maris, Bootle, with all the chaplains participating. The crews of Hoylake and New Brighton Stations were present. Over the years Merseysiders ever came together to meet the sadness of the sea and to mark the courage of the men of the lifeboats.

The story of the R.N.L.I. is familiar to most of us. In 1786 a London coach builder, Lionel Lukin, converted a fishing yawl into a more reliable vessel, making him the inventor of the first lifeboat. In 1789, a prize of two guineas was offered for a better design. The winner was given one guinea as his design required adjustments! It was left to a member of the Douglas, Isle of Man, lifeboat crew, William Hillary, to appeal for the founding of a national society and a meeting on 4th March, 1824 did just that. The annual expenditure today is in millions, but the real cost of the R.N.L.I. has been the lives lost.

I recall spending some time aboard a container ship. There were beautiful nights, a glassy sea under a near full moon, cold and crisp with clean visibility. The ship was on automatic, the engine console all green lights, Decca pin-pointing our position, radar screen showing all ships within 60 miles. All was well with the world. Yet just a months before, in Liverpool Bay, a hurricane force was sending waves some fifty feet over the bridge. The 'cruel sea'!

Peter carried the main pastoral care when, in July 1980, the *Derbyshire* was assumed missing in the China Seas. Together with a representative of Bibby Line, he visited all the mourning relatives on Merseyside. A Memorial Service was held in the Anglican Cathedral and I shall never forget the deep silence as I read out the names of those never to return.

At the time of that tragedy the families asked Peter to handle for them all contacts with the media. There was more to be done. Des and Vicky

King had lost their son and realised that they needed to meet the other families. This was achieved when they got together with Peter in the Swedish Church in Liverpool and the decision was taken to bring all the families together; out of this was born the Derbyshire Family Association.

Various official enquiries seemed to give no answers ... silence does not help grief. Eventually funds were found with the help of the International Transport Workers' Federation and the *Derbyshire* was located in 1994. The Government, at last, then provided two million pounds for a two stage search of the wreck. The truth may never be known, but as over one hundred and fifty bulk carriers have been lost or suffered serious structural damage at sea since the *Derbyshire*, it is imperative to search for the truth.

The Derbyshire Family Association has stayed together and now meets twice a year. At first they met regularly in the Mersey Mission to Seamen's Colonsay House, but a new pattern has evolved. Each Spring they hold an A.G.M. in Leeds and every September a Memorial Service takes place in Liverpool Parish Church ... the Seafarers' Church. Naturally, Peter continues to care and is accepted as chaplain to the Derbyshire Family Association.

The early 1980s were certainly a time of great decisions and changes in Liverpool. The Apostleship of the Sea closed Atlantic House in Hardman Street and concentrated their work in their Stella Maris in Bootle. The Merchant Navy Welfare Board sold Merchant Navy House in Canning Street and discontinued their work on Merseyside. The old Sailors' Home Building had long been demolished, although a Trust had been formed to continue the general care for the seafarer.

Peter and I tried to find a solution to our futures. We in the Mersey Mission to Seamen closed the residence and three floors of Kingston House in James Street and put the entire building on the market. The plan was simple. We adapted the bottom floor of Kingston House and created an 'International Seamen's' Centre'. This was a joint venture with the British Sailors' Society and the Mersey Mission to Seamen. Peter and I worked well together for eighteen months, but the experiment proved to be financially unsound. It could not continue. In time we sold the whole of Kingston House and relocated the Mersey Mission at Colonsay House almost four miles north of Pier Head in Crosby. That very quickly proved to be the right building in the right place. The centre of shipping had firmly moved to the extreme north end of the dock system. Peter reverted to his basic ship visiting and caring for the seafarers in their homes. In time the British Sailors' Society established a Centre in Birkenhead Docks. Much of Peter's work involved Birkenhead, Ellesmere Port. the Manchester Ship Canal and Runcorn. A new pattern of caring had emerged.

Peter McGrath is known and loved on Merseyside and can tell many a story about his work. He has shared some thoughts with me.

"The crew of the *M.V.Christianaki* were mostly Filipino, the officers were Greek and the Radio Officer was from Sudan. The 'sparks' had apparently bought a pair of shoes in Liverpool for some forty pounds and told me that he was delighted with them. We laughed and chatted happily about his purchase. Aboard the vessel were two Filipinos who were father and son ... that does not happen very often. They had been in the ship together for at least fifteen months. They, too, chatted excitedly to me as they explained that at the next port they would at last be able to go home. That's the magic word for the seafarer! It had been a good ship visit and I had enjoyed the welcome and friendship of the men.

"When I left the ship, I looked carefully at her. The thought came that, if she had been a car, there was no way in which she wouild have passed her M.O.T. The deck was eaten away with corrosion and rust. It was a sad sight.

"The *Christianaki* sailed on time loaded with scrap iron for South America. Sadly she never arrived. Two hundred miles from Landsend she met a Force Twelve gale and foundered. Aboard were twenty-seven·crewmen and not one survived. They had been my friends."

I knew that Peter had other stories, as we all have, as over the years and centuries seafarers have lost their lives. Too often the seaman is 'out of sight and out of mind'. He has no second chance.

Most of us had observed a Nigerian ship tied up for month after month in Elllesmere Port. The main motor-way was only a few hundred yards from her. Peter tells the story.

"When the Nigerian training ship, the *River Andoni,* arrived in Ellesmere Port it looked as though she had come through a war zone. Most of her deck plates were twisted and buckled. Apparently she had met the same Force Twelve as the *Christianaki,* but had survived. There were sixty-seven crew aboard. It was obvious, even to me, that she was in no condition to set to sea again without extensive repairs. The work was done. That was when it was discovered that the local repair company could not be paid. It was also revealed that the whole crew had not received pay for some time. Further investigation was to prove that some crew had received no wages for almost two years. We all have met this situation before ... too often!

(left) Peter McGrath and Bob Evans

"The International Transport Workers' Federation was called in and after extensive and almost endless negotiations, an agreement with the Nigerian Company was finally reached. This enabled most of the crew to go home with a percentage of their pay before they departed; there was a promise of full payment when they arrived at Lagos."

Peter and I talked about many other cases where such an agreement was reached. Sadly, in our experience, settlement was rarely made when the crews arrived at their destination and they would receive little compensation. Maybe the men off the *River Andoni* might have faired better than most, but at least they had received some back wages and had been flown home.

Peter continued with the story of the *River Andoni*.

"The ship remained in Ellesmere Port with ten crewmen aboard. It was to be a full two years before the accrued debts were payed. Eventually, the vessel was towed to Bidston Dry Dock for extensive repairs. Unfortunately, the engine room caught fire. The damage was irreparable and the *River Andoni* was sold for scrap!"

This had been yet another sad tale of ships and seamen and the sea. During all the protracted problems, the societies caring for the seafarer were in constant contact giving as much support as possible to the demoralised crewmen. There rarely is a happy ending.

Stranded crews are to be found in almost every port in the world ... almost turning the clock back two centuries! Of course, conditions have improved, but many men are being exploited. In some cases they have to pay a dishonest agent in order to get a berth aboard a ship and then be underpaid. Peter continued his observations.

"I have been aboard ships that have less than enough food. This is here in Britain. Our economy is built on this state of affairs! A cook showed me a fridge full of fish the crew had caught because they could not stomach the food in the pantry. A South American seaman showed Canon Peters ... he was with the Mersey Misson to Seamen then ... and me a bucket of yellow water taken from the Panama Canal to serve as drinking water for the crew. I was once aboard a small tanker shortly after a Japanese owner had told the Filipino crew that their families would come to physical harm if they caused any problems aboard the ship."

I could not help but reflect on the stories that I had uncovered in researching 'Mersey Mariners' and discovering the problems facing the caring Societies during the last two hundred years. The seafarer is still at risk. However, it is not all 'doom and gloom'. Peter continued his observations.

"Most ships are a delight to visit. I would put the Scandinavian and most of the European vessels into this càtagory. The ships are clean and the atmosphere is good, they are friendly and grateful for a visit from the Chaplain, no matter what organisation he represents. One of the saddest comments I hear is that there are no more Britiish ships. We still have a fleet though it is certainly much depleted."

The British Sailors' Society has quite recently been renamed and is now known as the British and International Sailors' Society. That seems rather heavy as a title for a modern society, especially as most of us call it 'The Sailors' Society'. Their motto is simple ... 'In Service for the Seafarer' ... and rightly implies that the British Sailors' Society has always been international, caring for the sailor whatever colour, creed, country or condition.

A recent and welcome addition to the port's facilities, provided by the British and International Sailors' Society, is the new 'drop-in' Centre in Birkenhead Docks. This is where the men can come to relax in a different environment, watch T.V., change their currency when other places are closed, phone home, talk about their families, tell of their problems and hopes, or just drink free coffee. The men always leave with free literature, mostly in their own language, and above all hopefully feeling much better for having paid a visit to the Centre.

A man who works in a factory or an office is able to escape at the end of his day, but for the seafarer his ship is his home and work-place. He remains with the same small group of shipmates for weeks and months. Most of us would find that a situation impossible for survival.

Perhaps the biggest danger for the British seafarer is the on-going decline in our own merchant fleet. In 1996 the world fleets grew by more than 4 per cent, whilst the U.K. owned and registered fleet shrunk by more than 20 per cent in deadweight tonnage terms. Also during that year seaborne trade rose by almost 4 percent to reach a new record, but the U.K. mainland-flagged-fleet fell from 251 to 237. This decline continues.

Yet, the Port of Liverpool continues to thrive ... a fact hard to communicate! Figures might help. The Port in 1996 handled more than 30 million tonnes of cargo for the first time in its history and the real strength of the port is the comprehensive nature of the cargoes. Inspite of recent labour problems, the performance record has seen a 50% increase of productivity since the new work-force was employed in 1995. One exciting development is the proposed £16.5 million river berth for Irish sea roll-on and roll-off ferries; this will speed up the turn-around of ships by enabling them to discharge and load in the River Mersey rather than entering the enclosed docks.

Even more exciting is the Euro Rail Link via the Channel Tunnel ... Liverpool to Paris 15 hours, Lyon 28 hours, Milan 36 hours. We are the major UK port for trade with the Eastern Seaboard of North America. The variety of the trade is almost endless ... grain and animal feed, timber and forest products, coal and stone, scrap metal, edible oils and fats, sulpher fossil fuels and every conceivable product tucked out of sight in the myriads of containers. The largest container ships are regularly turned around in 12 hours at Liverpool's Royal Seaforth Terminal. Massive Panamax sized, bulk carriers, discharge 20,000 tonnes of grain a day ... the vessels take three and a half days to empty! Another success is the Freeport as it handles £5 million worth of goods each week for hundreds of companies serving over 80 countries. The Freeport offers freedom from Import Duty, Import VAT, EU Levies and quotas. The latest companies to locate in the free zone include the world's largest manufacturer of fancy dress, based in New York! So much more could be said!

The care of the seafarer will continue into the millenium.

'They that go down to the sea in ships: and occupy their business in great waters;
These men see the works of the Lord: and his wonders in the deep.
For at his word the stormy wind ariseth: which lifteth up the waves thereof.
They are carried up to the heaven, and down again to the deep;
their soul melteth away because of the trouble.
They reel to and fro, and stagger like a drunken man: and are at their wits end.
So when they cry unto the Lord in their trouble;
he delivereth them out of their distress.
For he maketh the storm to cease: so that the waves thereof are still.
Then are they glad, because they are at rest:
and so he bringeth them unto the haven where they would be.'

Psalm 107

Mersey Mariners